Soups & Stews

Soups and stews

bay books

Contents

Introduction

Soup & Stew Secrets

There are no secret tricks to making wonderful soups and stews... no fancy techniques or difficult finishes... just a kitchen filled with delicious aromas and a tender, flavoursome meal that will satisfy the whole family from one pot.

Soups and stews are versatile, varied and above all delicious. Fish and fowl, meat and pulses, vegetables and even fruit can all be prepared in these ways. Once you have mastered the basics you will quickly realise that most soups or stews, from the humblest to the most exotic, are put together along similar lines. The differences lie in the ingredients and embellishments. We are all envious of those confident casual cooks who can just throw a few ingredients into the pot and produce a richly fragrant sauce packed with tender meat and flavoursome vegetables. But once you have gained confidence with the techniques you will find it easy to adapt them for your own variations. For example, many soups are blended in a food processor, (always let the soup cool a little first, so that you won't splash yourself with scalding liquid), but you may like to vary the textures by leaving some of the soup unpuréed.

Always pick the best ingredients. Your soup or stew is only as good as the sum of its parts. Use fresh bright-coloured meat and pick fresh firm vegetables that are in season.

CHEAP EATS

You may be using the freshest ingredients you can find but they certainly don't need to be the most expensive. One of the great advantages of soups and stews is that they are generally better made with the more economical cuts of meat. Unlike expensive cuts, which are usually cooked quickly, the cheaper cuts of meat are best when slowly simmered in liquid as the process tenderizes the meat. You can tell when the meat is cooked because the pieces will break up easily with a fork. Beef cuts such as blade, chuck, round or topside steak are ideal and generally have more flavour than fillet or rump.

COATING AND BROWNING MEAT

By coating the meat in seasoned flour and then browning it on all sides in oil or butter you will give it a crisp brown coating and delicious taste. The flour also helps to thicken the liquid—usually once you have coated the meat in flour you won't need to use another thickener. (If you find at the end of cooking you still need to thicken the soup or stew a little more it is always better to reduce the liquid by fast simmering for a while, uncovered, rather than adding more flour.)

Don't coat the meat until you are ready to start cooking or the moisture in the meat will absorb the flour. It will no longer be a coating and could change the whole texture of the dish. If the flour is absorbed for some reason, re-coat the meat just before use and shake off any excess.

To coat meat in flour you can lay the flour on greaseproof paper, sprinkle with a little seasoning and then turn the meat in the flour with your fingers or a pair of tongs. A cleverer and less messy method is to put the seasoned flour in a bag, add the meat cubes in batches, shake and then pick out the meat. Shake off any excess flour.

Browning the meat also seals in the juices and gives a good rich colour to the stew. Meat is browned quickly over fairly high heat and turned often to prevent sticking and to brown all sides. Oil is often used rather than butter, as butter burns at a lower temperature. However, a combination of the two means the oil prevents the butter burning and the butter adds flavour to the coating. It may be necessary to brown the meat in batches if there is a lot of it—too much meat crowded into the pan will merely stew in its own juices and become tough.

An easy way to coat meat with flour is to put them both in a bag and shake.

Brown meat quickly on all sides, over high heat, to seal in the juices.

Some of the lamb cuts which we rarely use are ideal for producing tasty stews—neck chops and lamb shanks are perfect and easy on the budget. Trim away any excess fat and sinew—these will toughen during cooking and can cause the meat to shrink. Cut the meat into even-sized pieces that will

cook at the same rate. About 2–3 cm (¾–1¼ inch) cubes are probably best, any smaller and the meat will fall into shreds while cooking and not look as appetizing. Any chicken pieces are suitable for stews, but take care they are simmered gently, not boiled, or the meat will toughen.

SIMMERING

Generally, when making soups or stews the ingredients are browned, liquid is added and then the food is brought to the boil. The heat is then reduced and the pan covered and left to simmer slowly until the ingredients are tender. Fish soups and stews are different in that the sauce is often prepared first and the fish added later to ensure it is not overcooked, tough or dry. Fast-cooking vegetables, such as snow peas (mangetout), broccoli or mushrooms, are also usually added towards the end of cooking to prevent them becoming too soft.

Soups and stews should never be boiled for long periods, or the meat will become tough and stringy and lose its flavour and any vegetables will break up. A lazy simmer is best—tiny bubbles will appear at a slower pace on the surface of the food.

By the time a stew is cooked there is quite likely to be a thin layer of fat on the surface which you can easily skim off with a spoon or some paper towels to make the dish healthier. This is even easier if you are refrigerating the dish overnight—the fat will set and can be lifted off.

A dish is boiling when large bubbles appear in quick succession.

Soups and stews are best cooked at a lazy simmer.

PANS

When choosing a pan for making soups and stews, buy one that can be taken straight from the freezer to the stove or oven. A pan with a heavy base ensures an even distribution of heat which is important when dishes are simmering in liquid for a long time. A tight-fitting lid is essential to keep in moisture. The size of the dish is important. If it's too small the liquid might overflow, too large and the food will dry out because the liquid will reduce too quickly. The food should come approximately three-quarters of the way up the dish for the best result.

SEASONING

When making both soups and stews it is best to add seasoning at the end of the cooking process. Often the liquid has been reduced during simmering which makes the flavours more concentrated. Chilled soups should be tasted after chilling and may need more seasoning than hot soups. Some dishes thicken if left to stand and may need to have water added to bring them back to the right consistency— don't forget to taste for seasoning.

Don't sprinkle salt directly onto raw meat before cooking as it draws out the moisture and can make the meat tough and dry.

FREEZING

For busy cooks, a great advantage of soups and stews is that both methods lend themselves to cooking in batches and storing. Fish soups and stews and the delicate oriental soups should be eaten immediately: their textures and flavours disintegrate on reheating. But most meat dishes, especially those which are highly spiced, such as curries, positively benefit from being refrigerated for a day or two before serving. This lets the flavours mature and also gives you the opportunity to easily lift off any fat which may have formed on the surface of the dish.

Many stews and some soups can be successfully frozen for 1 to 3 months. Don't add cream before freezing as it can curdle. Add it when you reheat to serve.

The food should be frozen as soon as it has cooled—and it should be cooled as quickly as possible to prevent bacteria forming. Skim any fat from the surface before freezing. The easiest way to freeze a soup or stew is to put a plastic bag inside a jug or bowl, spoon the food into it, tie loosely and then put the jug or bowl in the freezer. When the food is frozen, remove the bag from the container, squeeze out as much air as possible and seal securely. Label and date the bag before returning it to the freezer. If you are cooking in bulk it may be sensible to divide the food into small portions that can be thawed individually.

It is always best to thaw food completely before reheating but if you are in a hurry it is possible to reheat straight from the freezer. Remove the frozen food from the bag or container and heat slowly on the stovetop or in the microwave for about 20 minutes depending on the amount of food.

Line a jug or bowl with a plastic bag and spoon in the soup or stew.

Seal the bag and label with the date, then freeze and remove the jug.

Stock

FISH STOCK

Preparation time: 15 minutes
Total cooking time: 30 minutes
Makes 1.5 litres (6 cups)

15 g (½ oz) butter
2 medium onions, finely
   chopped
2 litres (8 cups) water
1.5 kg (3 lb 5 oz) fish bones,
   heads and tails
10 black peppercorns
1 bouquet garni

The secret to great soup is good stock. Home-made stock will give your soups a richer, more flavoursome base and, although the cooking time is long, the preparation couldn't be easier. Browning meat bones beforehand adds flavour and colour and a fresh bouquet garni of parsley, thyme and a bay leaf tied in muslin is preferable to the dried, bought variety. Make double the amount of stock and keep some frozen in an ice tray to be on hand whenever you need it. Stock should never be boiled: this will impair the flavour. Allow it to simmer gently.

1 Melt the butter in a large heavy-based pan and add the onion. Cook, stirring, over low heat for 10 minutes until the onion is soft and transparent, but not browned.
2 Add the water, fish, peppercorns and bouquet garni and bring slowly to the boil. Reduce the heat and simmer, uncovered, for 20 minutes, frequently skimming any froth from the surface. Strain through a fine sieve, discarding the bones and vegetables, and leave to cool before refrigerating.

Note: Use a white-fleshed fish for stock. Darker-fleshed, oily fish tends to make the stock greasy.

CHICKEN STOCK

Preparation time: 20 minutes
Total cooking time: 3 hours 50 minutes
Makes 1.5 litres (6 cups)

1.5 kg (3 lb 5 oz) chicken bones
2 large onions, unpeeled and
   roughly chopped
3 litres (12 cups) water
2 medium carrots, unpeeled and
   roughly chopped
2 sticks celery, leaves included,
   roughly chopped
1 bouquet garni
12 black or white peppercorns

1 Preheat the oven to 180°C (350°F/Gas 4). Bake the chicken bones and the onions in a large baking dish for 50 minutes, or until well browned. Transfer the bones and onion to a large heavy-based pan or stockpot.
2 Add the water, vegetables, bouquet garni and peppercorns to the pan. Bring slowly to the boil, then reduce the heat and simmer, uncovered, for 3 hours, skimming any froth from the top of the stock if necessary. Strain the stock through a fine sieve and discard the bones and vegetables.
3 Pour the stock into a shallow dish so that it cools quickly and then refrigerate until completely cold. Remove any fat that sets on the top.

VEGETABLE STOCK

Preparation time: 15 minutes
Total cooking time: 1 hour 30 minutes
Makes 1.5 litres (6 cups)

2 tablespoons oil
4 large brown onions, unpeeled and chopped
5 large carrots, unpeeled and chopped
2 large parsnips, unpeeled and chopped
5 sticks celery, including leaves, chopped
2 bay leaves
1 fresh bouquet garni
1 teaspoon whole black peppercorns
3 litres (12 cups) water

1 Preheat the oven to 200°C (400°F/ Gas 6). Heat the oil in a large baking dish, add the onion, carrot and parsnip and toss to coat in the oil. Bake for 30 minutes, until lightly golden.

2 Transfer the baked vegetables to a large heavy-based pan. Add the remaining ingredients and bring to the boil slowly. Reduce the heat and simmer, uncovered, for 1 hour, until reduced by half.

3 Strain the stock through a fine sieve, discarding the vegetables. Leave to cool before refrigerating. Remove any fat which sets on the top.

BEEF STOCK

Preparation time: 20 minutes
Total cooking time: 4 hours 50 minutes
Makes 1 litre (4 cups)

2 kg (4 lb 8 oz) beef bones
2 carrots, unpeeled and roughly chopped
2 brown onions, unpeeled and roughly chopped
3 litres (12 cups) water
2 sticks celery, leaves included, roughly chopped
1 bouquet garni
12 black peppercorns

1 Preheat the oven to 200°C (400°F/ Gas 6). Place the beef bones in a large baking dish and bake for 30 minutes, turning occasionally. Add the carrot and onion to the dish and cook for another 20 minutes.

2 Transfer the bones, carrot and onion to a stockpot or large heavy-based pan. Drain the excess fat from the baking dish, then pour 250 ml (9 fl oz/1 cup) of the water into the dish. Stir gently with a wooden spoon to dissolve any pan juices and then add to the stockpot.

3 Add the celery, remaining water, bouquet garni and peppercorns to the stockpot. Bring slowly to the boil and then reduce the heat and leave to simmer, uncovered, for 4 hours. Occasionally skim away any froth that forms on the top of the stock.

4 Strain the stock through a fine sieve and discard the vegetables and bones. Pour into a clean shallow dish so that the stock cools quickly (you could then leave this dish to stand in a larger oven tray of cold water if the weather is very warm), then put in the refrigerator. Once the stock is cold it is easier to lift off any fat which may set on the top.

Soups

Crostini and Croutons

Crostini (crisp thin slices of baked bread) and croutons (irresistibly crunchy cubes of browned bread) make wonderful accompaniments to any soup, whether it's a broth, creamy soup or chowder.

ROASTED GARLIC CROSTINI

Preheat the oven to 180°C (350°F/Gas 4). Wrap 2 garlic bulbs separately in foil. Bake for 1 hour, or until the garlic feels very soft to touch. Cool. Cut 1 long bread stick diagonally into twenty 2 cm (¾ inch) thick slices. Lay in a single layer on a large baking tray and brush with 3 tablespoons olive oil. Bake for 10 minutes, or until crisp and golden. Remove any that brown too quickly. Cut the tops off the garlic and squeeze out the flesh. Spread the garlic paste on the bread, sprinkle with a few thyme leaves, salt and freshly ground black pepper. Drizzle on a little extra olive oil, if you want. Serves 4.

Note: The garlic becomes very sweet when roasted. Roast an extra garlic bulb if you want more paste.

HERBED CROSTINI FINGERS

Preheat the oven to 180°C (350°F/Gas 4). Combine 80g (2¾ oz) of softened butter with 1 tablespoon each of chopped dill, flat-leaf (Italian) parsley and basil. Mix until well combined. Stir through 3 tablespoons finely grated Parmesan. Cut 1 long bread stick into diagonal slices, 2 cm (¾ inch) thick. Spread with the herbed butter. Cut each slice in half lengthways. Place the bread fingers on a baking tray and bake for 10–12 minutes, or until the butter has melted and the edges are crispy. Serves 4.

CRISPY CROSTINI

Preheat the oven to 180°C (350°F/Gas 4). Cut half a day-old crusty Italian loaf of bread (Ciabatta) into wafer-thin slices. Place the slices in a single layer on a baking tray and brush lightly on one side with a little olive oil. Cook for 8–10 minutes, or until lightly golden. Watch carefully as it is very easy for them to overbrown. Allow to cool. Serves 4.

ARTICHOKE AND GARLIC CROSTINI

Preheat the oven to 180°C (350°F/Gas 4). Finely chop 3 tablespoons marinated artichoke hearts and 3 teaspoons capers. Mix with 50 g (1¾ oz) softened butter and 2 crushed garlic cloves. Spread the mixture onto 8 thick slices of crusty Italian bread. Cut each slice in half diagonally. Lay on a baking tray and bake for 10–12 minutes, or until the edges are crispy. Serves 4.

GARLIC AND HERB CROUTONS

Preheat the oven to 180°C (350°F/Gas 4). Cut two 2 cm (¾ inch) thick slices from a loaf. Remove the crusts and cut each bread slice into 16 cubes. In a bowl, mix together 3 tablespoons olive oil, 2 crushed garlic cloves, 1 tablespoon chopped oregano, 2 teaspoons chopped thyme, 1 teaspoon chopped rosemary and a pinch of chilli flakes. Add the bread cubes to the herbed oil and toss until all the oil has been absorbed. Lay the bread cubes in a single layer on a baking tray and bake in the oven for 10–12 minutes, or until the croutons are golden brown. Turn once during baking. Serves 4.

Note: Croutons are best made with day-old bread, which holds together better than fresh bread.

PARMESAN TRIANGLE CROUTONS

Preheat the oven to 180°C (350°F/Gas 4). Lightly grease a baking tray. Remove the crusts from 4 slices of bread and cut the slices in half diagonally. Cut each triangle in half and then in half again so that you end up with 8 small triangles. Combine 4 tablespoons olive oil with ⅓ cup 4 tablespoons finely grated Parmesan. Add the triangles and toss in the mixture. When you add the Parmesan to the oil most of the oil will be absorbed, but you should have enough to coat the triangles. Place the triangles on a lightly greased baking tray. Bake for 10–15 minutes or until golden. Turn once during baking. Some triangles may be ready before others; if this is the case, remove the golden ones and continue to cook the rest. Serves 4.

SPICY CROUTONS

Preheat the oven to 180°C (350°F/Gas 4). Remove the crusts from 4 slices of bread and cut the slices into cubes or using a small round cutter, cut into circles. Combine 3 tablespoons olive oil, 1 teaspoon each of ground cumin and coriander, ½ teaspoon ground cinnamon and a pinch each of ground nutmeg and cloves. Add the bread to the oil and toss until all the oil has been absorbed. Lay the bread in a single layer on a baking tray and bake for 10–15 minutes, or until crisp and golden. Serves 4.

SUN-DRIED TOMATO AND OLIVE LAVASH BITES

Preheat the oven to 190°C (375°F/Gas 5). Soften 40 g (1¼ oz) butter and place in a small bowl. Add 2 tablespoons finely chopped sun-dried tomato, 1 tablespoon finely chopped olives, 2 crushed garlic cloves and 2 tablespoons shredded basil. Mix well. Spread the mixture over 1 slice of lavash bread. Cut the lavash into strips then into small triangles. Bake for 5–10 minutes. Watch carefully as they can overbrown quickly. Serves 4.

PEA AND HAM SOUP

Preparation time: 20 minutes +
  soaking
Total cooking time: 1 hour 30 minutes
Serves 8–10

500 g (1 lb 2 oz) green split peas
1 kg (2 lb 4 oz) ham hock or
  bacon bones, chopped into
  short pieces (ask your
  butcher to do this)
2 litres (8 cups) water
1 large onion, chopped
1 large carrot, chopped
1 stick celery, chopped
1 turnip or swede (rutabaga),
  peeled and chopped
1 parsnip, peeled and chopped
3 tablespoons chopped fresh
  parsley

1 Leave the peas to soak overnight or for a minimum of 4 hours in a large bowl of water. Drain, discarding the soaking water.
Put the hock or bones in a large heavy-based pan and add the water, peas, onion, carrot, celery, turnip or swede and parsnip. Bring slowly to the boil, reduce the heat and partially cover, then simmer for 1½ hours, or until the peas are reduced to a mush. Stir occasionally, and skim the surface regularly (with a spoon or paper towel) to remove any froth. Remove the pan from the heat and allow to cool a little.
2 Lift out the hock or bones with a pair of tongs or a slotted spoon. Leave them to cool a little before removing the meat. Discard the bones, dice the meat and set aside.
3 When the soup has cooled, purée it in small batches in a food processor or blender. Return the soup to the pan and add the diced meat. Stir in the parsley and reheat gently to serve.

COOK'S FILE

Hint: Ham hock will yield a larger amount of meat than bacon bones, however bacon bones have a more intense flavour.

Peel and chop the parsnip. Ask your butcher to chop the ham hock for you.

Simmer for 1½ hours until the peas are reduced to a mush.

Lift out the ham hock or bacon bones with a pair of tongs.

Return the chopped meat to the soup once it has been puréed.

SMOKED FISH CHOWDER

Preparation time: 20 minutes
Total cooking time: 30–35 minutes
Serves 4–6

500 g (1 lb 2 oz) smoked fish
1 large potato, peeled and diced
1 stick celery, diced
1 medium onion, finely chopped
50 g (1¾ oz) butter
1 rasher bacon, rind removed
    and finely chopped
2 tablespoons plain (all-purpose)
    flour
½ teaspoon Worcestershire
    sauce
½ teaspoon dried mustard
250 ml (9 fl oz/1 cup) milk
30 g (1 oz/½ cup) chopped fresh
    parsley
3 tablespoons cream, optional

1 Put the fish in a frying pan, cover with water and bring to the boil, then reduce the heat and simmer for 8 minutes, until the fish flakes easily when tested with a fork. Drain, reserving the fish stock, then peel, bone and flake the fish. Set aside.
2 Put the potato, celery and onion in a pan with enough reserved stock to cover the vegetables. Bring to the boil, reduce the heat and simmer for 8 minutes, or until tender. Set aside.

3 Melt the butter in a pan, add the bacon and cook, stirring, for 3 minutes. Add the flour, Worcestershire sauce and mustard and stir until smooth. Cook for 1 minute, gradually pour in the milk and stir, off the heat, until smooth. Return to the heat and stir for 5 minutes until smooth and thick. Stir in the vegetables and liquid, then add the parsley and fish. Simmer over low heat for 5 minutes to heat through. Add the cream, if using.

COOK'S FILE

Storage time: Can be kept covered and refrigerated for up to 3 days.

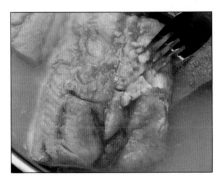
After simmering the fish, use a fork to test if it flakes easily.

Once the fish has been peeled and boned, use two forks to flake the flesh.

Add the parsley and flaked fish to the soup once it has thickened.

MULLIGATAWNY SOUP

Preparation time: 20 minutes
Total cooking time: 1 hour 15 minutes
Serves 4

30 g (1 oz) butter
375 g (13 oz) chicken thigh
  cutlets, skin and fat removed
1 large onion, finely chopped
1 apple, peeled, cored and diced
1 tablespoon curry paste
2 tablespoons plain (all-purpose)
  flour

750 ml (26 fl oz/3 cups) chicken
  stock
3 tablespoons basmati rice
1 tablespoon chutney
1 tablespoon lemon juice
3 tablespoons cream

1 Heat the butter in a large heavy-based pan and brown the chicken for 5 minutes; remove and set aside. Add the onion, apple and curry paste to the pan. Cook for 5 minutes, until the onion is soft. Stir in the flour; cook for 2 minutes then add half the stock. Stir until the mixture boils and thickens.

2 Return the chicken to the pan with the remaining stock. Stir until boiling, reduce the heat, cover and simmer for 1 hour. Add the rice for the last 15 minutes of cooking.
3 Remove the chicken; bone and dice the meat and return to the pan. Add the chutney, juice and cream. Season.

COOK'S FILE

Storage time: May be kept covered and refrigerated for up to 3 days.

Once the mixture has thickened, return the browned chicken thighs to the pan.

Add the basmati rice during the last 15 minutes of cooking

Add the chutney, lemon juice and cream at the end of cooking.

Cut the parsnip into even-sized strips, each about 4 cm (1½ inches) long.

Use a sharp knife to cut the stems from the beetroot.

You will need to let the beetroot cool before it can be peeled and grated.

Use a pair of tongs to lift the pieces of meat from the stock.

HOT BEEF BORSCHT

Preparation time: 30 minutes
Total cooking time: 2 hours
Serves 4–6

500 g (1 lb 2 oz) shin of beef,
  cut into large pieces
500 g (1 lb 2 oz) fresh beetroot
1 onion, finely chopped
1 carrot, cut into short strips
1 parsnip, cut into short strips
75 g (2½ oz/1 cup) finely
  shredded cabbage

1 Put the meat in a large heavy-based pan with 1 litre (4 cups) water and bring slowly to the boil; reduce the heat, cover and simmer for 1 hour. Skim the surface frequently to get rid of any froth.
2 Cut away the stems from the beetroot and place it in a large heavy-based pan with 1 litre (4 cups) water. Bring slowly to the boil, reduce the heat and simmer for 40 minutes, or until tender when pierced with a skewer. Drain, reserving the cooking liquid, leave the beetroot to cool, then peel and grate.
3 Use tongs to remove the meat from the stock, leave to cool and dice. Skim any fat from the stock. Return the meat to the stock and add the onion, carrot, parsnip and grated beetroot. Add 250 ml (9 fl oz/1 cup) of the beetroot liquid. Bring to the boil, reduce the heat, cover and simmer for 45 minutes. Add more beetroot liquid if a less thick soup is required.
4 Add the cabbage, stir and simmer for a further 15 minutes. Season to taste and serve hot. Borscht is a hearty main-meal soup and is good served with sour cream and chives.

COOK'S FILE

Storage time: May be kept covered and refrigerated for up to 4 days. Suitable to freeze for up to 1 month.

PUMPKIN SOUP

Preparation time: 30 minutes
Total cooking time: 50 minutes
Serves 6–8

4–5 kg (9 lb-11 lb 9 oz) whole
   pumpkin, with 5 cm (2 inch)
   stem
30 g (1 oz) butter
1 onion, chopped
1 carrot, peeled and chopped
1 teaspoon ground cumin
½ teaspoon ground nutmeg
1 teaspoon soft brown sugar
750 ml (26 fl oz/3 cups) chicken
   stock
125 ml (4 fl oz/½ cup) cream
cream and fresh chives, to serve

1 Preheat the oven to 160°C (315°F/
Gas 2–3). Use a small sharp knife to
cut a circle from the top of the
pumpkin. Scrape the seeds from inside
the pumpkin and lid and discard.
Scoop out the flesh with a spoon,
leaving a thick border. Dice the flesh
(you will have about 800 g/1 lb 12 oz)
and wash and dry the inside and
outside of the pumpkin.
2 Heat the butter in a large heavy-
based pan. Add the onion, pumpkin
flesh and carrot, cover and cook over
low heat for 10 minutes, stirring
occasionally. Add the cumin, nutmeg
and sugar and cook for 5 minutes.
3 Add the chicken stock and bring to
the boil, reduce the heat and cover.
Simmer for 30 minutes, stirring
occasionally. Meanwhile, put the
pumpkin shell, with its lid on, in the
oven for 30 minutes to heat through.
4 Purée the soup, in batches, and
return to the clean pan. Season to taste
and stir in the cream. Reheat gently
without boiling. Ladle into the
pumpkin shell, garnish with cream
and chives, replace the lid and serve.

COOK'S FILE

Storage time: May be kept covered
and refrigerated (not in the shell) for
up to 3 days. Freeze for up to 1 month.

*Cut a circle from the top of the pumpkin
using a small sharp knife.*

*Use paper towels to dry the pumpkin shell
inside and out.*

*Add the cumin, nutmeg and sugar and
cook for a further 5 minutes.*

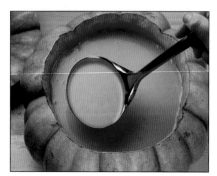

*Carefully ladle the soup into the warmed
pumpkin shell to serve.*

SCOTCH BROTH

Preparation time: 20 minutes
Total cooking time: 2 hours
  30 minutes
Serves 8–10

**750 g (1 lb 10 oz) best neck of
  lamb chops or lamb shanks**
**250 g (9 oz) pearl barley or soup
  mix**
1 carrot, peeled and diced
1 turnip, peeled and diced
1 parsnip, peeled and diced
1 onion, finely chopped

1 small leek, thinly sliced
**75 g (2½ oz/1 cup) finely
  chopped cabbage**
**30 g (1 oz/½ cup) chopped
  parsley**

1 Cut away any excess fat from the meat; place the meat in a large heavy-based pan with 2.5 litres (10 cups) water. Bring to the boil, reduce the heat and simmer, covered, for 1 hour. Skim any froth from the surface. Meanwhile, soak the barley or soup mix in a bowl of water for 1 hour.

2 Add the carrot, turnip, parsnip, onion and leek to the pan. Drain the

barley and add to the pan. Stir to combine, cover and simmer for 1½ hours. Stir in the cabbage 10 minutes before the end of cooking. (Add more water, according to taste.)

3 Remove the meat from the pan, and cool before removing from the bones. Chop the meat finely and return to the soup. Add the parsley and season.

COOK'S FILE

Storage time: May be kept covered and refrigerated for up to 3 days. Suitable to freeze for up to 1 month.
Note: Soup mix is a combination of pearl barley, split peas and lentils.

Instead of a spoon, use paper towels to skim any froth from the surface.

Drain the barley or soup mix and add to the pan.

Use tongs to hold the bones while removing the meat.

MEDITERRANEAN FISH SOUP

Preparation time: 25 minutes
Total cooking time: 25 minutes
Serves 6–8

1 kg (2 lb 4 oz) white fish fillets
3 tablespoons olive oil
2 large onions, chopped
1–2 garlic cloves, crushed
4 large tomatoes, peeled, seeded and chopped
2 tablespoons tomato paste (concentrated purée)
6 tablespoons chopped gherkins

1 tablespoon chopped capers
1 tablespoon pitted and chopped green olives
1 tablespoon pitted and chopped black olives
750 ml (26 fl oz/3 cups) fish stock
250 ml (9 fl oz/1 cup) white wine
1 bay leaf
3 tablespoons chopped fresh basil
60 g (2¼ oz/1 cup) chopped fresh parsley

1 Remove the skin and bones from the fish and chop into bite-sized pieces. Heat the oil in a large heavy-based pan and cook the onion and garlic for 8 minutes until soft.

2 Stir in the tomato and paste. Stir for 2–3 minutes, or until the tomato is soft. Stir in the gherkins and half the capers and olives.

3 Add the fish, stock, wine and bay leaf and season. Bring slowly to the boil, reduce the heat and simmer for 10–12 minutes, or until the fish is just cooked. Stir in the herbs. Add the remaining capers and olives. Serve.

COOK'S FILE

Note: Unsuitable to freeze.

Peel the tomatoes by soaking in boiling water. Remove the seeds with a spoon.

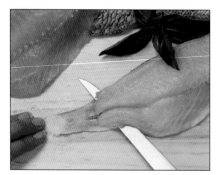

Use salt to help you keep a firm grasp on the fish while removing the skin.

Add the fish to the pan and pour in the stock and white wine.

SPICY LAMB SOUP

Preparation time: 40 minutes
Total cooking time: 1 hour 30 minutes
Serves 4–6

2 large onions, roughly chopped
3 red chillies, seeded, chopped
   (or 2 teaspoons dried chilli)
3–4 garlic cloves
2 cm (¾ inch) piece ginger,
   chopped
1 teaspoon ground black pepper
6 cm (2½ inch) piece lemon
   grass, white only, chopped
½ teaspoon ground cardamom

2 teaspoons ground cumin
½ teaspoon ground cinnamon
1 teaspoon ground turmeric
2 tablespoons peanut oil
1.5 kg (3 lb 5 oz) lamb neck
   chops
2–3 tablespoons vindaloo
   paste
580 ml (20 fl oz/2⅓ cups)
   coconut cream
3 tablespoons soft brown sugar
2–3 tablespoons lime juice
4 makrut (kaffir lime) leaves

1 Put the onion, chilli, garlic, ginger, pepper, lemon grass and spices in a food processor. Process to a paste.

Heat half the oil in a large pan and brown the chops in batches. Remove.
2 Add the remaining oil to the pan and cook the spice and vindaloo pastes for 2–3 minutes. Add the chops and 1.75 litres (7 cups) water, cover and bring to the boil. Reduce the heat; simmer, covered, for 1 hour. Remove the chops from the pan and stir in the coconut cream. Remove the meat from the bones, shred and return to the pan.
3 Add the sugar, lime juice and leaves. Simmer, uncovered, over low heat for 20–25 minutes, until slightly thickened. Garnish with chopped coriander (cilantro) leaves.

Wear disposable gloves when working with chillies to avoid smarting and burns.

Process the onions with the chilli, garlic and spices to make a paste.

Trim away any excess fat from the chops before cooking.

CARROT AND ORANGE SOUP

Preparation time: 20 minutes
Total cooking time: 30 minutes
Serves 4

60 g (2¼ oz) butter
500 g (1 lb 2 oz) carrots, peeled
   and sliced
1 large onion, thinly sliced
1–2 teaspoons grated orange zest
1 tablespoon plain (all-purpose)
   flour
125 ml (4 fl oz/½ cup) fresh
   orange juice
1.25 litres (5 cups) chicken
   stock
185 ml (6 fl oz/¾ cup) cream
chives and orange zest, to serve

1 Heat the butter in a large pan and add the carrot, onion and orange zest; stir over low heat until the onion is softened and translucent.
2 Stir in the flour. Gradually add the juice and stock, stirring until combined. Stir over the heat until the mixture boils and thickens. Reduce the heat and allow to simmer, covered, over low heat for 25 minutes, or until the carrot is tender.
3 Cool slightly before processing in batches until smooth. Return to the pan, stir in the cream and season. Stir over gentle heat until warmed through—do not boil. Garnish with chives and orange zest.

When grating oranges only grate the zest, not the bitter white pith.

Add the juice and stock gradually and stir to prevent lumps forming.

Allow the soup to cool a little before processing to avoid hot soup splashing.

CHICKEN AND SWEETCORN SOUP

Preparation time: 25 minutes
Total cooking time: 20 minutes
Serves 4–6

2 corn cobs
1.5 litres (6 cups) chicken
   stock
235 g (8½ oz/1⅓ cups) shredded
   cooked chicken
2 cm (¾ inch) piece fresh ginger,
   peeled and finely grated
2 tablespoons cornflour
   (cornstarch)
440 g (16 oz) can creamed corn
8 spring onions (scallions),
   finely chopped
½ teaspoon sesame oil

1 Steam the corn cobs until tender (about 10–15 minutes). Cool until they are easily handled, then cut the kernels from the cobs. Discard the cobs.
2 Heat the stock in a heavy-based pan and add the corn, chicken and ginger. Reduce the heat and simmer, uncovered, for 5 minutes.
3 Blend the cornflour with 4 tablespoons water until smooth. Add to the pan, stirring continuously, and stir over medium heat until the soup boils and thickens slightly. Reduce the heat, add the creamed corn, spring onion and oil and stir gently to combine. Season, leave to simmer for 2 minutes and serve immediately.

COOK'S FILE

Variation: Fresh corn adds texture and a distinctive taste but if it isn't available, use a drained can of corn kernels instead.

Once the corn is cooked it should be easy to cut the kernels from the cobs.

Add the corn, chicken and ginger to the stock in the pan.

Add the creamed corn and spring onion when the soup has thickened a little.

Carrot and Orange Soup (top) and Chicken and Sweetcorn Soup

BOUILLABAISSE

Preparation time: 40 minutes
Total cooking time: 1 hour 30 minutes
Serves 4–6

500 g (1 lb 2 oz) raw king
    prawns (shrimp)
1 lobster tail
1–2 fish heads
250 ml (9 fl oz/1 cup) red wine
1 small and 2 medium red
    onions, finely chopped
6 garlic cloves, crushed
3 bay leaves
3 tablespoons olive oil
1 small leek, finely sliced
4–6 ripe tomatoes, peeled and
    chopped
3 tablespoons tomato paste
    (concentrated purée)
5 cm (2 inch) piece orange zest
500 g (1 lb 2 oz) white fish,
    skinned and boned, cut into
    3 cm (1¼ inch) pieces
12 mussels, beards removed
200 g (7 oz) scallops with corals
30 g (1 oz/½ cup) chopped
    parsley
3 tablespoons shredded basil
    leaves

1 Peel and devein the prawns, reserving the heads and tails. Shell the lobster tail, keeping the shell and chopping the meat. Put the fish heads, prawn shells, heads and tails and the lobster shell in a large pan. Add the wine, small onion, 2 garlic cloves, 1 bay leaf and 500 ml (17 fl oz/2 cups) water. Bring to the boil, then reduce the heat and simmer for 20 minutes. Strain, reserving the liquid.
2 Heat the oil in a large heavy-based pan. Add the leek and remaining onion and garlic. Cover and simmer, stirring occasionally, over low heat for 20 minutes, or until browned. Add the tomato, paste, remaining bay leaves and zest, stir well and season. Uncover and cook for 10 minutes, stirring often. Add the reserved fish stock, bring to the boil and keep boiling for 10 minutes, stirring often.

3 Reduce the heat, add the seafood and simmer, covered, for 4–5 minutes. Discard any mussels which haven't opened. Remove the zest and the bay leaves. Sprinkle with the parsley and basil to serve.

Remove the large black veins from the backs of the prawns.

Pull away the beards from the mussels and discard any which are already open.

You need to be firm to pull the shell away from the lobster tail.

Cook the onions slowly until they are tender and deep golden.

Grill (broil) the slices of French bread for 2–3 minutes, turning once.

Spread the cheese mixture over the slices of French bread.

Grill until the cheese has just melted and serve immediately with the soup.

FRENCH ONION SOUP WITH CAMEMBERT EN CROUTE

Preparation time: 25 minutes
Total cooking time: 1 hour 15 minutes
Serves 4–6

6 onions (about 1 kg/2 lb 4 oz)
60 g (2¼ oz) butter
1 teaspoon soft brown sugar
3 tablespoons plain (all-purpose) flour
2.25 litres (9 cups) beef stock
½ stick French bread
1–2 garlic cloves, crushed
2 tablespoons grated Cheddar cheese
125 g (4½ oz) camembert cheese, chopped
1 tablespoon chopped fresh parsley

1 Peel the onions and slice into fine rings. Heat the butter in a large heavy-based pan, add the onion and sugar and cook slowly over low heat for about 30 minutes, or until the onion is very tender and deep golden. Add the flour and cook, stirring, for 1–2 minutes, or until the flour starts to turn golden.
2 Stir in the stock, cover and simmer over low heat for 1 hour. Season well.
3 Slice the bread thinly and grill (broil) for 2–3 minutes, turning once, until lightly golden. Mash the garlic, cheeses and parsley with a fork, spread over the bread and grill until the cheese has just melted.
4 Pour the soup into bowls and top with the bread, cheese-side-up.

COOK'S FILE

Variation: For a richer soup replace 250–500 ml (9–17 fl oz/1–2 cups) of the beef stock with a good red wine.

NORWEGIAN FISH SOUP

Preparation time: 20 minutes
Total cooking time: 25 minutes
Serves 4–6

30 g (1 oz) butter
2 carrots, diced
1 parsnip, peeled and diced
1 medium leek, white part only, sliced
1 teaspoon celery seeds
500 g (1 lb 2 oz) skinned and boneless white fish fillets
500 ml (17 fl oz/2 cups) milk
185 ml (6 fl oz/¾ cup) white wine
2 teaspoons cornflour (cornstarch)
1 tablespoon milk, extra
2 egg yolks
125 g (4½ oz/½ cup) sour cream
30 g (1 oz/½ cup) chopped fresh parsley

1 Heat the butter in a large heavy-based pan, add the vegetables and celery seeds and stir over medium heat for 3 minutes, without allowing the vegetables to brown. Chop the fish into bite-sized pieces and add to the vegetables in the pan.
2 Stir in the milk and wine. Bring to the boil, reduce the heat and simmer for 15 minutes. Remove from the heat.
3 Blend the cornflour and extra milk and mix together with the egg yolks and sour cream. Add to the pan, reduce the heat and stir continuously for 3–5 minutes, or until the soup thickens a little, but doesn't boil. Stir in the parsley and season to taste.

COOK'S FILE

Storage time: The soup is best served immediately, but will keep, covered and refrigerated for up to a day. It is unsuitable to freeze.

Variations: Replace the wine and/or some of the milk with fish stock. Use cream instead of sour cream. For a less chunky soup, finely chop the vegetables in a food processor.

Stir the vegetables and celery seeds over medium heat.

Stir in the milk and white wine and bring to the boil.

Mix the blended cornflour and milk with the egg yolks and sour cream.

CREAM OF TOMATO SOUP

Preparation time: 15 minutes
Total cooking time: 25 minutes
Serves 4

1 tablespoon olive oil
1 onion, chopped
2 garlic cloves, crushed
1.2 kg (2 lb 10 oz) canned
   crushed tomatoes
750 ml (26 fl oz/3 cups) chicken
   stock

1 tablespoon tomato paste
   (concentrated purée)
2 teaspoons soft brown
   sugar
250 ml (9 fl oz/1 cup) cream

1 Heat the oil in a heavy-based pan. Add the onion and cook for 5 minutes over medium heat until soft but not brown. Add the garlic and cook for a further minute.
2 Add the tomatoes to the pan with the stock, tomato paste and sugar. Season. Bring to the boil, reduce the heat and simmer, partially covered, for 20 minutes.
3 Cool slightly and purée in batches until smooth. Return to the pan, add the cream and reheat gently.

COOK'S FILE

Note: If available, use good, fresh tomatoes. Use 1 kg (2 lb 4 oz) ripe tomatoes and 1 litre (4 cups) chicken stock. Peel the tomatoes by plunging them first in boiling water, then cold.

Cook the onion until softened and translucent but not brown.

Add the crushed tomatoes with the stock and tomato paste.

Reheat gently after stirring in the cream, but do not boil.

STILTON AND APPLE SOUP

Preparation time: 20 minutes
Total cooking time: 30 minutes
Serves 8

40 g (1½ oz) butter
2 tablespoons plain (all-purpose) flour
750 ml (26 fl oz/3 cups) chicken stock

4 red apples
500 ml (17 fl oz/2 cups) milk
250 g (9 oz) Stilton cheese
2 tablespoons chopped chives

1 Melt the butter in a large heavy-based pan. Sprinkle with the flour and stir over low heat for 2 minutes, or until lightly golden. Gradually add the stock, stirring until smooth.

2 Peel, core and slice the apples and add to the pan. Cook, covered, over medium heat for 20 minutes, or until tender. Cool, then purée in a processor in batches until smooth.

3 Return the soup to the pan, add the milk and reheat, stirring. Simmer gently and add the crumbled Stilton and chives. Stir until the soup is smooth and serve immediately.

Add the stock gradually, stirring all the time to prevent lumps forming.

To test if the apples are tender insert the tip of a sharp knife.

Add the crumbled Stilton while the soup simmers and stir until smooth.

MINESTRONE

Preparation time: 30 minutes +
  overnight soaking
Total cooking time: 2 hours 45 minutes
Serves 6–8

250 g (9 oz) dried borlotti beans
2 tablespoons oil
2 onions, chopped
2 garlic cloves, crushed
80 g (2¾ oz/½ cup) chopped
  bacon pieces
4 Roma (plum) tomatoes, peeled
  and chopped
3 tablespoons chopped fresh
  parsley

2.25 litres (9 cups) beef stock
3 tablespoons red wine
1 carrot, peeled and chopped
1 swede (rutabaga), peeled and
  diced
2 potatoes, peeled and diced
3 tablespoons tomato paste
  (concentrated purée)
2 zucchini (courgettes), sliced
80 g (2¾ oz/½ cup) green peas,
  shelled
80 g (2¾ oz/½ cup) small
  macaroni
Parmesan and pesto, to serve

1 Soak the borlotti beans in water
overnight and drain. Add to a pan of
boiling water, simmer for 15 minutes
and drain. Heat the oil in a large
heavy-based pan and cook the onion,
garlic and bacon, stirring, until the
onion is soft and the bacon golden.
2 Add the tomato, parsley, borlotti
beans, stock and red wine. Simmer,
covered, over low heat for 2 hours.
Add the carrot, swede, potato and
tomato paste, cover and simmer for
15–20 minutes.
3 Add the zucchini, peas and pasta.
Cover and simmer for 10–15 minutes,
or until the vegetables and macaroni
are tender. Season to taste and serve
topped with grated Parmesan and a
little pesto.

*Soak the borlotti beans in a bowl of water
overnight and then drain.*

*Use a sharp knife to peel and dice the
swede and other vegetables.*

*Stir the onion and bacon over the heat until
soft and golden.*

LENTIL AND VEGETABLE SOUP

Preparation time: 30 minutes +
  2 hours soaking
Total cooking time: 1 hour
Serves 8–10

280 g (10 oz/1½ cups) green
  lentils
1 tablespoon olive oil
1 onion, finely chopped
1 teaspoon ground paprika
1 teaspoon ground oregano
2 litres (8 cups) vegetable
  stock

400 g (14 oz) can tomatoes,
  chopped
3 tablespoons tomato paste
  (concentrated purée)
3 sticks celery, thinly sliced
2 medium carrots, thinly sliced
2 bay leaves
3 small zucchini (courgettes),
  thinly sliced
150 g (5½ oz) beans, cut in half

1 Soak the lentils in cold water for 2 hours and then rinse and drain well. Heat the oil in a large heavy-based pan and cook the onion over medium heat until soft but not browned, stirring occasionally (this will take about 3 minutes). Stir in the paprika and oregano and cook for a further minute.
2 Add the lentils, stock, undrained tomatoes and tomato paste to the pan; bring to the boil and then reduce the heat to low and simmer, uncovered, for 5 minutes.
3 Add the celery, carrot and bay leaves and stir well. Bring to the boil, reduce the heat and simmer, covered, for 40 minutes until thickened.
4 Add the zucchini and beans and leave to simmer, covered, for a further 10–15 minutes, or until the vegetables are tender. Remove the bay leaves before serving with crusty bread.

Soak and rinse the lentils well and pick out any which are discoloured.

Add the celery, carrot and bay leaves before bringing to the boil again.

Leave the soup to simmer, covered, for 40 minutes until it has thickened.

CREAM OF CHICKEN SOUP

Preparation time: 15 minutes
Total cooking time: 20 minutes
Serves 4–6

60 g (2¼ oz) butter
4 tablespoons plain (all-purpose)
  flour
750 ml (26 fl oz/3 cups) chicken
  stock

250 ml (9 fl oz/1 cup) milk
2 chicken breast fillets, sliced
250 ml (9 fl oz/1 cup) cream
1 stick celery, finely sliced
3 tablespoons lemon thyme
  leaves
2 spring onions (scallions),
  finely sliced

1 Melt the butter in a large pan and add the flour. Stir over low heat for 2 minutes, or until lightly golden.
2 Gradually add the stock, stirring between each addition until smooth. Stir continuously over moderate heat until the mixture boils and thickens.
3 Reduce the heat and add the milk, chicken, cream and celery. Simmer over low for 5 minutes, until chicken is cooked but tender. Season. Sprinkle with thyme and spring onions. Serve.

Stir the flour and butter over low heat until lightly golden.

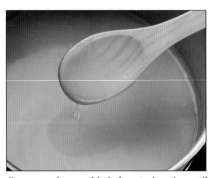

Once you have added the stock, stir until the mixture boils and thickens.

Reduce the heat and then add the milk, chicken, cream and celery.

*Lentil and Vegetable Soup (top) and
Cream of Chicken Soup*

CREAMY BEETROOT SOUP

Preparation time: 15 minutes
Total cooking time: 50 minutes
Serves 6

1 tablespoon oil
1 small onion, chopped
1.5 kg (3 lb 5 oz) beetroot,
  peeled, chopped

1.25 litres (5 cups) vegetable
  stock
2 teaspoons caraway seeds
2 tablespoons horseradish cream
250 g (9 oz) sour cream

1 Heat the oil in a heavy-based pan. Cook the onion over medium heat for 5 minutes until soft.
2 Add the beetroot, stock and seeds; bring to the boil. Simmer, partially covered, for 40 minutes.

3 Cool, then process in batches until smooth. Reheat gently and stir in the horseradish and sour cream to serve.

Storage time: Can be kept in the fridge for 1 day. Add the sour cream and horseradish when you reheat.

Peel the beetroot with a potato peeler before dicing the flesh.

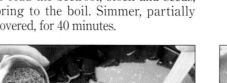

Add the beetroot, stock and caraway seeds and bring to the boil.

Stir in the horseradish and sour cream after processing the soup.

CHICKEN NOODLE SOUP

Preparation time: 20 minutes
Total cooking time: 20–25 minutes
Serves 4–6

2.25 litres (9 cups) chicken
 stock
175 g (6 oz) shredded cooked
 chicken

100 g (3½ oz) broken thin
 noodles
3 tablespoons chopped fresh
 chives
45 g (1½ oz/¾ cup) chopped
 fresh parsley

1 Put the stock in a pan and bring to the boil. Add the shredded chicken.
2 Add the noodles, chives and parsley to the pan and simmer over low heat for 15–20 minutes, or until the chicken is hot and noodles are tender. Season, then spoon into bowls. Serve immediately.

COOK'S FILE

Hint: The noodles must be added immediately before serving, otherwise they will soften too much and become soggy if left to stand.

To finely shred the cooked chicken pull it apart with two forks.

Add the thin noodles to the pan of stock and shredded chicken.

Simmer until the chicken is hot and the noodles tender.

35

WHOLE GREEN PEA SOUP

Preparation time: 20 minutes + 1 hour
soaking
Total cooking time: 40 minutes
Serves 6

1 kg (2 lb 4 oz) green peas in the
pod
1 litre (4 cups) vegetable stock
30 g (1 oz) butter
1 small onion, sliced
2 tablespoons finely chopped
flat-leaf (Italian) parsley
2 tablespoons olive oil
4 thick slices bread, cut into
1 cm (½ inch) cubes

1 Shell the peas and set aside. Cut the stringy tops from the pods and discard them. Wash the pods thoroughly and place in a large bowl. Cover with cold water and leave to stand for 1 hour. Drain the pods well and put them in a large heavy-based pan. Add the stock and bring to the boil, reduce the heat and simmer, covered, for 15 minutes, or until the pods are tender. Leave to cool slightly.

2 Put the pods and stock in batches into a food processor or blender and process for 30 seconds, until smooth. Strain the purée, discarding the pods.

3 Melt the butter in a pan, add the onion and cook over medium heat until soft. Add the peas, parsley and 250 ml (9 fl oz/1 cup) water, bring to the boil, reduce heat to low and cook, covered, for 15 minutes until tender.

4 Heat the oil in a frying pan, add the bread cubes and cook until lightly brown. Remove them from the pan and leave to drain on paper towels.

5 Add the purée of pea pods to the simmering peas and stir through. Bring to the boil, then reduce the heat and simmer for 5 minutes to heat through. Season and serve sprinkled with the croutons.

COOK'S FILE

Variation: Add 125 ml (4 fl oz/½ cup) of cream at the end and heat through.
Hint: If the pea pods seem quite tough remove the tails as well as tops.

Shell the peas and set them aside, but keep the pods.

Simmer the pods in stock for 15 minutes until they are tender.

Fry the bread cubes in hot oil until lightly brown and then drain on paper towels.

Add the strained purée of pea pods to the simmering peas.

ROASTED RED CAPSICUM SOUP

Preparation time: 50 minutes
Total cooking time: 1 hour
Serves 6

4 large red capsicums (peppers)
4 medium ripe tomatoes
2 tablespoons oil
1 red onion, chopped
1 garlic clove, crushed
1 litre (4 cups) vegetable stock
1 teaspoon sweet chilli sauce
Pesto and Parmesan, to garnish

1 Cut the capsicums into large flat pieces, removing the seeds and membrane. Place skin-side-up under a hot grill (broiler) until blackened. Leave covered with a tea towel until cool. Peel the skin and chop the flesh.
2 Cut a small cross in the base of each tomato, put in a large heatproof bowl and cover with boiling water. Leave for 1 minute, plunge into cold water and peel the skin from the cross. Cut in half, scoop out the seeds and roughly chop the flesh.
3 Heat the oil in a large heavy-based pan and add the onion. Cook over medium heat for 10 minutes, stirring frequently, until very soft. Add the garlic and cook for a further minute. Add the capsicum, tomato and stock; bring to the boil, reduce the heat and simmer for about 20 minutes.
4 Allow the soup to cool slightly before processing in batches until smooth. Return to the pan to reheat gently and stir in the chilli sauce (vary the amount according to your taste). This soup is delicious topped with pesto and shavings of Parmesan.

Once the skin of the capsicum has been blackened it should peel away easily.

Cutting a cross in the base of the tomato makes it easier to remove the skin.

Use a spoon to scoop out the seeds from the tomatoes once they have been peeled.

SPICY CHICKEN BROTH WITH CORIANDER PASTA

Preparation time: 40 minutes
Total cooking time: 50 minutes
Serves 4

350 g (12 oz) chicken thighs or
    wings, skin removed
2 carrots, finely chopped
2 sticks celery, finely chopped
2 small leeks, finely chopped
3 egg whites
1.5 litres (6 cups) chicken stock
Tabasco sauce

Coriander pasta
60 g (2¼ oz/½ cup) plain
    (all-purpose) flour
1 egg
½ teaspoon sesame oil
small bunch coriander (cilantro)
    leaves

1 Put the chicken, carrot, celery and leek in a large heavy-based pan. Push the chicken to one side and add the egg whites to the vegetables. Using a wire whisk, beat for a minute or so until frothy (take care not to use a pan that can be scratched by the whisk).
2 Warm the stock in another pan, then add gradually to the first pan, whisking continuously to froth the egg whites. Continue whisking while slowly bringing to the boil. Make a hole in the froth on top with a spoon and leave to simmer, uncovered, for 30 minutes without stirring.
3 Line a large strainer with a damp tea towel or double thickness of muslin and strain the broth into a clean bowl (discard the chicken and vegetables). Season with salt, pepper and Tabasco to taste. Set aside.

4 To make the coriander pasta, sift the flour into a bowl and make a well in the centre. Whisk the egg and oil together and pour into the well. Mix together to make a soft pasta dough and knead on a lightly floured surface for 2 minutes, until smooth.
5 Divide the dough into four even portions. Roll one portion out very thinly and cover with a layer of evenly spaced coriander leaves. Roll out another portion of pasta and lay on top of the leaves, then gently roll the layers together. Repeat with the remaining pasta and coriander.
6 Cut out squares of pasta around the leaves. The pasta may be left to sit and dry out if it is not needed immediately. When you are ready to serve, heat the chicken broth gently in a saucepan. As the broth simmers, add the pasta and cook for 1 minute. Serve immediately.

COOK'S FILE

Hint: Beg, borrow or steal a pasta machine for making this fine, delicate pasta. A rolling pin will suffice if necessary but try to roll the pasta as thinly as possible.
Note: The egg whites added to the vegetable and chicken stock make the broth very clear rather than leaving it with the normal cloudy appearance of chicken stock. This is called clarifying the stock. When you strain the broth through muslin or a tea towel, don't press the solids to extract the extra liquid or the broth will become cloudy. It is necessary to make a hole in the froth on top to prevent the stock boiling over.

Use a wire whisk to beat the egg whites and vegetables.

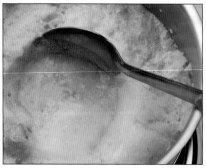

Use a metal spoon to make a hole in the froth on top of the soup.

Strain the broth through a damp tea towel or double thickness of muslin.

Knead the dough on a lightly floured surface until it is smooth.

Lay a second layer of thin pasta over the coriander leaves.

Cut out neat squares of pasta around each coriander leaf.

CLAM CHOWDER

Preparation time: 35 minutes
Total cooking time: 40 minutes
Serves 4

1.5 kg (3 lb 5 oz) fresh clams
    (vongole) in shell
1 tablespoon oil
3 rashers bacon, chopped
1 onion, chopped
1 garlic clove, crushed
4 potatoes, cubed
310 ml (10¾ fl oz/1¼ cups) fish
    stock
500 ml (17 fl oz/2 cups) milk
125 ml (4 fl oz/½ cup) cream
3 tablespoons chopped fresh
    parsley

1 Discard any clams which are already open. Put the remainder in a large heavy-based pan with 250 ml (9 fl oz/1 cup) water and simmer, covered, over low heat for 5 minutes, or until the shells open (discard any clams which do not open during cooking). Strain the liquid and reserve. Remove the clam meat from the shells, discarding the shells.

2 Heat the oil in a clean pan and then add the bacon, onion and garlic. Cook, stirring, until the onion is soft and the bacon golden. Add the potato and stir to combine.

3 Measure the reserved clam liquid and add enough water to make it up to 310 ml (10¾ fl oz/1¼ cups). Add this to the pan with the stock and milk. Bring to the boil and then reduce the heat, cover and simmer for 20 minutes, or until the potato is tender.

4 Uncover and leave to simmer for a further 10 minutes, or until reduced and slightly thickened. Add the cream, clam meat, salt and pepper to taste and parsley. Heat through before serving but do not allow to boil or the flavour will be impaired.

COOK'S FILE

Variation: Fresh clams, often available at fish markets, give the best flavour but you can use canned. Don't use the brine from the can—drain them before using and make up the liquid with fresh fish stock.

Use your fingers to remove the clam meat from the shells.

Add the potato cubes to the cooked bacon, onion and garlic.

Simmer the chowder for 20 minutes, or until the potato is tender.

Add the cream, clam meat and parsley and then heat through gently.

ROASTED PUMPKIN SOUP

Preparation time: 20 minutes
Total cooking time: 1 hour 35 minutes
Serves 6–8

1 kg (2 lb 4 oz) pumpkin, cut
  into small chunks, skin on
2 tablespoons olive oil
1 red onion, chopped
2 garlic cloves, crushed
4 potatoes, peeled and cut into
  2 cm (¾ inch) cubes
1.125 litres (4½ cups) vegetable
  stock

125 ml (4 fl oz/½ cup) cream
10 fresh basil leaves, shredded

1 Preheat the oven to 180°C (350°F/ Gas 4). Put the pumpkin on an oven tray, sprinkle with water and cook for 30–35 minutes, or until tender. Scoop out the flesh, discarding the skin. Mash and set aside.

2 Heat the oil in a heavy-based pan. Add the onion and garlic and cook over medium heat for 4 minutes until soft and lightly browned. Add the roasted pumpkin, potato, and 875 ml (30 fl oz/3½ cups) of the stock. Stir well and bring to the boil. Reduce the heat, cover and simmer for 45 minutes, or until the mixture breaks down and thickens. Season to taste.

3 Stir in the remaining stock. Bring to the boil and simmer for 10 minutes, or until the soup reaches the desired consistency. Serve with a swirl of cream and shredded basil leaves.

COOK'S FILE

Variation: Try using butternut or little golden nugget pumpkin: either of these will give a sweeter flavour.

Cut the pumpkin into chunks and put on an oven tray for roasting.

The roasted flesh should be soft and easy to scoop out with a spoon.

Leave the soup to simmer until the mixture has broken down and thickened.

VICHYSSOISE

Preparation time: 25 minutes
Total cooking time: 15–20 minutes
Serves 4–6

60 g (2¼ oz) butter
2 leeks, chopped
2 large potatoes, chopped
750 ml (26 fl oz/3 cups) chicken
   stock
250 ml (9 fl oz/1 cup) milk
sour cream, for serving
chives, chopped, for serving

1 Heat the butter in a medium pan and cook the leeks until soft.
2 Add the potato and chicken stock and simmer for 15–20 minutes, or until the potato is tender. Stir in the milk and season with salt and freshly ground black pepper.
3 Cool, then blend in batches until smooth. Vichyssoise is traditionally served well-chilled, but if you prefer, return to the pan and reheat gently without boiling. Whether hot or chilled, spoon sour cream on top and sprinkle with chives to serve.

COOK'S FILE

Note: Vichyssoise is a classic chilled cream soup created by the Ritz-Carlton Hotel in New York.

Cook the leeks in butter in a medium pan until they are soft.

Once the potato is tender, stir in the milk, and then season to taste.

Allow the soup to cool to make it easier and safer to process.

When hard-boiling eggs start them off in cold water to prevent the shells cracking.

To skin the tomatoes leave them in a bowl of boiling water for 2 minutes.

Chop the tomato flesh finely—it is best to do this in 2 batches.

Stir all the soup ingredients together in a large bowl before chilling.

GAZPACHO

Preparation time: 30 minutes
Total cooking time: Nil
Serves 4–6

750 g (1 lb 10 oz) ripe tomatoes
1 Lebanese (short) cucumber, diced
1 large green capsicum (pepper), diced
2–3 garlic cloves, crushed
2 tablespoons diced black olives
3 tablespoons olive oil
4 tablespoons red or white wine vinegar
1 tablespoon tomato paste (concentrated purée)

Accompaniments
1 red onion, diced
1 small red capsicum (pepper), diced
2 spring onions (scallions), finely sliced
2 hard-boiled eggs, chopped
1 Lebanese (short) cucumber, diced
chopped fresh marjoram, mint or parsley
croutons

1 Cut a cross in the base of each tomato and put in a bowl of boiling water. Leave for 2 minutes, then transfer to a bowl of cold water. Drain and peel away the skin from the cross. Chop the flesh so finely that it is almost a purée.
2 Put the tomato in a large bowl; stir in the remaining ingredients and season to taste. Mix well, cover and refrigerate for 2–3 hours.
3 Use 500–750 ml (17–26 fl oz/2–3 cups) of chilled water to thin the soup to your taste. Serve well chilled, with small bowls of red onion, capsicum, spring onion, boiled egg, cucumber, fresh herbs and croutons in the centre of the table. Diners can add their own choice of accompaniments to their individual bowls.

43

WON TON SOUP

Preparation time: 45 minutes
Total cooking time: 20 minutes
Serves 4–6

4 dried Chinese mushrooms
4 spring onions (scallions), very
    finely sliced, to garnish
125 g (4½ oz) minced (ground)
    pork and veal
60 g (2¼ oz) raw prawn
    (shrimp) meat, finely
    chopped
3 teaspoons soy sauce
1 teaspoon sesame oil
1 spring onion (scallion), finely
    sliced
2 teaspoons grated ginger
1 tablespoon finely chopped
    water chestnuts
24 won ton wrappers
1.25 litres (5 cups) chicken
    stock

1 Cover the mushrooms in hot water and soak for 30 minutes. Meanwhile, put the very fine strips of spring onion in a bowl of icy cold water (this makes the strips curl).

2 Squeeze the mushrooms dry with your hands. Remove the stems and chop the caps finely. Mix together the mushrooms, mince, prawn meat, soy sauce, sesame oil, spring onion, ginger, water chestnuts and salt to taste.

3 Working with one won ton wrapper at a time (cover the rest with a damp tea towel), place a teaspoon of the filling in the centre of each wrapper. Moisten the edges with a little water and bring the sides up to form a pouch. Set aside on a plate dusted with flour while making the rest.

4 Cook the won tons in batches in a large pan of rapidly boiling water for 4–5 minutes; remove and drain. Bring the stock to the boil in another pan. Put the won tons in small bowls, garnish with the curls of spring onion and pour in the hot stock.

COOK'S FILE

Note: Won ton wrappers are available from Asian food stores and can be frozen very successfully.

Slice the spring onions very finely and leave in iced water to make them curl.

Gently squeeze the excess liquid from the rehydrated mushrooms.

Moisten the edges of the wrapper and bring the sides up to make a pouch.

Cook the won tons in batches in a large pan of rapidly boiling water.

JERUSALEM ARTICHOKE SOUP

Preparation time: 20 minutes
Total cooking time: 55 minutes
Serves 4

1 kg (2 lb 4 oz) Jerusalem artichokes, peeled
25 g (1 oz) butter
1 onion, finely chopped

625 ml (21½ fl oz/2½ cups) chicken stock
250 ml (9 fl oz/1 cup) milk
170 ml (5½ fl oz/⅔ cup) cream

1 Cut any large artichokes so they are all an even size. Melt the butter in a large heavy-based pan and add the artichoke and onion. Cook over low heat, covered, for 10 minutes, stirring occasionally: they should not brown.

2 Add the stock and milk and bring to the boil. Reduce the heat, cover and simmer for 40 minutes, or until the vegetables are very soft.

3 Cool, then purée in batches until very smooth. Return to the pan, reheat gently, season and add the cream.

COOK'S FILE

Note: Jerusalem artichoke is related to the sunflower rather than the globe artichoke. 'Jerusalem' is derived from *girasole,* Italian for sunflower.

Scrub the artichokes well and peel with a potato peeler.

Cut the artichokes so that they are all an even size.

Leave the soup to simmer for 40 minutes until the vegetables are soft.

45

SPICY RED LENTIL SOUP

Preparation time: 15 minutes
Total cooking time: 35 minutes
Serves 4–6

2 tablespoons oil
1 medium onion, finely chopped
1 teaspoon ground cumin
1 teaspoon ground coriander
¼ teaspoon ground allspice
2 garlic cloves, crushed

An easy way to crush garlic is to bruise and scrape it with the side of a knife.

500 g (1 lb 2 oz) red lentils
1.25–1.5 litres (5–6 cups)
    vegetable stock
4 tablespoons thick plain
    yoghurt

1 Heat the oil in a heavy-based pan. Cook the onion over medium heat for 5 minutes, until soft. Stir in the spices and garlic for 1 minute.
2 Add the lentils, stirring to coat well with spices. Pour in the stock and stir well. Bring to the boil, then reduce the

Add the spices and garlic to the softened onion and cook for 1 minute further.

heat and simmer, partially covered with a loose-fitting lid, for 30 minutes.
3 Add a little more vegetable stock if you prefer a thinner soup and serve with a dollop of yoghurt on top.

Storage time: This soup will keep for 1 day in the fridge, but becomes quite thick on standing—thin it down with stock or water.
Note: Red lentils do not need soaking prior to cooking.

Add the lentils to the pan and stir them well to coat with spices.

TOM KHA GAI

Preparation time: 20 minutes
Total cooking time: 10 minutes
Serves 4

625 ml (21½ fl oz/2½ cups)
    chicken stock
2 makrut (kaffir lime) leaves
5 cm (2 inch) piece lemon grass,
    white part only, finely
    chopped
3 cm (1¼ inch) piece galangal,
    cut into 4 pieces lengthways
2 tablespoons fish sauce
2 tablespoons lime juice

Lemon grass, makrut leaves and galangal are available from Asian stores.

1 chicken breast fillet, finely
    sliced
120 g (4¼ oz) drained canned
    straw mushrooms
375 ml (13 fl oz/1½ cups)
    coconut milk
3–4 teaspoons palm sugar
    (jaggery)
2 small red chillies, split
hot chilli sauce, to serve

1 Heat the stock in a medium pan, add the lime leaves, lemon grass, galangal, fish sauce and lime juice. Bring to the boil.
2 Add the chicken, mushrooms and coconut milk. Reduce the heat and

Add the chicken, straw mushrooms and coconut milk.

simmer for 3–5 minutes, stirring all the time, until the chicken is cooked.
3 Add the sugar and chillies and cook for 1 minute. Serve garnished with hot chilli sauce.

Hint: When working with chillies avoid smarting by wearing a pair of disposable gloves (or wash your hands thoroughly with soapy water before touching your eyes or lips).

Add the palm sugar and small red chillies and cook for 1 minute further.

Spicy Red Lentil Soup (top) and Tom Kha Gai

CHEESE SOUP

Preparation time: 20 minutes
Total cooking time: 15 minutes
Serves 4–6

75 g (2½ oz) butter
3 spring onions (scallions),
    finely chopped
60 g (2¼ oz/½ cup) plain
    (all-purpose) flour

875 ml (30 fl oz/3½ cups)
    chicken stock
250 ml (9 fl oz/1 cup) milk
100 g (3½ oz) pumpkin,
    grated
150 g (5½ oz) grated Cheddar
crusty bread rolls, to serve

1 Melt the butter in a heavy-based pan and cook the spring onion for 3 minutes, until soft. Add the flour and stir for 2 minutes until smooth. Add the combined stock and milk gradually, stirring until smooth.
2 Add the pumpkin and bring to the boil, then reduce the heat and simmer for 10 minutes. Stir in the cheese until melted and smooth.
3 Cut the tops from the bread rolls and hollow out the centres. Heat in a preheated 180°C (350°F/Gas 4) oven until warm, then use as soup bowls.

Peel the pumpkin and finely grate it using the coarse side of a grater.

Add the stock and milk gradually and stir continuously to prevent lumps forming.

Add the grated cheese to the pan and stir until melted and smooth.

HOMESTYLE VEGETABLE SOUP

Preparation time: 25 minutes + overnight soaking
Total cooking time: 55 minutes
Serves 6

220 g (8 oz) dried soup mix
2 tablespoons oil
1 large onion, finely chopped
1 green capsicum (pepper), chopped

2 zucchini (courgettes), sliced
2 sticks celery, sliced
125 g (4½ oz) button mushrooms, sliced
2 carrots, sliced
1 large potato, chopped
500 g (1 lb 2 oz) pumpkin, peeled, chopped
2 litres (8 cups) vegetable stock

1 Soak the soup mix in water for 8 hours, then drain. Heat the oil in a large heavy-based pan and cook the onion for 5 minutes, until soft. Add the capsicum, zucchini, celery and mushrooms and cook for 5 minutes.

2 Add the sliced carrot, potato and pumpkin and stir to combine. Pour in the stock and add the soup mix; bring to the boil, then reduce the heat.

3 Partially cover the pan and simmer for 45 minutes, until the vegetables and soup mix are very soft.

COOK'S FILE

Storage time: Keep for 2 days in the refrigerator or freeze for 1 month.

Cover the soup mix with water and leave to soak and rehydrate.

Pour the stock into the pan over the chopped vegetables.

Partially cover the pan and simmer until the vegetables are very soft.

Stir-ins

Quick and easy to make, these vegetarian stir-ins are a fabulous way to dress up your soups. Serve them on the table for diners to help themselves, or add a generous dollop to each bowl when you're dishing up. Either way, they turn a simple bowl of soup into something quite special.

SPICED CARROT PURÉE

Melt 50 g (1¾ oz) butter in a medium pan. Peel and finely chop 500 g (1 lb 2 oz) carrots and add to the butter, stirring until they are well coated. Add 1 teaspoon each ground cumin and coriander, ½ teaspoon ground cinnamon and a pinch each of ground cloves and nutmeg. Cook over medium heat for 3–4 minutes. Cover and cook for a further 10 minutes. Remove the lid, add 125 ml (4 fl oz/½ cup) vegetable stock and simmer for 15 minutes. Place the carrots and the liquid into a blender and blend until smooth. Season to taste with salt and freshly cracked pepper. Shown here with Lentil and spinach soup (page 80) but also delicious with French onion or most meat soups. Serves 6.

ROUILLE

Cut 1 large red capsicum (pepper) in half and remove the seeds and white membrane. Place skin-side-up under a preheated hot grill (broiler). Cook for 5 minutes, or until the skin has charred and blackened. Place in a plastic bag and allow to cool, then peel away the skin. Roughly chop and place in a food processor. Cut 1 potato into cubes. Cook until tender and, while still warm, place in the food processor with 2 chopped garlic cloves and 1 egg yolk. Process until smooth. With the motor running, gradually pour in 125ml (4 fl oz/½ cup) olive oil in a thin stream, until you have a thick mixture. Shown here with Bouillabaisse (page 26) but also good with most fish soups. Serves 6.

From left to right: Spiced carrot purée; Rouille; Aïoli; Rocket and sun-dried tomato pesto; Coriander pesto; Yoghurt and herb stir-in.

AÏOLI

Crush 6–8 garlic cloves and place in a food processor. Add 2 egg yolks and a pinch of salt and process until well combined. With the motor running, very slowly add 250 ml (9 fl oz/1 cup) olive oil, in a thin stream. Shown here with Spicy tomato and chickpea soup (page 100). Serves 6.

ROCKET AND SUN-DRIED TOMATO PESTO

Add 70 g (2¼ oz/2 cups) finely shredded rocket (arugula) leaves to a food processor. Add 2 crushed garlic cloves and 50 g (1¾ oz/½ cup) finely grated Parmesan. Finely chop 3 tablespoons sun-dried tomatoes and add to the rocket. Process until finely chopped. Add 3 tablespoons olive oil and process again until well combined. Shown here with Roasted tomato soup (page 86) but good with most vegetable soups. Serves 6.

CORIANDER PESTO

Place 100 g (3½ oz/2 cups) chopped coriander (cilantro) leaves and stems into a food processor. Finely chop 3 garlic cloves and add to the processor along with 50 g (1¾ oz/ ½ cup) grated Parmesan and a pinch of salt. Process until finely chopped. With the motor running, gradually add 3 tablespoons olive oil, processing until all the ingredients are combined. Shown here with Spring vegetable soup (page 89) and good with vegetable broths. Serves 6.

YOGHURT AND HERB STIR-IN

Combine 185 g (6½ oz/¾ cup) thick plain yoghurt with 2 crushed garlic cloves, 3 tablespoons finely chopped mint and 2 tablespoons finely chopped coriander (cilantro). Stir through 1 tablespoon lemon juice and season well. Add a generous spoonful to Borscht, Mulligatawny or Roasted pumpkin soup (page 41), as shown here. Serves 6.

51

GARLIC SOUP

Preparation time: 20 minutes
Total cooking time: 25 minutes
Serves 4

1 garlic bulb (about 20 cloves)
2 large sprigs thyme
1 litre (4 cups) chicken stock
4 tablespoons cream
4 thick slices white bread
fresh thyme, to garnish

1 Crush each clove of garlic with the side of a knife. Discard the skin and place the garlic in a large pan with the thyme, stock and 250 ml (9 fl oz/1 cup) water. Bring to the boil, then reduce the heat and simmer gently for 20 minutes.
2 Strain the soup through a fine sieve into a clean pan. Add the cream and reheat gently, without allowing to boil. Season to taste.
3 Trim and discard the crusts from the bread and cut the bread into cubes about 3 cm (1¼ inch) square. Spread these out on a flat oven tray and cook in a preheated 180°C (350°F/Gas 4) oven for 5–10 minutes, until lightly golden. Put the bread into four serving bowls and pour the soup over the bread. Garnish with extra thyme and serve immediately.

COOK'S FILE

Storage time: Best served the same day. The bread cubes may be cooked up to 4 hours in advance and kept in an airtight container until required.
Note: The after-effects of the garlic are minimal as it has been boiled.

Bruise the cloves of garlic with the side of a knife and then discard the skin.

Strain the soup through a fine sieve into a clean pan.

Bake the bread in the oven until toasted and lightly golden.

AUTUMN GARDEN SOUP

Preparation time: 35 minutes
Total cooking time: 55 minutes
Serves 6

30 g (1 oz) butter
1 large leek, sliced
1 garlic clove, crushed
1 teaspoon grated ginger
2 parsnips, peeled and chopped
1 medium celeriac, peeled and
    chopped

2 large carrots, chopped
3 potatoes, chopped
2 turnips, peeled and chopped
1.125 litres (4½ cups) vegetable
    stock
2 tablespoons chopped
    chives

1 Melt the butter in a large heavy-based pan and add the leek. Cook over low heat for 15 minutes until very soft and lightly golden.
2 Add the garlic and ginger and cook, stirring, for 1 minute further. Add the vegetables and stock to the pan and bring to the boil.
3 Reduce heat to simmer, partially covered, for about 40 minutes until very soft. Stir in the chives and serve.

COOK'S FILE

Storage time: The soup will keep for up to 2 days in the refrigerator.
Hint: The soup becomes very thick on standing—thin with stock or water.

Peel away the outer rough surface of the celeriac with a potato peeler.

Cook the leek until soft and golden and then add the garlic and ginger.

Simmer for about 40 minutes, until the vegetables are very soft.

53

ZUCCHINI SOUP

Preparation time: 15 minutes
Total cooking time: 30 minutes
Serves 4

40 g (1½ oz) butter
1 onion, chopped
4 zucchini (courgettes), sliced
1 tablespoon plain (all-purpose)
    flour
500 ml (17 fl oz/2 cups) chicken
    stock

500 ml (17 fl oz/2 cups) milk
1 teaspoon chopped fresh thyme
125 ml (4 fl oz/½ cup) cream
4 tablespoons finely grated
    Parmesan cheese

1 Melt the butter in a large pan and cook the onion, covered, over low heat for 5 minutes, until soft but not browned. Add the zucchini and cook, covered, for a further 5 minutes.
2 Add the flour to the pan and stir over low heat for 1 minute. Gradually add the stock and milk, stirring after

each addition. Add the thyme and increase the heat to bring to the boil.
3 Reduce the heat and simmer for 15 minutes. Cool slightly, then purée in batches until smooth. Reheat gently and add the cream and Parmesan. Stir until the cheese has melted, but do not allow the soup to boil. Season to taste before serving.

COOK'S FILE

Storage time: Refrigerate for 1 day without the cream and cheese—add these when you reheat.

Add the stock and milk gradually, stirring after each addition.

Add the chopped fresh thyme and return to the heat.

Do not allow the soup to boil again once you have added the cream and cheese.

Add the spices to the pan with the onion and stir to thoroughly combine.

Add the stock to the mixture of spices and vegetables.

Saffron threads are expensive but will add a subtle flavour and golden colour.

Do not stir in the couscous until you are ready to serve the soup.

CHICKEN AND COUSCOUS SOUP

Preparation time: 25 minutes
Total cooking time: 30 minutes
Serves 6

1 tablespoon olive oil
1 onion, sliced
½ teaspoon ground cumin
½ teaspoon paprika
1 teaspoon grated ginger
1 garlic clove, crushed
2 sticks celery, sliced
2 small carrots, sliced
2 zucchini (courgettes), sliced
1.125 litres (4½ cups) chicken stock
2 chicken breast fillets, sliced
pinch of saffron threads, optional
95 g (3¼ oz/½ cup) instant couscous
2 tablespoons chopped parsley

1 Heat the oil in a large pan. Add the onion and cook over medium heat for 10 minutes until very soft, stirring occasionally. Add the spices, ginger and garlic and stir for 1 minute.
2 Add the celery, carrot and zucchini and stir to coat with spices. Stir in the stock. Bring to the boil, then reduce the heat and simmer, partially covered, for about 15 minutes, until the vegetables are tender.
3 Add the chicken and saffron threads to the pan and cook for about 5 minutes, until the chicken is just tender; do not overcook. Stir in the couscous and parsley and serve.

COOK'S FILE

Hint: Add the couscous to the soup just before serving: it absorbs liquid quickly and becomes very thick.

CARIBBEAN BLACK BEAN SOUP

Preparation time: 20 minutes +
 overnight soaking
Total cooking time: 1 hour 30 minutes
Serves 6

440 g (15½ oz) dried black
 beans
2 tablespoons oil
1 large onion, sliced
1 teaspoon ground coriander
2 teaspoons ground cumin
½ teaspoon chilli powder
2 garlic cloves, crushed
300 g (10½ oz) bacon bones
2 tablespoons red wine
 vinegar
1 tablespoon soft brown sugar
3 spring onions (scallions),
 finely chopped
1 tablespoon chopped parsley
2 hard-boiled eggs, chopped

1 Put the black beans in a large bowl, cover with water and leave to soak overnight. Drain.
2 Heat the oil in a large pan, cook the onion over medium heat for 5 minutes, until softened. Add the coriander, cumin, chilli powder and garlic to the pan and cook for 1 minute.
3 Add the bacon bones and 1.125 litres (4½ cups) water, stirring well to scrape the spices from the base of the pan. Add the drained black beans and bring to the boil, then reduce the heat and simmer, partially covered, for 1–1½ hours, until the beans are very soft.
4 Use a pair of tongs or forks to remove the bacon bones from the pan and discard. Stir in the vinegar and sugar. Season. For a thicker soup, mash the beans slightly with a potato masher. Garnish with spring onions, parsley and hard-boiled egg to serve.

COOK'S FILE

Note: Black beans are also known as turtle beans and are available at good delicatessens. They are not to be confused with Chinese black beans.
Storage time: Keeps, covered and refrigerated, for up to 2 days, but will become very thick. Thin down with chicken stock or water to reheat.

Add the cumin coriander, chilli powder and garlic to the softened onion.

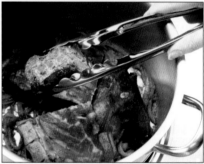

Add the bacon bones to the spices and onion in the pan.

Add the black beans to the pan and bring to the boil.

Use a pair of tongs to lift the bacon bones from the pan and discard.

CORN CHOWDER

Preparation time: 10 minutes
Total cooking time: 30 minutes
Serves 6

60 g (2¼ oz) butter
1 large onion, finely chopped
1 garlic clove, crushed
2 potatoes, cubed
1 litre (4 cups) chicken stock

420 g (15 oz) can creamed corn
420 g (15 oz) can corn kernels,
  drained
pinch cayenne pepper, optional
3 tablespoons cream
2 tablespoons chopped chives

1 Heat the butter in a large heavy-based pan and cook the onion, stirring, for 5 minutes, or until soft and lightly golden. Add the garlic and cook for a further minute.

2 Add the potato and stock and bring to the boil. Reduce the heat and leave to simmer for 10 minutes, add the cans of creamed corn and drained corn kernels and simmer for a further 10 minutes.

3 Season with salt, pepper and cayenne pepper to taste and stir in the cream and chives. Reheat gently, without allowing the soup to come to the boil, and serve immediately.

Stir-fry the onion in butter until it is soft and golden.

Add the cans of creamed corn and corn kernels to the simmering soup.

Stir in the cream and chives at the end of cooking time.

SEAFOOD LAKSA

Preparation time: 45 minutes
Total cooking time: 40–45 minutes
Serves 4–6

1 kg (2 lb 4 oz) medium raw
  prawns (shrimp)
125 ml (4 fl oz/½ cup) oil
2–6 large red chillies, seeded
1 large onion, roughly chopped
3 garlic cloves, peeled
2 cm (¾ inch) piece ginger or
  galangal
1 teaspoon turmeric
1 tablespoon ground coriander
3 x 6 cm (2½ inch) stalks lemon
  grass, white part only
1–2 teaspoons shrimp paste
600 ml (21 fl oz) coconut
  cream
4 makrut (kaffir lime) leaves
2 teaspoons salt
2 teaspoons palm sugar
  (jaggery)
200 g (7 oz) packet fish balls
190 g (6¾ oz) packet fried bean
  curd pieces
250 g (9 oz) thin fresh egg
  noodles
250 g (9 oz) fresh bean sprouts
4 tablespoons chopped fresh
  mint, to serve
3 tablespoons coriander
  (cilantro) leaves, to serve

1 Peel and devein the prawns (use a toothpick or large needle to remove the vein without having to cut the prawn). Leave the tails intact and reserve the heads and shells.
2 Heat 2 tablespoons of the oil in a large pan, add the prawn heads and shells and stir-fry until the heads are bright orange. Add 1 litre (4 cups) water, bring to the boil, then reduce the heat and simmer for 15 minutes. Strain the stock, discarding the shells.
3 Place the chillies, onion, garlic, ginger, turmeric, coriander, lemon grass and 3 tablespoons of the prawn stock in a food processor and process until almost smooth.
4 Heat the remaining oil in the clean pan, add the processed mixture and shrimp paste. Stir over low heat for 3 minutes, until fragrant. Add the prawn stock and leave to simmer for 10 minutes. Add the coconut cream, lime leaves, salt and sugar and allow to simmer, uncovered, for a further 5 minutes.
5 Add the prawns to the pan and simmer for 2 minutes until they are just pink. Lift the prawns out of the laksa with a slotted spoon and set aside. Add the fish balls and bean curd and simmer gently.
6 Bring a pan of water to the boil, add the noodles, cook for 2 minutes and drain. Remove the tails from the bean sprouts. Put the noodles in a large tureen or individual bowls and top with bean sprouts and prawns. Ladle the hot soup into the bowls and sprinkle with mint and coriander leaves to serve. For a really fiery soup, garnish with extra sliced red chilli.

COOK'S FILE

Note: Laksa originated in Singapore and can also be made using fresh or dried rice noodles. Shredded cucumber can be added with the bean sprouts.
Variation: Laksa can be made without the fish balls and bean curd. Instead, use a combination of seafood or replace the seafood with bite-sized pieces of chicken or pork.

Chopping chillies can lead to smarting eyes and skin so wear gloves.

Peel and devein the prawns, leaving the tails intact and reserving the heads.

Stir-fry the prawn heads and shells until they are bright orange.

Process the onion, garlic and spices with a little prawn stock until almost smooth.

Add the prawns and cook for 2 minutes until they are just pink.

Add the fish balls. Cut the bean curd into triangles for a traditional laksa.

59

GOULASH SOUP

Preparation time: 15 minutes
Total cooking time: 1 hour 15 minutes
Serves 4–6

650 g (1 lb 7 oz) blade steak
2 tablespoons oil
1 large leek, sliced
2 garlic cloves , crushed
1 teaspoon paprika
1 teaspoon caraway seeds
400 g (14 oz) can crushed
   tomatoes
1 litre (4 cups) beef stock
2 potatoes, diced
sour cream, to serve

1 Cut the meat into small cubes. Heat the oil in a—large pan, brown the meat in batches and set aside.

2 Add the leek to the pan and cook for 5 minutes until soft. Add the garlic and paprika and cook for 1 minute. Add the seeds, tomatoes, stock and meat. Bring to the boil, then simmer, partially covered, for 30 minutes.

3 Add the potatoes and simmer for 30 minutes, until very tender. Serve with sour cream.

COOK'S FILE

Storage time: The soup will keep for up to 2 days in the refrigerator.

Trim the blade steak of any fat and sinew when you cut it into small cubes.

Brown the meat in small batches so that it fries rather than stews.

Add the caraway seeds, tomatoes, stock and meat to the pan.

AVGOLEMONO

Preparation time: 20 minutes
Total cooking time: 10 minutes
Serves 4–6

1.5 litres (6 cups) chicken stock
150 g (5½ oz/¾ cup) long-grain
   rice
2 eggs, separated
125 ml (4 fl oz/½ cup) lemon
   juice

1 Bring the stock to the boil in a large heavy-based pan. Add the rice and allow to simmer for 8–10 minutes. until tender.
2 Beat the egg whites in a large dry mixing bowl until soft peaks form. Add the yolks and beat until they are combined.
3 Gradually pour in the lemon juice and then about 1–2 cups of the rice and stock soup, beating continuously. Gradually fold this into the pan of rice soup and serve immediately.

COOK'S FILE

Hint: Assemble all the ingredients and utensils beforehand , work quickly and serve this soup immediately—it does not reheat well.
Variation: Egg and lemon soup can also be made with fish stock instead of the chicken stock.

Beat the egg whites in a large dry mixing bowl until soft peaks form.

Beat continuously while you pour in the lemon juice and stock.

To keep the soup light and fluffy, use a large metal spoon to fold gently.

ASPARAGUS SOUP WITH PARMESAN CRISPS

Preparation time: 5 minutes
Total cooking time: 35 minutes
Serves 4

60 g (2 ¼ oz) butter
750 g (1 lb 10 oz) fresh
    asparagus spears, finely
    chopped
1 small onion, chopped
3 tablespoons plain (all-purpose)
    flour
750 ml (26 fl oz/3 cups) chicken
    stock
125 ml (4 fl oz/½ cup) cream
100 g (3½ oz) fresh Parmesan
    cheese

1 Heat the butter in a large heavy-based pan and cook the asparagus and onion, stirring, over medium heat for about 5 minutes, until the onion is soft. Sprinkle with the flour and stir for 1 minute to combine.
2 Remove from the heat and add the stock gradually, stirring until smooth. Return to the heat, bring to the boil, then reduce the heat and simmer, covered, for about 20 minutes, until the asparagus is tender.
3 Allow to cool a little for easier and safer handling, before processing in batches until smooth. Return to the pan, stir in the cream and then reheat gently without allowing the soup to boil. Season to taste and serve straight away with Parmesan crisps.
4 To make the Parmesan crisps, finely grate the cheese. Heat a non-stick frying pan until moderately hot. Sprinkle 3 tablespoons of the cheese into a 10 cm (4 inch) round in the pan. Cook until melted and bubbling, then remove the pan from the heat. When the bubbling subsides and the cheese hardens slightly, lift the crisp out with a spatula onto a paper towel. Repeat to make 4 large crisps.

COOK'S FILE

Note: If possible, buy a chunk of Parmigiano Reggiano from a good delicatessen—this is the best type of Parmesan cheese.

Choose tender young asparagus spears and chop them finely.

Cook the asparagus and onion, stirring over medium heat until the onion is soft.

Once the soup has been processed, stir in the cream.

Use a spatula to lift the Parmesan crisps out of the pan onto paper towels.

CURRIED SWEET POTATO SOUP

Preparation time: 20 minutes
Total cooking time: 40 minutes
Serves 6

1 tablespoon oil
1 large onion, chopped
2 garlic cloves, crushed
3 teaspoons curry powder
1.25 kg (2 lb 12 oz) orange sweet potato, peeled and cubed

1 litre (4 cups) chicken stock
1 large apple, peeled, cored and grated
125 ml (4 fl oz/½ cup) coconut cream

1 Heat the oil in a large pan and cook the onion over medium heat for 10 minutes, stirring occasionally, until very soft. Add the garlic and curry powder and cook for 1 minute.
2 Stir in the sweet potato, stock and apple. Bring to the boil, reduce heat and simmer, partially covered, for 30 minutes, until very soft.

3 Allow the soup to cool a little before processing in batches until smooth. Return to the pan, stir in the coconut cream and reheat gently without boiling. Delicious served with warmed pitta bread.

COOK'S FILE

Storage time: Can be kept in the fridge for 1 day without the coconut cream: add this before reheating.

Add the garlic and curry powder to the softened onion.

Stir in the stock with the cubed sweet potato and grated apple.

Once the soup has been processed stir in the coconut cream.

SPINACH AND POTATO SOUP

Preparation time: 20 minutes
Total cooking time: 45 minutes
Serves 6

30 g (1 oz) butter
1 large leek, sliced
2 garlic cloves, crushed
1 bunch English spinach
4 potatoes, chopped
1 litre (4 cups) vegetable stock
125 ml (4 fl oz/½ cup) sour
    cream

1 Melt the butter in a large heavy-based pan. Add the leek and cook over medium heat for 10 minutes, stirring occasionally, until very soft. Add the crushed garlic and cook for a further minute.
2 Wash the spinach very thoroughly to avoid any grittiness; discard the stalks and shred the leaves. Add to the pan with the potato and stock and bring to the boil. Reduce the heat and leave to simmer, partially covered, for about 30 minutes, until the potatoes are very soft.
3 Allow to cool a little for ease of handling, before processing in batches until smooth. Return to the pan and reheat gently without allowing to boil. Stir in the sour cream and add salt and pepper to taste.

COOK'S FILE

Storage time: If necessary, soup can be refrigerated for 1 day.
Note: If you can't find English spinach, use silverbeet (Swiss chard).

Cook the leek over medium heat until it is very soft.

Discard the stalks of the spinach and chop the leaves into shreds.

Partially cover with a loose-fitting lid and simmer until the potatoes are soft.

PIE-CRUST MUSHROOM SOUP

Preparation time: 25 minutes
Total cooking time: 35 minutes
Serves 4

400 g (14 oz) field mushrooms
60 g (2¼ oz) butter
1 small onion, finely chopped
1 garlic clove, crushed
3 tablespoons plain (all-purpose)
   flour
750 ml (26 fl oz/3 cups) chicken
   stock
2 tablespoons fresh thyme
   leaves
2 tablespoons sherry
250 ml (9 fl oz/1 cup) cream
1 sheet frozen puff pastry,
   thawed
1 egg, lightly beaten

1 Preheat the oven to 200°C (400°F/ Gas 6). Roughly chop the mushrooms. Melt the butter in a pan and cook the onion for 3 minutes, until soft. Add the garlic; cook for 1 minute. Add the mushrooms; cook until soft. Sprinkle with the flour and stir for 1 minute.

2 Stir in the stock, add the thyme and bring to the boil. Reduce the heat, cover and simmer for 10 minutes. Cool and process in batches. Return to the pan, stir in the sherry and cream and pour into four ovenproof bowls.

3 Cut rounds of pastry slightly larger than the bowl tops and cover each bowl with pastry (use small deep bowls rather than wide shallow ones or the pastry may sag into the soup).

4 Seal the pastry edges and brush lightly with the beaten egg. Bake for 15 minutes, until golden and puffed.

Stir gently as you sprinkle the flour over the mushrooms in the pan.

Stir in the sherry and cream after you have processed the soup.

Use a lid or cutter to cut pastry rounds a little larger than the bowls.

Seal the edges of the pastry and brush lightly with beaten egg.

RATATOUILLE AND PASTA SOUP

Preparation time: 25 minutes
Total cooking time: 40 minutes
Serves 6

1 medium eggplant (aubergine),
   chopped
1 tablespoon olive oil
1 large onion, chopped
1 large red and 1 large green
   capsicum (pepper), chopped
2 garlic cloves, crushed

3 zucchini (courgettes), sliced
2 x 400 g (14 oz) cans crushed
   tomatoes
1 teaspoon dried oregano leaves
½ teaspoon dried thyme leaves
1 litre (4 cups) vegetable stock
80 g (2¾ oz) pasta spirals

1 Place the eggplant in a colander and sprinkle generously with salt. Leave for 20 minutes; rinse and pat dry with paper towels.
2 Heat the oil in a large pan and cook the onion for 10 minutes, until soft and lightly golden. Add the capsicum,

garlic, zucchini and eggplant and cook for 5 minutes.
3 Add the tomatoes, herbs and stock. Bring to the boil, reduce the heat and simmer for 10 minutes, until tender. Add the pasta and cook for 15 minutes, until tender. Serve with Parmesan.

COOK'S FILE

Storage time: Soup will keep for up to 2 days in the refrigerator.

Put the chopped eggplant in a colander and sprinkle generously with salt.

Add the capsicum, garlic, zucchini and eggplant to the pan.

Once the vegetables are tender, add the pasta to the pan.

Use a sharp knife to chop the fennel.

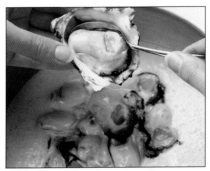

Remove the oysters from the shells with a small spoon, avoiding any grit.

The oysters are cooked when they just begin to curl at the edges.

Spread the pitta breads with butter and sprinkle with sesame seeds.

FENNEL AND OYSTER SOUP WITH SESAME PITTAS

Preparation time: 25 minutes
Total cooking time: 40 minutes
Serves 4–6

40 g (1½ oz) butter
1 medium onion, chopped
2 fennel bulbs (600 g/1 lb 5 oz), chopped
500 ml (17 fl oz/2 cups) fish stock
125 ml (4 fl oz/½ cup) dry white wine
125 ml (4 fl oz/½ cup) cream
½ teaspoon nutmeg
24 oysters, opened
1 teaspoon lemon juice
salt and white pepper
2 tablespoons chopped parsley, to serve

Sesame pittas
2 small pitta breads
60 g (2¼ oz) butter, melted
2 teaspoons sesame seeds

1 Melt the butter in a large heavy-based pan and cook the onion over medium heat for 5 minutes, until soft but not browned. Add the fennel and cook, covered, for 5 minutes. Add the stock, wine and 125 ml (4 fl oz/½ cup) water, bring to the boil, reduce the heat and simmer, partially covered, for 30 minutes, until the fennel is very soft.
2 Allow to cool before processing in batches until smooth. Return to the pan and reheat gently. Stir in the cream, nutmeg and oysters (and any liquid in the shells).
3 Simmer until the oysters just begin to curl at the edges (about 2 minutes). Do not overcook or the oysters will be tough. Stir in the lemon juice and add salt and pepper to taste . Garnish with chopped parsley.
4 To make sesame pittas, preheat the oven to 200°C (400°F/Gas 6). Split the pitta breads in half and brush both sides with melted butter. Place them on a baking tray and sprinkle with the sesame seeds. Bake for about 10 minutes, or until golden and crisp, and serve immediately.

JUNGLE SOUP

Preparation time: 10 minutes
Total cooking time: 35 minutes
Serves 4

2 teaspoons oil
1 medium onion, finely sliced
225 g (8 oz) butternut pumpkin, peeled and diced
225 g (8 oz) fresh pineapple or mango, chopped

1 garlic clove, crushed
1 dried red chilli, finely chopped
2 teaspoons grated ginger
1 litre (4 cups) chicken stock
2 tablespoons lime juice
350 g (12 oz) chicken breast, skinned, cut diagonally into thin strips

1 Heat the oil in a large heavy-based pan and cook the onion for 5 minutes, or until golden. Add the pumpkin and cook for 5 minutes, or until just brown.

Add the pineapple, garlic, chilli and ginger and toss together.
2 Add the stock and lime juice, bring to the boil and then reduce the heat to simmer for 20 minutes, or until the pumpkin is nearly tender.
3 Add the chicken and simmer for 5 minutes, or until the chicken is cooked. Serve immediately.

Peel and chop the pineapple or mango into bite-sized pieces.

Add the pumpkin to the onion in the pan and cook until browned.

Use two wooden spoons to toss together the contents of the pan.

68

MEXICAN CORN SOUP

Preparation time: 20 minutes
Total cooking time: 30 minutes
Serves 4–6

800 g (1 lb 12 oz/4 cups)
fresh corn kernels, off
the cob
1.125 litres (4½ cups) vegetable
stock
30 g (1 oz) butter
1 teaspoon paprika

30 g (1 oz/½ cup) chopped
spring onions (scallions)
½–1 teaspoon Tabasco
125 g (4½ oz/½ cup) sour cream
2 green chillies, chopped

1 Put 600 g (1 lb 5 oz/3 cups) of the corn and the stock in a blender or food processor. Process for 30 seconds, until the mixture is smooth.
2 Heat the butter in a large pan, stir in the paprika and spring onion and cook over medium heat for 2 minutes, or until the spring onion is soft.

3 Add the corn purée to the pan and bring to the boil. Reduce the heat to low and simmer for 10 minutes. Add the remaining cup of whole corn kernels and return to the boil. Reduce the heat to low and leave to simmer, for 15 minutes, or until the soup is thick. Stir in the Tabasco sauce and serve topped with a dollop of sour cream and the chopped chillies.

Use a food processor to purée the corn and stock until smooth.

Stir-fry the spring onions in the butter and paprika until soft.

Add the remaining cup of whole corn kernels to give texture to the soup.

HEARTY CHICKEN NOODLE SOUP

Preparation time: 30 minutes
Total cooking time: 15 minutes
Serves 6

10 g (¼ oz/½ cup) dried Chinese
   mushrooms
150 g (5½ oz) fresh Chinese egg
   noodles
200 g (7 oz) choy sum
1 tablespoon peanut oil
2 tablespoons sesame oil
1 medium onion, chopped
1.5 litres (6 cups) chicken stock
2 tablespoons soy sauce
1 tablespoon thinly shredded
   fresh ginger
1 garlic clove, crushed
500 g (1 lb 2 oz) chicken breast
   fillets, thinly sliced
salt, to taste
425 g (15 oz) can baby corn,
   drained, chopped
1 large red capsicum (pepper),
   thinly sliced

1 Soak mushrooms in boiling water
for 20 minutes. Drain and squeeze out
excess liquid. Slice finely. Cook noodles
in rapidly boiling water until just
tender. Rinse; drain well.

2 Cut leaves from stems of choy sum.
Cut stems into 4 cm (1½ inch) lengths.
Cut leaves into 1 cm (½ inch) slices.
Heat oils in large heavy-based pan.
Add onion and choy sum stems; cook
over medium heat, stirring, for
3 minutes or until onion and stems are
just tender.

3 Add chicken stock, soy sauce,
ginger and garlic to pan. Bring to boil,
stirring occasionally. Add chicken.
Reduce heat and simmer, stirring,
4 minutes, or until chicken is just
cooked through. Season.

4 Add corn, capsicum, choy sum
leaves and mushrooms to pan. Bring
to the boil; reduce heat and simmer for
3 minutes or until capsicum and leaves
are tender. Do not overcook. To serve,
place drained, cooked noodles in the
base of each serving bowl. Pour soup
over the noodles. Serve immediately.

COOK'S FILE

Storage time: Soup and noodles can
be prepared one day in advance. Store
separately in airtight containers in the
refrigerator. Bring noodles to room
temperature and reheat soup gently
just before serving.

1

2

3

CHICKEN AND COCONUT MILK SOUP

Preparation time: 30 minutes
Total cooking time: 12 minutes
Serves 8

150 g (5½ oz) rice vermicelli
1 lime
4 small fresh red chillies, seeded, chopped
1 medium onion, chopped
2 garlic cloves, crushed
4 thin slices fresh ginger, finely chopped
2 stalks lemon grass root, roughly chopped
1 tablespoon chopped fresh coriander (cilantro)
1 tablespoon peanut oil
750 ml (26 fl oz/3 cups) chicken stock
685 ml (24 fl oz/2¾ cups) coconut milk
500 g (1 lb 2 oz) chicken tenderloins, cut into thin strips
4 spring onions (scallions), chopped
150 g (5½ oz) fried bean curd or tofu, sliced
90 g (3¼ oz/1 cup) bean sprouts
salt, to taste
3 teaspoons soft brown sugar

1 Pour boiling water over vermicelli to cover. Stand 5 minutes or until tender; drain. Cut into shorter lengths with scissors and set aside.
2 Peel the lime rind and cut into long, thin strips.
3 Place chillies, onion, garlic, ginger, lemongrass and coriander in a food processor bowl or blender. Using pulse action, process for 20 seconds or until the mixture is smooth.
4 Heat oil in a large heavy-based pan. Add chilli mixture; cook for 3 minutes until fragrance is released, stirring frequently. Add stock, coconut milk and lime rind and bring to the boil. Add the chicken and cook, stirring, for 4 minutes or until it is tender.
5 Add spring onion, bean curd, bean sprouts, salt and sugar. Stir over medium heat for 3 minutes or until the spring onion is tender. Divide noodles among serving bowls and pour the soup over. Garnish with thinly sliced chillies and coriander leaves, if liked.

POTATO AND CHEESE SOUP

Preparation time: 20 minutes
Total cooking time: 40 minutes
Serves 4–6

30 g (1 oz) butter
4 rashers bacon, cut into strips
1 onion, finely chopped
½ teaspoon sweet paprika
1 kg (2 lb 4 oz) potatoes,
    chopped
750 ml (26 fl oz/3 cups) chicken
    stock
125 g (4½ oz/1 cup) grated
    Cheddar
chopped chives, to serve

1 Melt the butter in a large pan, add the bacon and cook until crisp. Remove the bacon from the pan with a slotted spoon, leaving as much fat as possible. Add the onion to the same pan and cook for 5 minutes, or until very soft and golden. Add the paprika and cook for a further 30 seconds.

2 Return the bacon to the pan and add the potato and stock. Bring to the boil, then reduce the heat and simmer for 30 minutes, or until the potato is very soft. Stir or mash lightly to break up the potato. Add the Cheddar and stir well, until it is melted through. Season with salt and pepper to taste and serve topped with a sprinkling of chopped chives.

Trim the rind and excess fat from the bacon and cut into strips.

Cook the bacon until crisp and remove from the pan with a slotted spoon.

Stir with a wooden spoon or mash lightly to break up the potato.

MOROCCAN CHICKPEA SOUP

Preparation time: 35 minutes
+ overnight soaking
Total cooking time: 1 hour 10 minutes
Serves 4

250 g (9 oz) dried chickpeas
2 tablespoons olive oil
1 onion, finely sliced
2 teaspoons ground cumin
2 teaspoons sweet paprika
1 teaspoon ground ginger
1 teaspoon ground cinnamon
¼ teaspoon allspice
250 g (9 oz) boneless lamb leg steaks, cut into strips
500 g (1 lb 2 oz) tomatoes, finely chopped
2 litres (8 cups) vegetable stock or water
2 teaspoons grated lemon zest
110 g (3½ oz/½ cup) short-grain rice
3 tablespoons chopped parsley
2 tablespoons chopped coriander (cilantro)

1 Soak the chickpeas in cold water overnight. Drain. Heat the oil in a large pan over low heat and add the onion and spices. Cook for 15 minutes, covered, stirring occasionally.

2 Add the chickpeas, lamb, tomato and stock. Bring to the boil, reduce the heat and simmer for 35 minutes. Skim the surface as required. Add the lemon zest and rice and cook for 12 minutes, or until the rice is tender. Add the herbs and season to taste.

COOK'S FILE

Note: Short-grain rice is plump and sticks together when cooked.

Soak the chickpeas in plenty of cold water and leave overnight. Drain well.

Use a sharp knife to cut the lamb leg steaks into strips.

Add the onion, cumin, paprika, ginger, cinnamon and allspice to the pan.

73

CREAMY SPINACH AND CHICKEN SOUP

Preparation time: 40 minutes
Total cooking time: 55 minutes
Serves 6

1 tablespoon oil
1 kg (2 lb 4 oz) chicken pieces
1 carrot, chopped
2 celery sticks, chopped
1 onion, chopped
6 black peppercorns
2 garlic cloves, chopped
1 bouquet garni
800 g (1 lb 10 oz) white sweet
   potato, chopped
2 bunches (about 500 g/1 lb
   2 oz) English spinach
125 ml (4 fl oz/½ cup) cream

1 Heat the oil in a large pan, add the chicken in batches and brown well. Drain on paper towels. Pour off the excess fat, leaving 1 tablespoon in the pan. Return the chicken to the pan with the carrot, celery, onion, peppercorns, garlic, bouquet garni and 1.5 litres (6 cups) of water. Bring to the boil, reduce the heat and simmer for 40 minutes. Strain, returning the stock to the pan. Pull the chicken meat from the bones, shred and set aside.

2 Add the sweet potato to the stock in the pan. Bring to the boil, reduce the heat and simmer until tender. Add the spinach leaves and cook until wilted. Process in batches in a food processor until finely chopped.

3 Return to the pan, add the chicken and stir in the cream. Season to taste. Reheat gently before serving but do not allow the soup to boil.

To make a bouquet garni, tie parsley, thyme and a bay leaf with string.

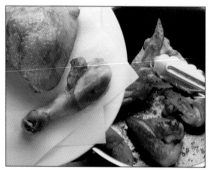

Brown the chicken in batches then drain on paper towels.

Add the spinach leaves to the soup and cook, stirring, until just wilted.

STEAMED BEEF BALLS IN LONG SOUP

Preparation time: 1 hour
Cooking time: 20 minutes
Serves 6

500 g (1 lb 2 oz) lean minced
    (ground) beef
2 egg whites, lightly beaten
1 tablespoon iced water
2 tablespoons soy sauce
1 teaspoon sesame oil
2 teaspoons cornflour
    (cornstarch)
2 tablespoons finely chopped
    fresh coriander (cilantro)
2 spring onions (scallions),
    finely chopped

¼ teaspoon ground white pepper
¼ teaspoon five-spice powder

Long soup
1 litre (4 cups) beef stock,
    preferably homemade
2 cups assorted Chinese
    vegetables, sliced very finely
    for rapid cooking
375 g (13 oz) fresh, thin egg
    noodles, cooked

1 Place small batches of mince in a food processor bowl. Using the pulse action, press button for 30 seconds or until mixture is a fine paste. Transfer to a bowl and repeat. Mix in the remaining ingredients.
2 Roll level tablespoonfuls of mixture into balls with wet hands. Half-fill a wok with water, cover, bring to the boil. Place mince balls in a steamer lined with lightly oiled greaseproof paper over the boiling water. Cover, steam for 20 minutes.
3 To make long soup, bring stock to the boil in a separate pan, add the vegetables, cook 2 minutes. Pour into a tureen, add noodles and beef balls.

COOK'S FILE

Storage time: Beef balls can be made 1 day ahead and reheated in the boiling stock just before serving.
Variation: For combination long soup, add 125 g (4½ oz) each of peeled, cooked prawns (shrimp), sliced barbecued pork and cooked chicken.

FENNEL, ASPARAGUS AND PEA SOUP

Preparation time: 20 minutes
Total cooking time: 40 minutes
Serves 4

30 g (1 oz) butter
1½ tablespoons olive oil
1 leek, white part only, sliced
1 fennel bulb, sliced
375 g (12 oz) asparagus, cut into
    pieces
1 garlic clove, crushed
8 mint leaves, chopped
150 g (5 oz) shelled or frozen
    peas (400 g/13 oz in pods)
200 g (6½ oz) potatoes, cubed
1 litre (4 cups) chicken or
    vegetable stock
pinch of cayenne pepper
pinch of ground nutmeg

Mint and garlic croutons
20 g (¾ oz) butter
1 tablespoon olive oil
2 slices day-old white bread,
    crusts removed, cut into four
mint leaves
2 garlic cloves, sliced, soaked in
    cold water for 15 minutes

1 Heat the butter and oil in a large pan and add the leek and fennel. Cook over medium heat for 8–10 minutes, then stir in the asparagus, garlic, mint, peas and potato. Cook for 1 minute.
2 Add enough stock to cover the vegetables, and bring to the boil. Remove 4 asparagus tips, plunge into a bowl of iced water and set aside. Reduce the heat and simmer for 15–20 minutes, or until the vegetables are tender. Cool slightly then purée in a food processor. Return to the pan with the remaining stock, cayenne pepper and nutmeg and season.
3 Preheat the oven to 190°C (375°F/ Gas 5). To make the croutons, melt the butter and oil and brush over both sides of the bread. Lay on a baking tray. Tear the mint leaves in half, and place on the bread; dry the garlic and place on the mint. Drizzle the remaining butter mixture over the top. Bake for 5–6 minutes, or until the bread is toasted and the garlic golden.
4 Gently reheat the soup and serve garnished with the croutons and the reserved asparagus tips.

Split the pods to remove the peas; or string the pod by pulling from the top.

Using tongs, remove 4 asparagus tips and plunge into iced water.

Lay the mint leaves and garlic slices on the slices of bread.

CHICKPEA, CHORIZO AND PORK RIB SOUP

Preparation time: 20 minutes +
  overnight soaking
Total cooking time: 40 minutes
Serves 6–8

180 g (6 oz) dried chickpeas
300 g (10 oz) smoked bacon ribs
2 tablespoons olive oil
1 onion, finely chopped
1 garlic clove, crushed
2 tomatoes, peeled, seeded and
  finely chopped

1 potato, cubed
1 carrot, sliced
200 g (6½ oz) pumpkin, chopped
150 g (5 oz) chorizo or
  pepperoni sausage, sliced
¼ teaspoon dried oregano
1.5 litres (6 cups) chicken stock

1 Soak the chickpeas in cold water overnight. Drain.
2 Blanch the bacon ribs in boiling water for 30 seconds, then plunge into iced water. Drain and slice into pieces.
3 Heat the oil in a large, heavy-based pan and cook the onion over medium heat for 3–4 minutes, stirring continuously. Add the garlic and tomato and cook for a further 5 minutes.
4 Add the chickpeas, ribs, potato, carrot, pumpkin, chorizo, dried oregano and stock. Bring to the boil, then reduce the heat and simmer, covered, for 30 minutes, or until the chickpeas are tender. Season to taste

COOK'S FILE

Note: If bacon ribs are unavailable, use 150 g (5 oz) smoked bacon instead.

Halve the peeled tomatoes and scoop out the seeds using a teaspoon.

Use chorizo, pepperoni or another type of spicy sausage.

Drain the blanched ribs, then cut into smaller sections.

VEGETABLE AND WATERCRESS SOUP

Preparation time: 40 minutes
Total cooking time: 1 hour
Serves 4

1 kg (2 lb 4 oz) chicken bones
8 cm (3 inch) piece of ginger,
    roughly chopped
several celery leaves
2 carrots, roughly chopped
6 spring onions (scallions),
    roughly chopped
2 carrots, extra
2 sticks celery
2 leeks
200 g (6½ oz) whole baby corn
1 head broccoli
50 g (1¾ oz) baby beans or
    whole beans, cut into short
    lengths
100 g (3½ oz) sugar snap peas
2–3 tablespoons soy sauce
1–2 tablespoons sesame oil
60 g (2 oz/2 cups) watercress
    sprigs, to serve

1 To make the chicken stock, place the chicken bones, ginger, celery leaves, chopped carrot, spring onion and a teaspoon of salt in a large pan. Cover with 2 litres (8 cups) of water and bring to the boil. Reduce the heat to low and simmer for 45 minutes, skimming the surface as required.
2 Cut the extra carrots and celery into matchsticks and the leeks into strips. Cut the corn in half lengthways and trim the broccoli into florets.
3 Strain the stock and discard the bones and vegetables. Strain again through a very fine sieve and bring the stock to a simmer. Add the carrot, corn and baby beans and cook for 3 minutes. Add the celery, leek, broccoli and sugar snap peas and cook for a further 3–4 minutes. Do not overcook the vegetables: they should be tender but crisp.
4 Add the soy sauce and sesame oil and season to taste with salt and pepper. Add the watercress and serve immediately with some extra sesame oil and soy sauce, if you want.

Trim the coarse stems from the watercress.

Cut the carrots and celery into matchsticks, and the leeks into strips.

Using a sharp knife, cut the broccoli into small florets.

Strain the stock a second time through a fine sieve.

MANHATTAN-STYLE SEAFOOD CHOWDER

Preparation time: 30 minutes
Total cooking time: 30 minutes
Serves 4–6

60 g (2 oz) butter
3 rashers bacon, chopped
2 onions, chopped
2 garlic cloves, finely chopped
2 sticks celery, sliced
3 potatoes, diced
1.25 litres (5 cups) fish or
    chicken stock

3 teaspoons chopped thyme
1 tablespoon tomato paste
    (concentrated purée)
425 g (14 oz) can chopped
    tomatoes
375 g (12 oz) boneless white
    fish fillets, cut into chunks
12 large raw prawns (shrimp),
    peeled, deveined and halved
310 g (10 oz) can baby clams
    (vongole), undrained
2 tablespoons chopped parsley
grated orange zest, to garnish

1 Melt the butter in a large pan and cook the bacon, onion, garlic and celery over low heat, stirring occasionally, for 5 minutes, or until soft but not brown. Add the potato, stock and thyme and bring to the boil.

2 Reduce the heat and simmer, covered, for 15 minutes. Stir in the tomato paste and tomato and return to the boil. Add the fish pieces, prawns and clams and simmer for 3 minutes.

3 Season to taste and stir in the parsley. Serve garnished with grated orange zest, if you want.

COOK'S FILE

Note: Prawns are not in a traditional chowder but are an excellent addition.

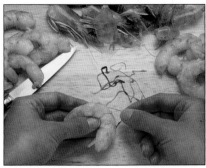

Devein the prawns by gently making a slit down the back and removing the vein.

Cook the bacon and vegetables over low heat until softened.

Add the potato, stock and chopped thyme and bring to the boil.

LENTIL AND SPINACH SOUP

Preparation time: 25 minutes
Total cooking time: 1 hour
Serves 8

95 g (3 oz/½ cup) brown lentils
2 tablespoons vegetable oil
1 leek, chopped
1 onion, chopped
1 stick celery, chopped
600 g (1¼ lb) potatoes, chopped
1 litre (4 cups) chicken stock
250 g (9 oz) English spinach

1 Put the lentils in a pan. Cover with water and bring to the boil, reduce the heat and simmer for 20 minutes, or until tender; drain.
2 Heat the oil in a large pan. Cook the leek, onion and celery for 5 minutes, or until softened. Add the potato and cook, stirring frequently, for 10 minutes. Add the stock and bring to the boil. Reduce the heat and simmer, covered, for 20 minutes, or until the potato is tender.
3 Remove the stalks from the spinach, wash the leaves well, add to the soup and cook for 1–2 minutes. Purée in a food processor, return to the pan, add the lentils and reheat.

Place the lentils in a pan and cover with plenty of cold water.

Cook the leek, onion and celery until soft, then add the chopped potato.

Add the cooked and drained lentils to the puréed soup in the pan.

RICH OXTAIL SOUP

Preparation time: 35 minutes
+ 2 hours refrigeration
Total cooking time: 2 hours
25 minutes
Serves 4

2 oxtails, cut into pieces (ask
your butcher to do this)
2 tablespoons olive oil
3 onions, chopped
4 garlic cloves, finely chopped
1 tablespoon plain (all-purpose)
flour
1 litre (4 cups) beef stock
2 bay leaves, torn in half

2 tablespoons tomato paste
(concentrated purée)
2 teaspoons Worcestershire
sauce
4 potatoes, chopped
2 parsnips, chopped
2 carrots, chopped
3 tomatoes, chopped
2 tablespoons chopped parsley

1 Cut the excess fat from the oxtail. Heat the oil in a heavy-based pan over medium heat. Add the oxtail, onion and garlic and cook for 8 minutes, turning regularly, or until well browned. Add the flour and cook for 1 minute, stirring. Mix in 500 ml (17 fl oz/2 cups) of the stock and bring to the boil, stirring continuously. Remove from the heat and refrigerate for 2 hours, or until the fat can be spooned off the surface.

2 Add the remaining stock, 1 litre (4 cups) of water, the bay leaves, ½ teaspoon each of salt and pepper, tomato paste and Worcestershire sauce. Bring to the boil, reduce the heat to low and simmer, covered, for 2 hours, stirring occasionally.

3 Add the potato, parsnip and carrot and simmer for 10 minutes, or until tender. Remove the bay leaves and discard. Serve with the chopped tomato and parsley.

Using a sharp knife, trim away the excess fat from the oxtail.

Sprinkle the flour over the browned oxtail and cook, stirring, for 1 minute.

Add the parsnip, carrot and potato and simmer for 10 minutes.

CREAM OF CHICKEN AND VEGETABLE SOUP

Preparation time: 20 minutes
Total cooking time: 1 hour 45 minutes
Serves 6

1.1 kg (2 lb 7 oz) chicken

Stock
1.5 litres (6 cups) water
½ stick celery, chopped
6 peppercorns
1 bay leaf
1 garlic clove, sliced
1 small onion, chopped

Soup
1 medium carrot
1 tablespoon oil
1 medium onion, sliced
200 g button mushrooms, sliced
3 tablespoons plain (all-purpose) flour
170 ml (5½ fl oz/⅔ cup) milk
250 ml (9 fl oz/1 cup) cream
100 g (3½ oz) snow peas (mangetout), thinly sliced
3 medium tomatoes, peeled, seeded, chopped
1 tablespoon soy sauce
salt and freshly ground black pepper, to taste

1 Wipe over and dry chicken. To make stock, using poultry shears, cut chicken into breasts, thighs, legs and wings. Place in a large heavy-based pan with water, celery, peppercorns, bay leaf, garlic and onion. Bring to the boil, then reduce heat and simmer, covered, for 1 ¼ hours. Remove from heat; cool slightly. Strain, reserve stock and chicken; discard onion mixture. (You need 1.25 litres/5 cups of stock for this recipe.)

2 To make the soup, cut the carrot into matchstick strips. Heat oil in a large heavy-based pan; add onion, carrot and mushrooms. Cook, stirring, over low heat until onion is tender, stir in stock and blended flour and milk. Bring to boil. Reduce heat and simmer, stirring, until slightly thickened.

3 Cut the reserved chicken into thin strips. Add the chicken, cream, snow peas, tomatoes and soy sauce to the soup. Stir until heated through. Season to taste. Serve hot.

WATERCRESS AND POTATO SOUP

Preparation time: 30 minutes
Total cooking time: 50 minutes
Serves 6–8

30 g (1 oz) butter
2 onions, chopped
1–2 garlic cloves, chopped
1 kg (2 lb 4 oz) potatoes,
    chopped into chunks
2 litres (8 cups) chicken stock
250 g (9 oz) watercress,
    trimmed
4 tablespoons cream

Parmesan croutons
2 slices bread, crusts removed
1 tablespoon olive oil
1 tablespoon grated Parmesan

1 Heat the butter in a large pan. Cook the onion and garlic for 2–3 minutes, or until softened. Add the potato and stir for 1–2 minutes Add the stock and bring to the boil. Reduce the heat and simmer for 30 minutes, or until the potato is cooked. Strain, reserving the cooking liquid.

2 Transfer the potato mixture to a food processor, pour in about half the cooking liquid and process until smooth. Return to the pan.

3 In a food processor, process the watercress and 500 ml (17 fl oz/2 cups) of the cooking liquid until smooth. Pour the watercress mixture, cream and any remaining cooking liquid into the pan and combine. Stir over low heat for 3 minutes, or until warmed through, but do not allow the soup to boil. Season to taste.

4 To make the croutons, preheat the oven to 180°C (350°F/Gas 4). Cut the bread into cubes and mix with the oil and grated Parmesan. Bake for 10 minutes, or until golden. Serve the croutons on top of the soup.

Pour in half the cooking liquid over the potato mixture.

Process the watercress and liquid until smooth and pour into the pan.

Quickly mix the bread cubes in the oil and Parmesan until well coated.

SAFFRON FISH SOUP

Preparation time: 20 minutes
Total cooking time: 30 minutes
Serves 4

1 kg (2 lb 4 oz) white fish bones
    (heads and trimmings),
    chopped
500 ml (17 fl oz/2 cups) dry
    white wine
1 onion, chopped
1 carrot, chopped
1 stick celery, chopped
1 bay leaf
6 black peppercorns
¾ teaspoon saffron threads
50 g (1¾ oz) butter
3 tablespoons plain (all-purpose)
    flour
12 scallops, trimmed
250 g (9 oz) boneless white fish
    fillets, cut into cubes
250 ml (9 fl oz/1 cup) cream

To make the saffron fish stock, place the fish bones, 750 ml (26 fl oz/ 3 cups) of water, the wine, onion, carrot, celery, bay leaf and peppercorns in a large pan. Bring to the boil slowly, skimming the surface as required. Simmer, covered, for 20 minutes. Strain and discard the fish and vegetables. Take 1 litre (4 cups) of the hot stock and stir in the saffron threads. (If you have any stock leftover, freeze it for another use.)

1 Melt the butter in a large pan and stir in the flour. Cook, stirring continuously, over low heat for 3 minutes but do not allow the mixture to colour. Remove from the heat and gradually pour in the reserved fish stock. Return to the heat and stir continuously until the mixture boils and thickens slightly. Add the scallops and fish cubes, bring back to the boil and simmer for 1–2 minutes.

2 Stir in the cream and reheat gently, but do not allow the soup to boil. Season to taste with salt and freshly ground white pepper. Garnish with sprigs of chervil, if you want.

Using a sharp knife, remove the dark vein from the scallops.

Add the bay leaf and peppercorns.

Combine the reserved hot fish stock and saffron threads in a jug or bowl.

Add the scallops and fish cubes to the soup and simmer for 1–2 minutes.

COCK-A-LEEKIE

Preparation time: 10 minutes +
2 hours refrigeration
Total cooking time: 1 hour 40 minutes
Serves 4–6

1.5 kg (3 lb) chicken
250 g (9 oz) chicken giblets
(optional), (see Note)
1 onion, sliced
2 litres (8 cups) chicken stock
4 leeks, thinly sliced

¼ teaspoon ground coriander
pinch of nutmeg
1 bouquet garni
12 pitted prunes
pinch of cayenne pepper
3 sprigs thyme
thyme sprigs, extra, to serve

1 To make the chicken stock, put the chicken in a large pan and add the giblets (if using), onion and stock. Bring to the boil, skimming the surface as required. Add the leek, coriander, nutmeg and bouquet garni.

Reduce the heat, cover and simmer for 1¼ hours.
2 Remove the chicken and bouquet garni and lift out the giblets with a slotted spoon. Cool the stock, then refrigerate for 2 hours. Spoon off the fat from the surface and discard. Remove the meat from the bones and shred. Discard the skin and carcass.
3 Return the meat to the soup with the prunes, cayenne pepper and thyme. Simmer for 20 minutes. Season to taste and garnish with the extra thyme sprigs, if you want.

Trim the ends from the leeks and slice thinly, including some green parts.

Add the chicken stock to the pan with the chicken, giblets (if using) and onion.

Add the prunes and thyme sprigs to the soup and stir to combine.

85

ROASTED TOMATO SOUP

Preparation time: 20 minutes
Total cooking time: 1 hour 10 minutes
Serves 4

1 kg (2 lb 4 oz) Roma (plum)
   tomatoes
5 garlic cloves, unpeeled
5 tablespoons olive oil
1 teaspoon dried basil
3 tablespoons olive oil, extra
1 onion, finely chopped
1 red chilli, finely chopped
2 tablespoons balsamic vinegar

2 teaspoons soft brown sugar
1 tablespoon plain (all-purpose)
   flour
1 litre (4 cups) vegetable stock
3 tablespoons chopped flat-leaf
   (Italian) parsley, to serve

1 Preheat the oven to 200°C (400°F/ Gas 6). Halve the tomatoes and lay cut-side-up in a baking tray with the garlic. Add the oil, some seasoning and the basil. Roast for 30 minutes. Take the garlic out after 20 minutes if it is drying out.

2 Heat the extra oil in a heavy-based pan. Add the onion and chilli and cook, covered, for 10 minutes over medium heat, stirring frequently.

3 Chop the tomatoes and squeeze the garlic pulp from their skins. Add to the pan along with the vinegar and sugar. Cook, stirring, for 1 minute. Stir in the flour and cook for 30 seconds.

4 Remove from the heat and add the stock. Return to the heat and bring to the boil, stirring occasionally. Simmer for 5 minutes. Season to taste and add the parsley.

Sprinkle the dried basil over the halved tomatoes and unpeeled garlic cloves.

Squeeze the garlic pulp from their skins and add to the pan.

Add the chopped parsley to the soup just before serving.

Halve the tomatoes and scoop out the seeds with a teaspoon.

Brown the shanks in 2 batches, remove with tongs and drain on paper towels.

Stir the paprikas and flour into the onion mixture until it just begins to colour.

Spoon off the fat that forms on the surface of the soup.

RUSTIC HOT POT

Preparation time: 40 minutes +
  1 hour refrigeration
Total cooking time: 2 hours
Serves 4

2 tablespoons olive oil
8 lamb shanks
2 onions, sliced
4 garlic cloves, finely chopped
3 bay leaves, torn in half
1–2 teaspoons hot paprika
2 teaspoons sweet paprika
1 tablespoon plain (all-purpose)
  flour
3 tablespoons tomato paste
  (concentrated purée)
1.5 litres (6 cups) vegetable
  stock
4 potatoes, chopped
4 carrots, sliced
3 sticks celery, thickly
  sliced
3 tomatoes, seeded and
  chopped

1 To make the lamb stock, heat 1 tablespoon of the oil in a large, heavy-based pan over medium heat. Brown the shanks well in two batches and drain on paper towels.

2 Add the remaining tablespoon of oil to the pan and cook the onion, garlic and bay leaves over low heat for 10 minutes, stirring regularly. Add the paprikas and flour and cook, stirring continuously, for 2 minutes. Gradually add the combined tomato paste and stock. Bring to the boil, stirring continuously, and return the shanks to the pan. Reduce the heat to low and simmer, covered, for 1½ hours, stirring occasionally.

3 Remove the bay leaves and discard. Remove the shanks, allow to cool slightly and then cut the meat from the bone. Discard the bones. Cut the meat into pieces and refrigerate. Refrigerate the stock for about 1 hour, or until fat forms on the surface and can be spooned off.

4 Return the meat to the soup along with the potato, carrot and celery and bring to the boil. Reduce the heat and simmer for 15 minutes. Season and add the chopped tomato to serve.

87

BEEF CONSOMME

Preparation time: 30 minutes +
  overnight refrigeration
Total cooking time: 5 hours
Serves 4–6

1 kg (2 lb 4 oz) gravy beef, cut
  into small pieces
500 g (1 lb 2 oz) beef bones
  including marrow, cut into
  small pieces (ask your
  butcher to do this)
1 leek, cut into small pieces
2 onions, quartered
2 carrots, chopped
2 sticks celery, chopped
6 black peppercorns
6 whole cloves
3 sprigs thyme
3 sprigs parsley
3 bay leaves
1 egg shell, crumbled
1 egg white, lightly beaten
2 tablespoons chopped parsley

1 Preheat the oven to 180°C (350°F/
Gas 4). Place the gravy beef and beef
bones in a single layer in a baking
dish. Bake for 45 minutes, or until
lightly browned, turning once.
2 Put the meat, bones, vegetables,
peppercorns, cloves, herbs, bay leaves
and 1 teaspoon of salt in a large pan.
Add 3 litres (12 cups) of water and
slowly bring to the boil. Reduce the
heat to low, cover and simmer for
4 hours. Set aside to cool slightly.
Remove the larger pieces of meat and
discard. Ladle the liquid through a
muslin-lined sieve into a bowl. Discard
the remaining meat and vegetables.
3 Cover the liquid and refrigerate for
several hours, or overnight. Spoon off
the fat from the surface. Return to a
clean pan with the egg shell and the
lightly beaten egg white.
4 Slowly heat the stock to simmering
and simmer for 10 minutes. A frothy
scum will form on the surface. Remove
from the heat and leave for 10 minutes.
Skim the surface and ladle the stock
through a muslin-lined sieve. Reheat,
season if needed, and serve with the
chopped parsley.

*Lay the gravy beef and bones in a single
layer in a large baking dish.*

*Gently stir in the egg shell and egg white
with a balloon whisk or wooden spoon.*

*Carefully ladle the stock into the muslin-
lined sieve placed over a bowl.*

*A froth will form on the surface as the
stock gently simmers.*

SPRING VEGETABLE SOUP

Preparation time: 30 minutes +
 overnight soaking
Total cooking time: 1 hour 15 minutes
Serves 8

105 g (3½ oz/½ cup) pinto beans
2 teaspoons olive oil
2 onions, finely chopped
2 garlic cloves, finely chopped
2.5 litres (10 cups) vegetable
 stock
2 sticks celery, finely chopped
2 carrots
2 potatoes
150 g (5 oz) green beans
2 zucchini (courgettes)
100 g (3½ oz) shelled peas (see
 Hint)
2 tablespoons chopped flat-leaf
 (Italian) parsley

1 Soak the pinto beans in plenty of cold water overnight. Drain.
2 Heat the oil in a large pan, add the onion and cook over low heat until soft and translucent. Add the garlic and cook for 1 minute further. Add the pinto beans, stock and celery and bring to the boil. Reduce the heat to low and simmer, covered, for 45 minutes, or until the beans are almost cooked.
3 Finely chop the carrots, potatoes, green beans and zucchini and add to the pan. Simmer gently for 15 minutes, or until the vegetables are almost cooked. Stir in the peas and simmer for a further 10 minutes.
4 Season well and stir through the chopped parsley.

COOK'S FILE

Note: If pinto beans are hard to find, you can easily substitute them with borlotti beans or the smaller haricot beans.
Hint: If you can't find fresh peas, use frozen peas. Thaw and add during the last 5 minutes of cooking.

Add the drained pinto beans to the pan and stir in with a wooden spoon.

Chop all of the vegetables into small, even-sized dice.

CHICKEN AND VEGETABLE SOUP

Preparation time: 1 hour +
  refrigeration
Total cooking time: 1 hour 25 minutes
Serves 6–8

1.5 kg (2½ lb) chicken
2 carrots, roughly chopped
2 sticks celery, roughly chopped
1 onion, quartered
4 parsley sprigs
2 bay leaves
4 black peppercorns
50 g (1¾ oz) butter
2 tablespoons plain (all-purpose)
  flour
2 potatoes, chopped
250 g (9 oz) butternut pumpkin
  (squash), chopped into bite-
  sized pieces
2 carrots, extra, cut into
  matchsticks
1 leek, cut into matchsticks
3 sticks celery, extra, cut into
  matchsticks
100 g (3½ oz) green beans, cut
  into short lengths or baby
  green beans, halved
200 g (6½ oz) broccoli, cut into
  small florets
100 g (3½ oz) sugar snap peas,
  trimmed
50 g (1¾ oz) English spinach
  leaves, shredded
125 ml (4 fl oz/½ cup) cream
3 tablespoons chopped parsley

1 To make the chicken stock, place the chicken in a large pan with the carrot, celery, onion, parsley, bay leaves, 2 teaspoons of salt and the peppercorns. Add 3 litres (12 cups) of water. Bring to the boil, reduce the heat and simmer for 1 hour, skimming the surface as required. Allow to cool for at least 30 minutes. Strain and reserve the liquid.

2 Remove the chicken and allow to cool enough to handle. Discard the skin, then cut or pull the flesh from the bones and shred into small pieces. Set the chicken meat aside.

3 Heat the butter in a large pan over medium heat and, when foaming, add the flour. Cook, stirring, for 1 minute. Remove from the heat and gradually stir in the stock. Return to the heat and bring to the boil, stirring continuously. Add the potato, pumpkin and extra carrot and simmer for 7 minutes. Add the leek, extra celery and beans and simmer for a further 5 minutes. Finally, add the broccoli and sugar snap peas and cook for a further 3 minutes.

4 Just before serving, add the chicken meat, spinach, cream and chopped parsley. Reheat gently but do not allow the soup to boil. Keep stirring until the spinach has wilted. Season to taste with plenty of salt and freshly ground black pepper. Serve immediately.

COOK'S FILE

Hint: Do not overcook the vegetables, they should be tender yet crispy.
Note: The chicken stock (up to the end of Step 1) can be made 1 day ahead and kept, covered, in the refrigerator. This can, in fact, be beneficial—before reheating the stock, spoon off the fat which will have formed on the surface.

Cut the extra celery into short lengths, then into matchsticks.

Using a knife, trim the tops from the peas, pulling down to remove the string

Add the parsley sprigs and bay leaves to the pan.

Remove the skin from the chicken, then shred the meat.

Add the potato, pumpkin and extra carrot to the boiling soup.

Pour in the cream and stir until the spinach has wilted. Reheat gently.

ROASTED LEEK, GARLIC AND BACON SOUP

Preparation time: 25 minutes
Total cooking time: 1 hour 30 minutes
Serves 4–6

1 tablespoon olive oil
20 g (¾ oz) butter
2 rashers bacon, chopped
3 leeks, chopped
2 garlic cloves, chopped
1 stick celery, coarsely chopped
2 zucchini (courgettes), coarsely chopped
2 bay leaves
1.5 litres (6 cups) chicken stock
4 tablespoons cream
3 tablespoons finely chopped parsley
2 rashers bacon, extra, to serve

1 Preheat the oven to 160°C (315°F/Gas 2–3). Heat the oil and butter in a large roasting tin. Add the bacon rashers and stir over medium heat for 1–2 minutes. Add the leek, garlic, celery, zucchini and bay leaves and cook, stirring, for 2–3 minutes, without allowing to brown.
2 Transfer the roasting tin to the oven and roast the vegetables and bacon for 40 minutes, turning a couple of times. Cover with foil if starting to brown. Transfer to a large pan, pour on the stock and bring to the boil. Lower the heat and simmer for 30 minutes. Cool slightly, strain and return the liquid to the pan. Remove the bay leaves.
3 Put the vegetables and bacon in a food processor with a ladleful of the cooking liquid and process until smooth, adding more liquid if necessary. Return the purée to the pan with the liquid and add some pepper, the cream and parsley. Reheat gently.
4 To make the bacon garnish, trim off the rind and excess fat from the bacon and grill (broil) until crisp. Drain on paper towels, then crumble and serve on top of the soup.

Turn the vegetables during cooking and cover with foil to prevent browning

Process the vegetables and bacon until smooth. Add more liquid if necessary.

Grill (broil) the bacon until it is very crisp, then crumble to make a garnish.

PORK BALL AND VEGETABLE SOUP

Preparation time: 45 minutes
Total cooking time: 10 minutes
Serves 6–8

90 g (3 oz) stale white bread,
    crusts removed
500 g (1 lb 2 oz) minced
    (ground) pork
2 teaspoons chopped coriander
    (cilantro) roots and stems
3 teaspoons chopped coriander
    (cilantro) leaves
½ teaspoon five-spice powder
1 teaspoon grated ginger
1 egg white

270 g (9 oz/3 cups) bean sprouts
2 teaspoons sesame oil
2.25 litres (9 cups) chicken
    stock
1 small red chilli, chopped
2 carrots, cut into strips
2 sticks celery, cut into strips
6 spring onions (scallions),
    cut into strips
1½ tablespoons lime juice
coriander (cilantro) leaves,
    to serve

1 Line a baking tin with baking paper. Cover the bread with cold water, then squeeze out the liquid. Mix with the mince, coriander, five-spice powder, ginger, egg white and ¼ teaspoon each of salt and pepper.

2 Roll ½ tablespoons of the mixture into balls and lay in the tin. Divide the bean sprouts among bowls. Mix the sesame oil and stock in a large pan, bring to the boil and add the balls in batches. Return to the boil and, when they float, divide among the bowls.

3 Add the chilli, carrot, celery and spring onion to the stock, bring to the boil and simmer for 1 minute. Remove from the heat, season to taste and add the lime juice. Ladle into bowls and top with a few coriander leaves.

COOK'S FILE

Note: Five-spice is a mixture of Sichuan pepper, star anise, fennel, cloves and cinnamon.

Coarsely chop the roots and stems from the coriander and then chop finely.

Cut the vegetables into short lengths, then cut into fine (julienne) strips.

Soak the bread in water, then squeeze out the liquid.

MEXICAN BEAN CHOWDER

Preparation time: 20 minutes +
  overnight soaking
Total cooking time: 1 hour 10 minutes
Serves 6

155 g (5 oz/¾ cup) dried red
    kidney beans
165 g (5½ oz/¾ cup) dried
    Mexican black beans
1 tablespoon oil
1 onion, chopped
2 garlic cloves, crushed
½–1 teaspoon chilli powder
1 tablespoon ground cumin
2 teaspoons ground coriander
2 x 400 g (13 oz) cans chopped
    tomatoes
750 ml (26 fl oz/3 cups)
    vegetable stock
1 red capsicum (pepper),
    chopped
1 green capsicum (pepper),
    chopped
440 g (14 oz) can corn kernels
2 tablespoons tomato paste
    (concentrated purée)
grated Cheddar, to serve
sour cream, to serve

1 Soak the kidney beans and black beans in separate bowls in plenty of cold water overnight. Drain. Place all the beans in a large pan, cover with water and bring to the boil. Reduce the heat and simmer for 45 minutes, or until tender. Drain.
2 Heat the oil in a large pan, add the onion and cook over medium heat until soft. Add the garlic, chilli powder, cumin and coriander and cook for 1 minute. Stir in the tomato, stock, capsicum, corn and tomato paste. Cook, covered, for 25–30 minutes. Add the beans during the last 10 minutes of cooking. Stir occasionally.
3 Serve topped with grated Cheddar and a spoonful of sour cream.

COOK'S FILE

Note: Mexican black beans are also known as black turtle beans.

Soak the red kidney beans and black beans in separate bowls overnight.

Add the tomato, stock, capsicum, corn and tomato paste.

TOM YAM GOONG

Preparation time: 25 minutes
Total cooking time: 45 minutes
Serves 4–6

500 g (1 lb 2 oz) raw prawns
   (shrimp)
1 tablespoon oil
2 tablespoons Thai red curry
   paste
2 tablespoons tamarind purée
2 teaspoons turmeric
1 teaspoon chopped red chillies
4 makrut (kaffir lime) leaves,
   shredded

2 tablespoons fish sauce
2 tablespoons lime juice
2 teaspoons soft brown sugar
coriander (cilantro) leaves,
   to serve

1 Peel and devein the prawns, leaving the tails intact. Heat the oil in a large pan and cook the prawn shells and heads for 10 minutes over medium-high heat, tossing frequently, until the heads are deep orange.

2 Add 250 ml (9 fl oz/1 cup) water and the curry paste. Boil for 5 minutes, or until reduced slightly. Add another 2 litres (8 cups) of water and simmer for 20 minutes. Strain, discarding the shells and heads, and return the stock to the pan.

3 Add the tamarind, turmeric, chilli and kaffir lime leaves; bring to the boil and cook for 2 minutes. Add the prawns and cook for 5 minutes, or until pink. Mix in the fish sauce, lime juice and sugar. Serve sprinkled with coriander leaves.

COOK'S FILE

Hint: If you can't find tamarind purée, soak one-quarter of a block of tamarind in warm water for 10 minutes, work the mixture with your fingertips and remove the stones.

Add the red curry paste and 1 cup of water to the pan.

Add the tamarind, turmeric, chilli and makrut leaves.

Add the prawns to the boiling soup mixture and cook until pink.

THAI-STYLE CHICKEN AND BABY CORN SOUP

Preparation time: 30 minutes
Total cooking time: 15 minutes
Serves 4

150 g (5 oz) whole baby corn
1 tablespoon oil
2 stalks lemon grass, white part only, very finely sliced
2 tablespoons finely grated ginger
6 spring onions (scallions), chopped
1 red chilli, finely chopped

1 litre (4 cups) chicken stock
375 ml (13 fl oz/1½ cups) coconut milk
250 g (9 oz) chicken breast fillets, thinly sliced
130 g (4¼ oz) creamed corn
1 tablespoon soy sauce
2 tablespoons finely chopped chives, to serve
1 red chilli, thinly sliced, to serve

1 Cut the baby corn in half or quarters lengthways, depending on their size. Set aside.

2 Heat the oil in a pan over medium heat and cook the lemon grass, ginger, spring onion and chilli for 1 minute, stirring continuously. Add the stock and coconut milk and bring to the boil—do not cover or the coconut milk will curdle.

3 Stir in the corn, chicken and creamed corn and simmer for 8 minutes, or until the corn and chicken are just tender. Add the soy sauce, season well and serve garnished with the chives and chilli.

COOK'S FILE

Note: Canned baby corn can be substituted for fresh corn. Add during the last 2 minutes of cooking.

Grate the peeled ginger on the fine side of the grater.

Cut the baby corn lengthways into halves or quarters, depending on size.

Add the corn, chicken and creamed corn to the pan.

PARSNIP AND MUSTARD SOUP

Preparation time: 25 minutes
Total cooking time: 30 minutes
Serves 4–6

30 g (1 oz) butter
1 onion, chopped
750 g (1½ lb) parsnips, chopped
1 litre (4 cups) chicken stock
125 ml (4 fl oz/½ cup) milk
125 ml (4 fl oz/½ cup) cream
2–3 tablespoons wholegrain
    mustard
2 tablespoons chopped flat-leaf
    (Italian) parsley, to serve

1 Melt the butter in a large pan, add the onion and cook over moderate heat, stirring occasionally, until soft but not brown.
2 Add the parsnip and stock and bring to the boil. Simmer, covered, for 25 minutes, or until the parsnip is tender. Set aside to cool slightly.
3 Blend the soup in batches, in a blender or food processor. Return to the pan, add the milk and cream and reheat gently, but do not allow the soup to boil. Stir in the wholegrain mustard and season to taste with salt and freshly ground black pepper. Serve topped with the parsley.

Cut the peeled parsnips into strips, then chop into small pieces.

Add the parsnip and stock to the pan.

Using a wooden spoon, stir in the wholegrain mustard.

Breads and Dampers

Nothing transforms a humble bowl of soup or stew into a complete meal as successfully, or tastily, as a hunk of warm, freshly baked bread. The wonderful advantage to damper is that it can be cooked up quickly from a few store-cupboard standbys. Originally a staple food for early European settlers in outback Australia, it was a simple dough of flour and water cooked directly in the hot ashes of an open fire. These days the term refers to round leavened bread with a crunchy crust and a taste and texture similar to that of fresh white bread. The name comes from a British dialect word meaning 'something that takes the edge off the appetite'. The following recipes all serve 4 people.

HERB DAMPER

Sift 375 g (13 oz/3 cups) of self-raising flour and 1 teaspoon salt into a large bowl. Stir in 30 g (1 oz/½ cup) of chopped fresh herbs of your choice: try chives, parsley, oregano or coriander (cilantro). Make a well in the centre; combine 90 g (¾ oz) melted butter, 125 ml (4 fl oz/½ cup) of water and 125 ml (4 fl oz/½ cup) of milk and pour onto the dry ingredients. Stir with a knife until just combined and turn onto a lightly floured surface; knead briefly until just smooth. Shape the dough into a ball, put it on a greased oven tray and press into a 20 cm (8 inch) round. Using a sharp-pointed knife, score into 8 sections, without cutting all the way through. Brush with a little extra milk and dust lightly with extra flour. Bake in a preheated 210°C (415°C/ Gas 6–7) oven for 10 minutes, then reduce the heat to 180°C (350°F/Gas 4) and bake for a further 15 minutes, or until the damper is golden and sounds hollow when tapped.

Clockwise from top left: Herb Damper; Pumpkin Rounds; Onion Bread; Cheese, Olive and Rosemary Dampers

CHEESE, OLIVE AND ROSEMARY DAMPERS

Sift 250 g (9 oz/2 cups) of self-raising flour and 1 teaspoon salt into a large mixing bowl. Add 30 g (1 oz) chopped butter and use your fingertips to rub the butter into the flour until it resembles fine breadcrumbs. Stir in 50 g (1¾ oz/½ cup) of freshly grated Parmesan cheese, 60 g (2¼ oz/½ cup) of sliced black pitted olives and 1 tablespoon chopped fresh rosemary. Make a well in the centre and pour in the combined 125 ml (4 fl oz/½ cup) milk and 3 tablespoons buttermilk. Mix to form a soft dough using a knife. Turn the dough onto a lightly floured surface and knead briefly until just smooth. Divide the dough into 4 equal portions, shape each into a round ball and then flatten out to a 2 cm (¾ inch) thick round. Place on a greased oven tray, leaving room to expand. Brush with a little extra milk and score a cross on the top of each. Sprinkle with a little extra grated Parmesan and bake in a preheated oven 210°C (415°C/Gas 6–7) for 20 minutes, or until golden brown and crusty.
Variation: Try other chopped herbs such as oregano, parsley or chives in place of rosemary.

PUMPKIN ROUNDS

Sift 310 g (11 oz/2½ cups) of self-raising flour and ½ teaspoon ground nutmeg into a bowl. Add 60 g (2¼ oz) chopped butter and use your fingertips to rub the butter into the flour until it resembles fine breadcrumbs. Make a well in the centre. Mix together 1 egg, 250 g (9 oz/1 cup) of cooked mashed pumpkin (350 g/12 oz raw) and 1–2 tablespoons milk and pour onto the dry ingredients. Stir with a knife until just combined, then turn onto a lightly floured surface and knead gently until just smooth. Press the mixture out gently until about 2 cm (¾ inch) thick, then cut into 7 cm (2¾ inch) rounds. Place closely together on a greased oven tray and brush with a little extra milk. Bake in a preheated 210°C (415°C/Gas 6–7) oven for 15–20 minutes, or until the tops are lightly golden. Serve warm or cold with soup or stew.
Variations: Add 4 tablespoons of grated Cheddar cheese to the combined egg and pumpkin mixture or 4 tablespoons of chopped fresh herbs of your choice.

ONION BREAD

Heat a little olive oil in a frying pan, add a large, finely chopped onion and cook over medium heat until golden. Sift 375 g (13 oz/3 cups) of self-raising flour into a large mixing bowl and stir in a 35 g (1¼ oz) sachet French onion or tomato soup mix and the cooked onion. Make a well in the centre and stir in 500 ml (17 fl oz/2 cups) of buttermilk to form a soft sticky dough. Turn onto a well-floured surface, taking care to flour your hands and the surface of the dough. Gently and quickly mix in enough extra flour to form a smooth ball. Place the dough on a greased baking tray and shape into a long loaf. Score a criss-cross pattern on top, brush the top with milk and sprinkle with a little rock or sea salt. Bake in a preheated 180°C (350°F/Gas 4) oven for 50–60 minutes, or until the bread is browned and sounds hollow when tapped on the base. Serve warm or cold.

SPICY TOMATO AND CHICKPEA SOUP

Preparation time: 20 minutes +
  overnight soaking
Total cooking time: 1 hour 25 minutes
Serves 4

220 g (7 oz/1 cup) dried
  chickpeas
1 tablespoon oil
1 onion, finely chopped
2 garlic cloves, crushed
½–1 teaspoon chopped chilli
425 g (14 oz) can chopped
  tomatoes
500 ml (17 fl oz/2 cups)
  vegetable stock
2 teaspoons balsamic vinegar

1 Soak the chickpeas overnight in cold water. Drain. Cook the chickpeas in a large pan of boiling water for 1 hour, or until tender. Drain well.

2 Heat the oil in a large pan, add the onion and cook for 5 minutes, or until very soft and lightly golden. Add the garlic and chilli and cook for 1 minute, then add the tomato and stock.

3 Take 250 ml (9 fl oz/1 cup) of the soup mixture and transfer the rest to a food processor. Process until smooth, and return to the pan with the reserved soup mixture and chickpeas. Bring to the boil and simmer for 15 minutes. Stir in the vinegar and season to taste.

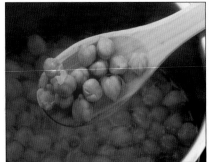

Cook the chickpeas in plenty of boiling water for 1 hour, or until tender.

Add the chopped garlic and chilli (to your taste) to the onion in the pan.

Pour the reserved soup mixture back into the pan.

SNOW PEA AND PRAWN SOUP

Preparation time: 10 minutes
Total cooking time: 25 minutes
Serves 4

350 g (11 oz) snow peas
    (mangetout), topped and
    tailed
45 g (1½ oz) butter
1 leek, chopped
1 garlic clove, crushed
2 teaspoons grated fresh ginger
1½ tablespoons plain
    (all-purpose) flour
1 litre (4 cups) chicken or fish
    stock
12 raw prawns (shrimp), peeled,
    deveined and chopped
coriander (cilantro) leaves,
    to serve

1 Roughly chop the snow peas. Melt the butter in a large saucepan and add the leek, garlic and ginger. Cook over medium heat until the leek is soft but not brown. Stir in the flour and cook for 1 minute.
2 Remove the pan from the heat and gradually stir in the stock. Return to the heat and bring to the boil, stirring continuously, until the mixture thickens slightly. Reduce the heat, cover the pan and simmer for 5 minutes. Add the snow peas and simmer for 5 minutes.
3 Puree the soup in batches in a blender or food processor. Return to a clean pan, bring to the boil and add the prawns. Simmer for 2 minutes, or until the prawns turn pink and are cooked through.
4 Season with salt and freshly ground black pepper to taste. Serve immediately, sprinkled with fresh coriander leaves.

COOK'S FILE

Hint: If you have one, it is best to purée this soup in a blender rather than a food processor. A food processor will give the soup a slightly granular and inferior texture.

Starting from the tail end, pull the string from the snow peas and trim the tops.

Remove the head, then peel away the shell from the body and tail of each prawn.

LOBSTER BISQUE

Preparation time: 1 hour
Total cooking time: 1 hour
Serves 4

400 g (13 oz) raw lobster tail
100 g (3½ oz) butter, softened
7 spring onions (scallion),
    chopped
1 onion, chopped
1 carrot, chopped
1 litre (4 cups) fish stock
4 sprigs parsley
1 bay leaf
4 peppercorns
4 tablespoons plain (all-purpose)
    flour
440 ml (14 fl oz/1¾ cups)
    tomato purée
1 tablespoon sherry, optional
125 ml (4 fl oz/½ cup) cream
pinch of nutmeg
2 teaspoons chopped tarragon

1 Carefully cut the lobster tail in half lengthways.
2 Melt half the butter in a pan, add the spring onion and onion and cook for 5 minutes, or until soft but not coloured. Add the carrot and cook for a further 2 minutes. Add the lobster halves, fish stock, parsley, bay leaf, peppercorns and 600 ml (20 fl oz/ 2½ cups) of water. Bring to the boil, then reduce the heat and simmer for 20 minutes, skimming the froth from the surface as required.
3 Remove the lobster from the stock, cool slightly and remove the meat from the shells. Crush the shells and return to the pan. Continue simmering for a further 40 minutes. Strain the stock, then strain again through a sieve lined with 2 layers of damp muslin.

4 Cut some thin slices from the lobster to use as a garnish and set aside. In a blender, blend the remaining lobster flesh with a little of the strained stock until smooth. Mix the flour and remaining butter to a paste. Add the puréed lobster to the pan along with the flour paste, tomato purée, sherry, cream, nutmeg and salt and pepper, to taste. Mix well.

5 Add the tarragon and remaining stock and cook, stirring continuously, over high heat until the soup boils and thickens. Reduce the heat and simmer gently for 5 minutes. Season to taste and serve garnished with the reserved lobster and some sprigs of tarragon, if you want.

Lift the meat out of the lobster shells and lightly crush the shells with a mallet.

Add the puréed lobster, flour paste, tomato purée, sherry, cream and nutmeg.

Add the chopped tarragon and remaining stock to the pan.

GRILLED CAPSICUM SOUP WITH HERB OMELETTE

Preparation time: 20 minutes
Total cooking time: 50 minutes
Serves 4–6

1 yellow or green capsicum (pepper), quartered
4 red capsicums (peppers), quartered
1 tablespoon olive oil
1 red onion, chopped
1 garlic clove, crushed
1 potato, diced
170 ml (5½ fl oz/⅔ cup) tomato juice

1 tablespoon balsamic vinegar

Herb omelette
3 eggs, lightly beaten
1 tablespoon milk
2 tablespoons chopped parsley
2 teaspoons oil
3 spring onions (scallions), finely chopped

1 Grill the capsicums skin-side-up under a hot grill (broiler) until blackened. Place in a plastic bag and cool. Peel away the skin and dice the yellow and one of the red capsicums. Set aside the remaining red capsicum.
2 Heat the oil and cook the onion, stirring, over medium heat until translucent. Add the garlic and potato and cook, stirring, for 1 minute. Add the tomato juice and 750 ml (26 fl oz/ 3 cups) of water and bring to the boil, then reduce the heat and simmer, covered, for 25 minutes, or until the potato is tender.
3 Blend the soup until smooth, in batches, with the reserved red capsicum. Return to the pan and add the diced capsicum, vinegar and seasoning. Reheat gently to serve.
4 To make the herb omelette, whisk the eggs, milk and parsley and season. Heat the oil in a frying pan. Add the spring onion and cook until just soft. Pour in the egg mixture and cook over medium heat until set. Cool on a wire rack and cut into diamonds. Serve on top of the soup.

Dice the yellow capsicum and one of the red capsicums.

Add the reserved red capsicum to the blender or food processor.

It is best to use a non-stick frying pan, if you have one.

OSSO BUCO, BARLEY AND VEGETABLE SOUP

Preparation time: 25 minutes
Total cooking time: 50 minutes
Serves 6

500 g (1 lb 2 oz) veal shanks
    with bones (osso buco), cut
    into 5 cm (2 inch) pieces (ask
    your butcher to do this)
2 tablespoons olive oil
1 onion, diced
1–2 garlic cloves, crushed
425 g (14 oz) can chopped
    tomatoes
1 tablespoon tomato paste
    (concentrated purée)
½ teaspoon dried oregano
1.5 litres (6 cups) beef stock
300 g (10 oz) potatoes, cubed
300 g (10 oz) pumpkin, cubed
165 g (5½ oz/¾ cup) pearl
    barley
200 g (6½ oz) zucchini
    (courgette), sliced

1 Trim the meat from the bones and cut into cubes. Scrape out the marrow from the bones, if you want to use it, and discard the bones. Heat the oil in a heavy-based pan and brown the meat and marrow, in batches if necessary, until a rich brown. Remove and drain on paper towels. Set the fried marrow aside, to garnish.

2 Add the onion to the pan and cook for 4–5 minutes over low heat; then add the garlic and cook for 1 minute longer. Add the meat, tomato, tomato paste, oregano, stock, potato and pumpkin to the pan.

3 Wash the barley in a sieve until the water runs clean, then drain and add to the soup. Bring to the boil, reduce the heat to low and simmer, covered, for 20 minutes. Add the zucchini and cook, covered, for 10 minutes, or until the barley is cooked. Serve garnished with the fried marrow.

COOK'S FILE

Note: Osso buco (or *ossobuco*) is Italian for marrowbone. It is a stew made with the knuckle of veal, usually served in a tomato sauce.

Trim the meat from the bones and then cut it into cubes.

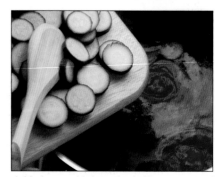

Add the meat, tomato, tomato paste, oregano, stock, potato and pumpkin.

Wash the barley in a sieve under running water until the water runs clear.

Add the zucchini to the boiling soup and cook for 10 minutes.

ROASTED VEGETABLE SOUP

Preparation time: 30 minutes
Total cooking time: 1 hour 35 minutes
Serves 6

500 g (1 lb 2 oz) unpeeled pumpkin, cut into large pieces
350 g (11 oz) unpeeled sweet potato, cut into large pieces
2 carrots, cut into large pieces
1 parsnip, cut into large pieces
1 red capsicum (pepper), cut into large pieces
2 onions, halved
4 garlic cloves, unpeeled
750 ml (24 fl oz/3 cups) vegetable stock
sour cream and thyme, to serve

1 Preheat the oven to 180°C (350°F/ Gas 4). Put the vegetables in a large greased baking dish and brush lightly with some olive oil.
2 Bake for 1 hour, turning often.

Remove the capsicum. Bake for 30 minutes longer; cool the vegetables slightly. Remove the skin from the capsicum; place in a food processor with the carrot, parsnip and onion.
3 Scrape the pumpkin and sweet potato flesh into the processor and squeeze in the garlic pulp. Add half the stock and purée until smooth. Place in a pan with the remaining stock and heat through. Season and serve with sour cream and thyme.

Cut the carrots, parsnip, pumpkin and sweet potato into large pieces.

Using your fingers, carefully peel away the blackened capsicum skin.

Using a teaspoon, scrape the flesh from the sweet potato and pumpkin.

MINESTRONE PRIMAVERA

Preparation time: 15 minutes
Total cooking time: 40 minutes
Serves 4–6

3 tablespoons olive oil
45 g (1½ oz) pancetta, finely
  chopped
2 onions, chopped
2 garlic cloves, thinly sliced
2 small sticks celery, sliced
2 litres (8 cups) chicken stock

4 tablespoons macaroni
2 zucchini (courgettes), chopped
150 g (5 oz/2 cups) shredded
  savoy cabbage
185 g (6 oz/1½ cups) green
  beans, chopped
155 g (5 oz/1 cup) frozen peas
40 g (1¼ oz/1 cup) shredded
  English spinach leaves
3 tablespoons chopped basil
grated Parmesan, to serve

1 Put the oil, pancetta, onion, garlic and celery in a large pan and stir occasionally over low heat for 8 minutes, or until the vegetables are soft but not brown. Add the stock and bring to the boil. Simmer, covered, for 10 minutes.
2 Add the macaroni and boil for 12 minutes, or until almost tender. Stir in the zucchini, cabbage, beans and peas and simmer for 5 minutes. Add the spinach and basil and simmer for 2 minutes. Season to taste and serve with the grated Parmesan.

Using a sharp knife, cut the pancetta into strips and then chop finely.

Chop the zucchini and finely shred the savoy cabbage.

Add the spinach and basil to the soup.

COUNTRY LENTIL, BACON AND GARLIC SOUP

Preparation time: 35 minutes
Total cooking time: 1 hour 5 minutes
Serves 4–6

3 tablespoons olive oil
3 onions, finely chopped
6 garlic cloves, thinly sliced
150 g (5 oz) speck or bacon,
 finely chopped
3 carrots, finely chopped
2 parsnips, finely chopped
3 sticks celery, sliced
200 g (6½ oz) red lentils, rinsed
1 litre (4 cups) vegetable stock
3 tablespoons tomato paste
 (concentrated purée)
3 tablespoons risoni (rice-shaped
 pasta)
4 spring onions (scallions),
 finely chopped
3 tablespoons chopped parsley
2 teaspoons finely grated lemon
 zest
100 g (3½ oz/1 cup) grated
 Parmesan, to serve

1 Heat the oil in a large pan. Add the onion, garlic and speck and cook, stirring occasionally, over low–medium heat for 15 minutes, or until a deep golden brown.
2 Add the carrot, parsnip and celery, stir well, cover and cook for 5 minutes, or until softened. Stir in the lentils, stock, tomato paste and 1 litre (4 cups) of water. Bring to the boil, then reduce the heat and simmer, uncovered, for 30 minutes, or until the lentils are tender; skim the surface as required.
3 Stir in the risoni and 500 ml (17 fl oz/ 2 cups) of water. Return to the boil and simmer for 10 minutes.
4 Add the spring onion, parsley and lemon zest and season to taste. Serve with the grated Parmesan.

Using a sharp knife, slice the garlic and finely chop the speck.

Add the well-drained lentils to the pan and stir well to combine.

CREAM OF ASPARAGUS SOUP

Preparation time: 20 minutes
Total cooking time: 55 minutes
Serves 4–6

1 kg (2 lb 4 oz) asparagus
   spears
30 g (1 oz) butter
1 onion, finely chopped
1 litre (4 cups) chicken stock
3 tablespoons basil leaves,
   chopped
1 teaspoon celery salt
250 ml (9 fl oz/1 cup) cream

1 Break off the woody ends from the asparagus and trim off the tips. Blanch the tips in boiling water for 1–2 minutes, refresh in cold water and set aside. Chop the remaining asparagus spears into large pieces.
2 Melt the butter in a large pan and cook the onion for 3–4 minutes over low–medium heat, or until it is soft and golden. Stir in the chopped asparagus and cook for 1–2 minutes, stirring continuously.
3 Add the chicken stock, basil and celery salt. Bring to the boil, then reduce the heat and simmer gently, covered, for 30 minutes.
4 Check that the asparagus is well cooked and soft. If not, simmer for a further 10 minutes. Set aside and allow to cool slightly.
5 Pour into a processor and process in batches until smooth, then sieve into a clean pan. Return to the heat, pour in the cream and gently reheat. Do not allow the soup to boil. Season to taste with salt and white pepper.
6 Serve immediately, with the asparagus tips placed on top.

COOK'S FILE

Hint: If you are not using home-made stock, always taste before adding seasoning to your soup—shop-bought stock can be very salty.

Break off the woody ends from the asparagus spears.

Test whether the asparagus is well cooked by piercing it with a fork.

BARLEY SOUP WITH GOLDEN PARSNIPS

Preparation time: 30 minutes +
  overnight soaking
Total cooking time: 2 hours
  20 minutes
Serves 6

200 g (6½ oz) pearl barley
1 tablespoon oil
2 onions, chopped
2 garlic cloves, finely chopped
2 carrots, chopped
2 potatoes, chopped
2 sticks celery, chopped
2 bay leaves, torn in half

2 litres (8 cups) chicken
  stock
125 ml (4 fl oz/½ cup) milk
40 g (1¼ oz) butter
3 parsnips, cubed
1 teaspoon soft brown sugar
chopped parsley, to serve

1 Soak the barley in water overnight. Drain. Place in a saucepan with 2 litres (8 cups) of water. Bring to the boil, reduce the heat and simmer, partially covered, for 1 hour 15 minutes, or until tender. Drain.

2 Heat the oil in a large saucepan, add the onion, garlic, carrot, potato and celery and cook for 3 minutes. Stir well, cover and cook for 15 minutes over low heat, stirring occasionally.

3 Add the barley, bay leaves, chicken stock, milk and 2 teaspoons of salt and 1 teaspoon of pepper. Bring to the boil, then reduce the heat and simmer the soup, partially covered, for 35 minutes. If it is too thick, add cold water, a little at a time, until the soup reaches your preferred consistency.

4 While the soup is simmering, melt the butter in a frying pan, add the parsnip and toss in the butter. Sprinkle with the sugar and cook until golden brown and tender. Serve the parsnip on top of the soup and sprinkle with the parsley.

Using a sharp knife, chop the potatoes, carrots and celery.

Add the drained barley to the cooked vegetables and stir in.

Sprinkle the soft brown sugar over the parsnip in the frying pan.

SAFFRON AND MUSSEL SOUP

Preparation time: 15 minutes
Total cooking time: 35 minutes
Serves 4

500 g (1 lb 2 oz) mussels
1 stick celery, chopped
1 carrot, chopped
1 onion, chopped
3 black peppercorns
3–4 parsley stalks
100 g (3½ oz) butter, softened
10 spring onions (scallions), finely chopped
40 g (1¼ oz/⅔ cup) finely chopped parsley
2 garlic cloves, crushed
185 ml (6 fl oz/¾ cup) dry white wine
4 tablespoons plain (all-purpose) flour
250 ml (9 fl oz/1 cup) cream
pinch of saffron threads

1 To make the mussel stock, scrub the mussels, remove their beards and discard any open or damaged mussels. Place the mussels, celery, carrot, onion, peppercorns and parsley stalks in a large saucepan with 1.5 litres (6 cups) of water and bring to the boil. Reduce the heat to low and simmer, covered, for 6 minutes.

2 Discard any unopened mussels. Strain the stock through a sieve lined with 2 layers of damp muslin. Rinse out the pan and reserve the mussels. Return the stock to the pan and simmer for 15 minutes. Set aside.

3 Melt half the butter in a pan, add the spring onion and cook over medium heat for 3–4 minutes, or until softened. Add the parsley, garlic and wine and season well with salt and freshly ground black pepper.

4 Mix the flour and remaining butter to a paste. Add the reserved stock to the pan and stir in the flour paste, cream and saffron threads, stir until the soup boils and thickens slightly. Simmer for 2–3 minutes. Add the mussels and stir gently until reheated.

Discard any unopened mussels with a pair of tongs.

Strain the stock through a sieve lined with damp muslin over a bowl.

Saffron is expensive, but only a pinch is needed to give the colour and flavour.

CREAM OF BROCCOLI SOUP

Preparation time: 15 minutes
Total cooking time: 25 minutes
Serves 4–6

750 g (1½ lb) broccoli
600 ml (20 fl oz/2½ cups)
    chicken stock
pinch of nutmeg
250 ml (9 fl oz/1 cup) cream

1 Cut the broccoli stems and florets into chunks. Place in a large pan with 250 ml (9 fl oz/1 cup) of the stock, cover and bring to the boil. Reduce the heat to low and simmer, covered, for 10 minutes, or until the broccoli is tender. Stir occasionally.
2 Transfer half the mixture to a food processor and process until finely chopped. Add a little of the remaining stock and blend to a purée. Transfer to a clean pan.
3 Transfer the remaining broccoli mixture and stock to the food processor and process until finely chopped. Return all the puréed soup to the pan, add the nutmeg and cream and stir over medium heat until heated through, but do not allow the soup to boil. Before serving, season with salt and freshly ground black pepper.

COOK'S FILE

Variation: Use vegetable stock for a vegetarian meal.

Using a sharp knife, cut the broccoli stems and florets into chunks.

Process the broccoli mixture until finely chopped, then add a little stock.

Add a pinch of nutmeg and pour on the cream, stirring until heated through.

111

ROASTED APPLE AND PUMPKIN SOUP

Preparation time: 20 minutes
Total cooking time: 1 hour 30 minutes
Serves 4

2 red apples, unpeeled
3 tablespoons olive oil
1 onion, finely chopped
2 teaspoons ground cumin
¼ teaspoon chilli powder
1 kg (2 lb 4 oz) butternut
   pumpkin (squash), roughly
   chopped
2 potatoes, chopped
2 teaspoons plain (all-purpose)
   flour
1 litre (4 cups) vegetable stock
315 ml (10 fl oz/1¼ cups) cream

1 Preheat the oven to 200°C (400°F/ Gas 6). Cut the unpeeled apples into thick wedges and cut away the core. Lay in a baking dish and pour over 1 tablespoon of the oil. Roast for 25–30 minutes, turning occasionally, until golden brown. Set aside.

2 Heat the remaining oil in a large pan, add the onion, cumin and chilli and cook for 10 minutes over low heat, or until the onion is very soft and golden. Add the pumpkin and potato and cook for 15 minutes, over medium–high heat, tossing regularly, or until slightly brown. Add the flour and cook, stirring, for 1 minute.

3 Remove from the heat and gradually pour in the stock, stirring. Return to the heat, bring to the boil, then reduce the heat and simmer, covered, for 30 minutes. Drain, reserving the vegetables and stock.

4 Set aside 8 pieces of the roasted apple. Put the rest in a food processor, with half the vegetables and 250 ml (9 fl oz/1 cup) of the reserved stock. Puree until smooth and return to the pan. Repeat with the remaining vegetables and the same amount of stock, then add to the pan with any remaining stock and the cream. Reheat and season well. Serve the remaining roasted apple as a garnish.

Using a sharp knife, seed and roughly chop the pumpkin.

Lay the unpeeled apples in the baking tray and drizzle with the olive oil.

Cook the vegetables until they begin to brown a little.

Add some of the reserved stock to the vegetables and apple.

PASTA AND WHITE BEAN SOUP

Preparation time: 30 minutes
Total cooking time: 20 minutes
Serves 6

4 tablespoons pine nuts
50 g (1¾ oz/1 cup) basil
    leaves
50 g (1¾ oz) rocket (arugula)
    leaves
2 garlic cloves, chopped
4 tablespoons finely grated
    Parmesan

4 tablespoons olive oil
185 g (6 oz) spiral pasta
1.5 litres (6 cups) chicken stock
2 x 300 g (10 oz) cans cannellini
    beans, drained

1 Put the pine nuts in a frying pan and dry-fry them over medium heat for 1–2 minutes, or until golden brown. Remove and allow to cool.
2 To make the pesto, mix the pine nuts, basil, rocket, garlic and Parmesan in a food processor and process until finely chopped. With the motor running, add the oil in a thin stream until well combined. Season to

taste with salt and pepper. Set aside.
3 Cook the pasta until just underdone. Heat the chicken stock in a large pan until it begins to boil. Reduce the heat to simmering point. Drain the pasta and add to the stock with the cannellini beans. Reheat and serve with a spoonful of pesto.

COOK'S FILE

Note: Cannellini beans are small, white and slightly kidney-shaped and are used a lot in Italian cooking, particularly in Tuscany.

Dry-fry the pine nuts until golden brown, but take care not to let them burn.

Put the pine nuts, basil, rocket, garlic and Parmesan in a food processor.

Add the drained cannellini beans to the simmering stock.

ORANGE-SCENTED, CURRIED PARSNIP SOUP

Preparation time: 25 minutes
Total cooking time: 40 minutes
Serves 6–8

50 g (1¾ oz) butter
1 onion, chopped
800 g (1 lb 10 oz) parsnips, diced
2 teaspoons curry powder

4 tablespoons orange juice
½ teaspoon grated orange zest
1.5 litres (6 cups) chicken stock
strips of orange zest, to garnish

1 Melt the butter in a large pan. Cook the onion for 2–3 minutes, then stir in the parsnip. Cover the pan and cook over low heat, stirring occasionally, for 20 minutes, or until the parsnip has softened but not browned.
2 Add the curry powder and cook for a further 2–3 minutes. Add the orange juice and grated zest. Put the parsnip mixture in a blender and blend in batches until smooth. Return to the pan and pour on the stock. Bring to the boil and simmer for 15 minutes.
3 Season to taste and garnish with the strips of orange zest. Serve with a spoonful of cream stirred through.

Peel and cut the parsnips into strips, then finely dice.

Peel the orange, remove the white pith, then cut the zest into thin strips.

Add the curry powder to the onion and parsnip and mix in well.

POTATO, PEA AND PARMESAN SOUP

Preparation time: 45 minutes
Total cooking time: 1 hour
Serves 4

750 g (1½ lb) unshelled peas
3 tablespoons olive oil
30 g (1 oz) butter
3 garlic cloves, thinly sliced
2 onions, very thinly sliced
500 g (1 lb 2 oz) potatoes, chopped
2 teaspoons plain (all-purpose) flour

500 ml (17 fl oz/2 cups) beef stock
2 teaspoons grated lemon zest
3 tablespoons chopped flat-leaf (Italian) parsley
125 ml (4 fl oz/½ cup) cream
100 g (3½ oz/1 cup) grated Parmesan

1 Shell the peas and set aside.
2 Heat the oil and butter in a large, heavy-based pan. Add the garlic, onion and potato and cook, stirring regularly, for 15–20 minutes, or until the potato is golden. Add the flour and stir for 2 minutes. Add the stock and 750 ml (24 fl oz/3 cups) of water and bring to the boil, stirring until the mixture thickens slightly. Reduce the heat and simmer, covered, for 20 minutes.
3 Add the peas, lemon zest and parsley. Simmer for 10 minutes, or until the peas are just tender. Stir in the cream, half the Parmesan and season to taste. Serve the remaining Parmesan with the soup.

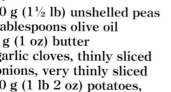

Using a sharp knife, slice the garlic and onion very thinly.

Cook the onion, garlic and potato until golden brown, stirring regularly.

Stir in the peas, grated lemon zest and chopped parsley.

Orange-scented, curried parsnip soup (top) with Potato, pea and Parmesan soup

Using a fine strainer, drain the liquid from the crab meat.

Using a sharp knife, peel the ginger, cut into strips, then chop finely.

Fold over the wrapper to enclose the filling and press firmly.

Cut the spring onions into lengths, then into thin strips.

LARGE CRAB DUMPLING SOUP

Preparation time: 25 minutes
Total cooking time: 20 minutes
Serves 4

170 g (5½ oz) can crab meat, drained
2 tablespoons finely chopped spring onions (scallions)
2 garlic cloves, finely chopped
2 teaspoons sesame oil
3 teaspoons chopped ginger
12 small gowgee or won ton wrappers
2 spring onions (scallions), extra
1.25 litres (5 cups) chicken stock
1 tablespoon soy sauce
1 tablespoon mirin (see Note)
1 teaspoon sugar

1 To make the crab filling, mix the crab with the spring onion, 1 clove of garlic, 1 teaspoon of sesame oil and 1 teaspoon of the ginger.

2 Place 2 teaspoons of filling on one half of each wrapper. Moisten the edge with some water and fold over to form a crescent. Press the edges together firmly. Lay the dumplings on a lightly floured surface.

3 Cut the extra spring onions into thin strips and set aside. Heat the remaining sesame oil in a pan, add the remaining garlic and ginger and cook over medium heat for 3–4 minutes, or until the garlic is lightly golden. Add the stock, soy sauce, mirin and sugar. Bring to the boil, add the spring onion strips and simmer for 2–3 minutes.

4 Bring a large pan of water to the boil, add 3–4 dumplings at a time and cook for 5 minutes, or until just cooked. Place in bowls, ladle the stock over the dumplings and serve.

COOK'S FILE

Note: Mirin is a Japanese sweetened rice wine which is used frequently in cooking.

ZUCCHINI CORN CHOWDER

Preparation time: 15 minutes
Total cooking time: 25 minutes
Serves 4

500 g (1 lb 2 oz) desiree
  potatoes, diced
1 onion, chopped
2 sticks celery, finely chopped
1 litre (4 cups) chicken stock
200 g (6½ oz/1 cup) corn
  kernels (either fresh or
  frozen)

4 zucchini (courgettes),
  chopped
125 g (4 oz/1 cup) grated
  Cheddar
70 g (2¼ oz/1½ cups) roughly
  chopped rocket (arugula)
  leaves
250 ml (9 fl oz/1 cup) milk
4 slices prosciutto, chopped,
  to serve

1 Place the potato, onion, celery and stock in a large pan and bring to the boil. Simmer, covered, for 20 minutes, or until the vegetables are tender. Leave to cool slightly.

2 Process the vegetables in a food processor until smooth. Return to a clean pan and then bring gently to the boil.
3 Reduce the heat, add the corn and zucchini and cook until the zucchini is tender but still firm. Stir in the Cheddar, rocket leaves and milk Reheat gently, while stirring, but do not allow the soup to boil.
4 Adjust the consistency of the soup with extra stock if necessary. Season to taste with salt and freshly ground black pepper and serve topped with the chopped prosciutto.

Using a sharp knife, roughly chop the rocket leaves.

Using a sharp knife, chop the prosciutto into small pieces.

Add the grated Cheddar and rocket leaves to the soup.

CABBAGE AND HAM SOUP WITH CHEESE DUMPLINGS

Preparation time: 40 minutes
Total cooking time: 1 hour 10 minutes
Serves 6

3 tablespoons olive oil
350 g (11 oz) piece of Kasseler
   or double-smoked ham,
   chopped into cubes
2 teaspoons soft brown sugar
2 onions, thinly sliced
2 leeks, thinly sliced
3 garlic cloves, finely
   chopped
1 tablespoon plain (all-purpose)
   flour
500 ml (17 fl oz/2 cups) chicken
   stock
250 g (9 oz) bacon bones
3 potatoes, chopped
½ savoy cabbage, finely
   shredded
1 tablespoon white wine vinegar

Cheese dumplings
30g (1 oz) cold butter, cut into
   small pieces
250 g (9 oz/2 cups) self-raising
   flour
60 g (2 oz/½ cup) finely grated
   Cheddar
2 teaspoons finely chopped
   thyme
2 teaspoons finely grated lemon
   zest, optional

1 Heat 1 tablespoon of the oil in a large pan and add the ham and sugar. Sauté over high heat, stirring continuously, for 5 minutes, or until just golden. Remove with a slotted spoon and drain on paper towels. Take care not to overcook or the ham will become dry.

2 Add the remaining oil, onion, leek and garlic and cook for 15 minutes over low heat, stirring regularly. Add the flour and cook for 1 minute, stirring. Remove from the heat and gradually add the stock, bacon bones and 1.5 litres (6 cups) of water. Return to the heat and cook, stirring, until the mixture comes to the boil and thickens slightly. Reduce the heat and simmer for 30 minutes, skimming the surface as required.

3 Remove the bacon bones, cut off the meat and discard the bones. Shred the meat into small pieces. Return to the pan with the potato and simmer for 10 minutes, or until heated through and the potato is tender. Add the ham, cabbage and vinegar and season with pepper, cover and cook over very low heat for 5–10 minutes while preparing the dumplings.

4 To make the dumplings, rub the butter into the flour until crumbly. Mix in the Cheddar, thyme and about 125 ml (4 fl oz/½ cup) of water, or enough to bind the mixture together. Roll 2 level teaspoons of the mixture into balls. Place into the soup and simmer, covered, for 8 minutes, or until the dumplings are plump. Season to taste and scatter with the lemon zest. Serve immediately.

COOK'S FILE

Note: Kasseler ham is cured and smoked ham—a traditional German speciality.

Hint: Avoid crusty-looking bacon bones as they are extremely salty. Taste before adding any extra salt to this recipe.

Using a sharp knife, cut the ham into slices and then into cubes.

Remove the ham with a slotted spoon and drain on paper towels.

Add the water, stock and bacon bones to the pan.

Add the peeled chopped potato to the pan and simmer until tender.

With a flat-bladed knife, mix in the cheese and thyme, then add the water.

The dumplings are ready when they are plump and float to the surface.

CREAM OF MUSHROOM SOUP

Preparation time: 30 minutes
Total cooking time: 15 minutes
Serves 4

500 g (1 lb 2 oz) large field
    mushrooms
50 g (1¾ oz) butter
4 spring onions (scallions),
    finely chopped
3 garlic cloves, finely chopped
1 teaspoon chopped lemon
    thyme

2 teaspoons plain (all-purpose)
    flour
1 litre (4 cups) chicken or
    vegetable stock
250 ml (8 fl oz/1 cup) cream
chives and thyme, to garnish

1 Thinly slice the mushroom caps, discarding the stalks. Melt the butter in a heavy-based pan and cook the spring onion, garlic and lemon thyme, stirring, for 1 minute, or until the garlic is golden. Add the mushroom and ½ teaspoon each of salt and white pepper. Cook for 3–4 minutes, or until the mushroom just softens. Add

the flour and cook, stirring, for a further minute.

2 Remove the pan from the heat and add the stock, stirring continuously. Return to the heat and bring to the boil, stirring. Reduce the heat and simmer gently for 2 minutes more, stirring occasionally.

3 Whisk the cream into the soup, then reheat gently, stirring. Do not allow the soup to boil. Season to taste with salt and pepper, and garnish with the chopped chives and thyme.

Pull the lemon thyme leaves from the stems and chop them.

Remove the stalks from the mushrooms and thinly slice the caps.

Whisk in the cream, then reheat the soup gently without boiling.

CAULIFLOWER SOUP WITH CHEDDAR FINGERS

Preparation time: 25 minutes
Total cooking time: 1 hour
Serves 4

20 g (¾ oz) butter
1 onion, chopped
1 stick celery, chopped
1 potato, chopped
½ teaspoon ground nutmeg
750 g (1½ lb) cauliflower,
  cut into florets
1 litre (4 cups) chicken or
  vegetable stock
250 ml (9 fl oz/1 cup) cream

Cheddar fingers
4 slices white bread, crusts
  removed
20 g (¾ oz) butter, melted
1 garlic clove, crushed
60 g (2 oz/½ cup) finely grated
  Cheddar

1 Melt the butter in a large pan. Cook the onion for 1–2 minutes. Add the celery, potato and nutmeg. Cook, stirring, for 2–3 minutes, then add the cauliflower.

2 Pour on the stock and bring to the boil, then reduce the heat and simmer for 20 minutes, or until the vegetables are tender. Stir occasionally.

3 Place in a food processor in batches and process until smooth. Return to the pan, add the cream and season to taste. Reheat gently, but do not allow the soup to boil.

4 To make the Cheddar fingers, preheat the oven to 180°C (350°F/Gas 4). Brush the bread on both sides with the combined butter and garlic. Cut each slice into 4 fingers. Lay on a baking tray and bake for 10 minutes, or until crisp. Sprinkle with the Cheddar and bake for 10 minutes more, or until golden and the cheese has melted. Float two fingers on top of the soup for each person and serve the rest alongside.

Using a sharp knife, trim the cauliflower into florets.

Add the ground nutmeg to the pan and mix in with a wooden spoon.

Sprinkle the grated Cheddar onto the crisp bread fingers.

CREAM OF CELERY SOUP

Preparation time: 40 minutes
Total cooking time: 25 minutes
Serves 4

600 ml (20 fl oz/2½ cups) milk
1 onion, studded with 3 cloves
410 ml (13 fl oz/1⅔ cups)
    vegetable stock
4 celery tops and leaves
2 bay leaves, torn in half
3 sticks celery
60 g (2 oz) butter
1 onion, finely chopped
3 tablespoons plain (all-purpose)
    flour
125 ml (4 fl oz/½ cup) cream

Blue cheese croutons
4 slices bread
80 g (2¾ oz) blue cheese, at
    room temperature
40 g (1¼ oz) finely grated
    mozzarella cheese

1 Put the milk, studded onion, stock, celery tops and leaves, bay leaves and ½ teaspoon each of salt and white pepper in a pan. Bring to the boil, then reduce the heat and simmer gently for 8 minutes. Allow to cool, then strain. Set aside, discarding the flavourings.

2 Cut the celery into matchsticks. Heat the butter in a large pan and, when foaming, add the onion and cook for 5 minutes, or until softened. Add the celery and cook for a further 2 minutes. Add the flour and cook for 1 minute, stirring continuously.

3 Remove from the heat and gradually stir in the stock. Return to the heat and cook, stirring, until the mixture boils and thickens. Simmer for 2 minutes. Stir in the cream and season. Set aside and keep warm.

4 To make the blue cheese croutons, lightly toast the bread, then trim away the crusts. Spread the bread with the blue cheese and sprinkle with the mozzarella. Grill (broil) for 1–2 minutes, or until golden. Cut into 8 triangles and float a couple on top of the soup. Serve the rest alongside.

Peel the onion and stud with the cloves, pressing firmly to secure.

Using a sharp knife, cut the celery into even-sized lengths, then into matchsticks.

Remove the pan from the heat and pour in the stock.

Trim the crusts from the toasted bread and spread with the blue cheese.

LEMON CHICKEN SOUP

Preparation time: 10 minutes
Total cooking time: 10 minutes
Serves 4

2 chicken breast fillets
1 lemon
1 litre (4 cups) chicken stock
2 sprigs lemon thyme, plus
    extra, to garnish (see Note)

1 Trim any excess fat from the chicken. Using a vegetable peeler, cut 2 strips of rind from the lemon and remove the pith. Place the stock, rind and thyme in a shallow pan and slowly bring almost to the boil Reduce to simmering point, add the chicken and cook, covered, for 7 minutes, or until the meat is tender.
2 Remove the chicken from the pan, transfer to a plate and cover with foil.
3 Strain the stock through a sieve lined with 2 layers of damp muslin into a clean pan. Finely shred the chicken and return to the stock. Reheat gently and season to taste with salt and freshly ground black pepper. Serve immediately, garnished with the extra sprigs of thyme.

COOK'S FILE

Note: You can use ordinary thyme if lemon thyme is not available.
Hint: If you don't have time to make your own stock, poultry shops or butchers sometimes sell their own. These may have more flavour and contain less salt than stock cubes.

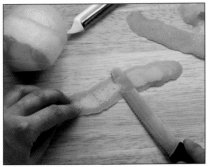

Using a small knife, remove the white pith from the lemon rind.

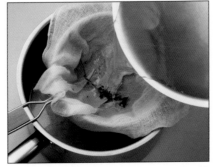

Pour the stock through a sieve lined with damp muslin into a clean pan.

Finely shred the chicken into thin pieces and return to the soup.

CHILLI, CHICKPEA AND CORIANDER SOUP

Preparation time: 20 minutes
Total cooking time: 25 minutes
Serves 2–4

30 g (1 oz) butter
1 onion, roughly chopped
3 garlic cloves, crushed
2 red chillies, seeded and finely
    chopped
2 teaspoons ground cumin
1 teaspoon ground turmeric
1 teaspoon ground coriander
425 g (14 oz) can chickpeas
1 teaspoon grated lemon zest

4 tablespoons chopped coriander
    (cilantro) leaves and stalks
600 ml (20 fl oz/2½ cups)
    chicken or vegetable stock

Crispy gremolata
2 slices of bread
30 g (1 oz) butter, melted
2 tablespoons chopped parsley
1 tablespoon grated lemon zest

1 Heat the butter in a large pan. Cook the onion, garlic and chilli for 2–3 minutes, or until softened but not browned. Add the spices and cook for 1–2 minutes, then add the chickpeas.
2 Process in a food processor until smooth. Add the lemon zest and coriander, pour on the stock and process until smooth. Reheat gently for 15 minutes, stirring frequently, but do not allow the soup to boil. Season to taste with salt and freshly ground black pepper.
3 To make the crispy gremolata, preheat the oven to 180°C (350°F/ Gas 4). Put the bread in a food processor and chop roughly. Lay the crumbs on a baking tray and mix in the butter. Bake for 5 minutes, or until crisp. Mix the parsley and lemon rind together and add to the gremolata just before serving. Serve the gremolata sprinkled on top of the soup.

Using a sharp knife, chop the coriander leaves and stalks.

Add the ground cumin, turmeric and coriander to the pan.

Mix through the melted butter with the breadcrumbs on the baking tray.

POTATO AND GARLIC SOUP

Preparation time: 15 minutes
Total cooking time: 1 hour 5 minutes
Serves 4–6

2 garlic bulbs
500 g (1 lb 2 oz) potatoes
2 tablespoons olive oil
1 onion, finely chopped
2 litres (8 cups) chicken stock
snipped chives, to serve

1 Separate the garlic bulbs into cloves and gently crush with the flat side of a knife to split the skin. Peel the cloves and cut in half. Chop the potatoes into small cubes.

2 Heat the olive oil in a large frying pan, add the onion and garlic and cook over low–medium heat for 5–10 minutes, or until the garlic is lightly golden. Add the potato and cook over low heat for 5 minutes. Add the chicken stock and simmer for 40–45 minutes, or until the garlic is very soft and the stock has reduced. Set aside to cool slightly.

3 Process the soup in batches in a food processor until smooth. Return to the pan and add ½ teaspoon of salt; taste before adding any more seasoning. Reheat gently before serving. Serve with a sprinkling of snipped chives.

COOK'S FILE

Note: If you don't have time to make stock, butchers or poultry shops may sell their own. Or try the carton stocks from supermarkets, which contain less salt and additives than cubes. If you are not using home-made stock, make sure you taste the soup before seasoning—some shop-bought stocks can be extremely salty. Season after cooking, as long simmering tends to concentrate the flavours of the soup.

Two bulbs may seem a lot, but once it is cooked garlic takes on a mellow flavour.

Crush each clove with the flat side of a knife to split the skin.

Simmer the stock until the garlic cloves are very soft.

125

POTAGE BONNE FEMME

Preparation time: 20 minutes
Total cooking time: 45 minutes
Serves 6

30 g (1 oz) butter
1 tablespoon olive oil
2 leeks, thinly sliced
500 g (1 lb 2 oz) potatoes, finely
    chopped
2 carrots, finely chopped
1.75 litres (7 cups) vegetable
    stock
finely chopped flat-leaf (Italian)
    parsley, to garnish

1 Melt the butter and oil in a large pan. Add the leek and cook over low heat for 5 minutes, or until softened. Add the potato and carrot and cook over medium heat for 5 minutes, stirring continuously.
2 Add the stock and slowly bring to the boil. Simmer, covered, for 25–30 minutes, or until the vegetables are tender. Allow to cool slightly.
3 Process the soup in a food processor in batches until smooth and return to the pan. Reheat gently over low heat and season well with salt and freshly cracked pepper. Serve sprinkled with chopped parsley.

COOK'S FILE

Hint: If you don't have time to make your own stock, ask your butcher or poultry shop if they make their own. Alternatively, buy supermarket stock in cartons—these tend to be less salty than the cubes.

When using shop-bought stock be careful with the amount of seasoning you add, as they can be rather salty. Always taste before seasoning.

Note: Potage Bonne Femme is a traditional French soup. *Potage* is the French word for soup and *bonne femme* (literally, 'good wife') is the term applied to dishes prepared in a simple, family or rustic fashion.

Thinly slice the leeks and finely chop the potatoes and carrots.

Process the soup in batches in a food processor until smooth.

TORTELLINI VEGETABLE SOUP WITH PISTOU

Preparation time: 30 minutes
Total cooking time: 55 minutes
Serves 6–8

1 tablespoon olive oil
1 leek, finely chopped
1 onion, finely chopped
2 carrots, finely chopped
2 potatoes, finely chopped
2 zucchini (courgettes), finely
   chopped
1 stick celery, finely chopped

2 tomatoes, chopped
2.5 litres (10 cups) vegetable
   stock
375 g (12 oz) tortellini pasta
100 g (3¼ oz/2 cups) basil
   leaves
3 garlic cloves, chopped
100 g (3¼ oz/1 cup) finely
   grated Parmesan
5 tablespoons olive oil, extra

1 Heat the oil in a very large pan, add the leek and onion and cook over low heat for 5 minutes, or until just soft. Add the carrot, potato, zucchini and celery and cook over medium heat for 5 minutes, stirring continuously. Add the tomato and stock and bring to the boil. Simmer, covered, over low heat for 20–30 minutes, or until the vegetables are tender.

2 Bring a large saucepan of salted water to the boil and cook the pasta for 6–8 minutes, until *al dente*. Drain, add to the soup and season well.

3 To make the pistou, place the basil in a food processor with the garlic and Parmesan. Process until chopped. With the motor running, add the extra oil. Add a spoonful to each bowl.

Add the chopped tomato and stock to the softened vegetables.

Add the al dente (semi-firm) tortellini to the soup.

Process the basil, garlic and Parmesan until finely chopped.

127

Stews

BOMBAY LAMB CURRY

Preparation time: 25 minutes
Total cooking time: 1 hour 25 minutes
Serves 4–6

1.5 kg (3 lb 5 oz) leg of lamb,
   boned (ask your butcher
   to do this)
2 tablespoons ghee or oil
2 onions, finely chopped
2 garlic cloves, crushed
2 small green chillies, finely
   chopped
5 cm (2 inch) piece ginger,
   grated
1½ teaspoons turmeric
2 teaspoons ground cumin
3 teaspoons ground coriander
½–1 teaspoon chilli powder
1–½ teaspoons salt
425 g (15 oz) can crushed
   tomatoes
2 tablespoons coconut cream

1 Cut the meat into cubes, removing any skin and fat. You will have about 1 kg (2 lb 4 oz) meat remaining. Heat the ghee or oil in a large heavy-based frying pan (with a lid). Add the onion and cook, stirring frequently, over medium–high heat for 10 minutes, until golden brown. Add the garlic, chilli and ginger and stir for 2 minutes, taking care not to burn them.

2 Mix together the spices and chilli powder in a small bowl. Stir to a smooth paste with 2 tablespoons water and add to the frying pan. Stir constantly for 2 minutes, taking care not to burn them.

3 Add the meat a handful at a time, stirring well to coat with spices—make sure all the meat is well coated and browned.

4 Add the salt to taste and stir in the tomatoes. Bring to the boil, cover and reduce the heat to low. Simmer for 45–60 minutes, until the lamb is tender. Stir in the coconut cream 30 minutes before the end of the cooking time.

COOK'S FILE

Storage time: Keep covered and refrigerated up to 3 days. The flavour improves after at least 1 day.

Cut the meat into bite-sized chunks, about 3 cm (1¼ inch) square.

Once the onion is golden brown, stir in the garlic, chilli and ginger.

Blend the ground spices to a smooth paste with a little water.

Add the meat a handful at a time to make sure it is thoroughly coated.

PERSIAN CHICKEN

Preparation time: 20 minutes
Total cooking time: 1 hour
Serves 6

1.5 kg (3 lb 5 oz) small chicken
  thighs
60 g (2¼ oz/½ cup) plain
  (all-purpose) flour
2 tablespoons olive oil
1 large onion, chopped
2 garlic cloves, chopped
½ teaspoon ground cinnamon
4 ripe tomatoes, chopped

6 fresh dates, pitted and halved
2 tablespoons currants
500 ml (17 fl oz/2 cups) rich
  chicken stock
2 teaspoons finely grated lemon
  zest
80 g (2¾ oz/½ cup) almonds,
  toasted and roughly chopped
2 tablespoons chopped fresh
  parsley

1 Coat the chicken pieces with flour and shake off any excess. Heat the oil in a large heavy-based pan over medium heat. Brown the chicken on all sides, turning regularly, and then remove from the pan. Drain any excess oil from the pan.

2 Add the onion, garlic and cinnamon and cook for 5 minutes, stirring regularly, until the onion is soft.

3 Add the tomatoes, dates, currants and stock. Bring to the boil, return the chicken to the pan, cover with sauce, lower the heat and simmer, uncovered, for 30 minutes. Add the lemon zest and season to taste. Bring back to the boil and boil for 5 minutes, or until thickened. Garnish with almonds and parsley and serve with buttered rice.

An easy way to coat the chicken with flour is to toss them both in a bag.

Brown the chicken on all sides, turning it regularly to prevent sticking.

Add the tomatoes, dates, currants and stock to the softened onion.

HUNGARIAN VEAL GOULASH

Preparation time: 20 minutes
Total cooking time: 2 hours
Serves 4

2 tablespoons olive oil
2 medium onions, chopped
500 g (1 lb 2 oz) stewing veal, cubed
1 tablespoon Hungarian paprika
¼ teaspoon caraway seeds

425 g (15 oz) can chopped tomatoes
500 ml (17 fl oz/2 cups) beef stock
1 large potato, diced
1 large carrot, sliced
1 green capsicum (pepper), chopped
125 g (4½ oz/½ cup) sour cream

1 Heat the oil in a large heavy-based pan. Fry the onion for 10 minutes, stirring often, until soft and golden brown. Remove the onion, increase the heat and brown the veal in batches. Return the veal and onion to the pan.
2 Add the paprika, caraway seeds, tomatoes and stock. Bring to the boil, reduce the heat, cover and simmer for 1¼ hours.
3 Add potato, carrot and capsicum and cook, uncovered, for 20 minutes, or until the vegetables are tender. Season to taste with salt and freshly ground black pepper, then stir in the sour cream. Serve with rice or pasta.

Brown the meat in small batches so that it browns but doesn't stew in the liquid.

Stir in the paprika, caraway seeds, undrained tomatoes and stock.

Add the potato, carrot and capsicum for the last 20 minutes of cooking.

Use the prawn shells and trimmings to make a good base stock.

Use a slotted spoon to lift the sausage from the oil in the pan.

Add the canned tomatoes and their juice to the pan with the herbs.

After 25 minutes the rice should have absorbed most of the liquid.

SEAFOOD JAMBALAYA

Preparation time: 20 minutes
Total cooking time: 1 hour 10 minutes
Serves 6

1 kg (2 lb 4 oz) raw king prawns
    (shrimp)
1 small onion, chopped
1 stick celery, chopped
250 ml (9 fl oz/1 cup) dry white
    wine
3 tablespoons vegetable oil
200 g (7 oz) spicy sausage,
    chopped
1 medium onion, chopped
1 red capsicum (pepper),
    chopped
1 stick celery, chopped
425 g (15 oz) can crushed
    tomatoes
½ teaspoon cayenne pepper
½ teaspoon cracked black pepper
¼ teaspoon dried thyme
¼ teaspoon dried oregano
400 g (14 oz/2 cups) long-grain
    rice

1 Shell the prawns, remove the back veins and set the prawns aside. Put the trimmings in a pan with the small onion, celery, wine and 1 litre (4 cups) of water. Bring to the boil, then reduce the heat and simmer for 20 minutes. Strain, reserving the stock.
2 Heat the oil in a large heavy-based pan and cook the sausage for 5 minutes, until browned. Remove from the pan and set aside.
3 Add the onion, capsicum and celery to the pan and cook, stirring often, for 5 minutes. Add the tomato, pepper and herbs, bring to the boil and then reduce the heat and simmer, covered, for 10 minutes.
4 Return the sausage to the pan and add the rice and prawn stock. Bring back to the boil, reduce the heat and simmer, covered, for 25 minutes, until almost all the liquid has been absorbed and the rice is tender. Add the prawns, cover and cook for a further 5 minutes. Serve immediately.

PORK AND APPLE BRAISE

Preparation time: 20 minutes
Total cooking time: 40 minutes
Serves 4

2 tablespoons oil
1 large onion, thinly sliced
1 garlic clove, chopped
2 teaspoons soft brown sugar
2 green apples, cut into wedges
4 pork loin steaks or medallions
2 tablespoons brandy

2 tablespoons wholegrain
  mustard
250 ml (9 fl oz/1 cup) rich
  chicken stock
110 g (3¾ oz/½ cup) pitted
  prunes
185 ml (6 fl oz/¾ cup) cream

1 Heat the oil in a large heavy-based pan. Cook the onion and garlic for 10 minutes over low heat, stirring often, until softened and golden brown. Add the sugar and apple and cook, stirring regularly, until the apple begins to brown. Remove from the pan.

2 Reheat the pan and lightly brown the pork steaks, two at a time; return to the pan. Add the brandy and stir until it has nearly all evaporated. Add the mustard and stock. Simmer over low heat, covered, for 15 minutes.
3 Return the apple to the pan with the prunes and cream and simmer for 10 minutes, or until the pork is tender. Season to taste before serving.

COOK'S FILE

Hint: Take care not to overcook pork or it can become tough and dry.

Stir the apple regularly over the heat until it begins to brown.

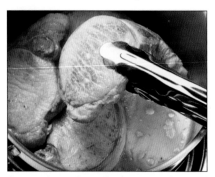

Brown the pork steaks two at a time and then return them all to the pan.

Put the browned apple back in the pan with the prunes and cream.

VEGETABLE STEW WITH COUSCOUS

Preparation time: 30 minutes
Total cooking time: 40 minutes
Serves 4

2 tablespoons olive oil
1 onion, sliced
2 teaspoons mustard seeds
2 teaspoons ground cumin
1 teaspoon paprika
1 garlic clove, crushed
2 teaspoons grated ginger
2 sticks celery, thickly sliced
2 small carrots, thickly sliced
2 small parsnips, peeled, cubed
300 g (10½ oz) pumpkin, diced
2 zucchini (courgettes), sliced
375 ml (13 fl oz/1½ cups)
   vegetable stock
185 g (6½ oz/1 cup) instant
   couscous
30 g (1 oz) butter

1 Heat the oil in a large pan. Add the onion and cook over medium heat for 10 minutes, until very soft and lightly golden, stirring occasionally. Add the mustard seeds, spices, garlic and ginger and stir for 1 minute. Add the vegetables and stir to coat with spices.
2 Add the stock and bring to the boil. Reduce the heat and simmer, partially covered, for 30 minutes, until tender.
3 Put the couscous in a heatproof bowl. Add 185 ml (6 fl oz/¾ cup) of boiling water and stand for 2 minutes. Add the butter and stir until melted, then fluff up the grains with a fork. Serve with the vegetables.

Add the mustard seeds, cumin, paprika, garlic and ginger.

Simmer until the vegetables are tender but not breaking up.

Separate the grains of couscous and fluff them up with a fork.

FAMOUS IRISH STEW

Preparation time: 20 minutes
Total cooking time: 1 hour 15 minutes
Serves 4

8 lamb neck chops
4 thick rashers bacon
30 g (1 oz) dripping or butter
1 kg (2 lb 4 oz) potatoes,
    sliced
3 carrots, sliced
3 medium onions, thickly
    sliced

500 ml (17 fl oz/2 cups) beef
    stock
4 thyme sprigs

1 Trim the chops, removing any excess fat, and cut the bacon into short strips. Heat the dripping or butter in a pan and cook the chops until brown on both sides; remove from the pan. Add the bacon and cook until crisp. Remove from the pan and leave to drain on paper towels.
2 Layer half the potato, carrot and onion in a deep, heavy-based pan. Season with pepper and add half the

bacon. Layer the chops over this and cover with the rest of the potato, carrot, onion and bacon.
3 Add the stock and thyme. Cover and bring to the boil, then reduce the heat and simmer for 1 hour, or until the lamb is very tender.

COOK'S FILE

Note: Traditionally, Irish Stew was made from mutton with no potatoes or carrots. The addition of vegetables makes the dish a satisfying one-pot meal. Try using lemon thyme for a slightly different flavour.

Use a sharp knife to remove any excess fat from the chops.

Spread the chops in one layer over the vegetables and bacon.

Once all the ingredients are layered, pour the stock and thyme over them.

VEAL BRAISED WITH LEMON THYME

Preparation time: 15 minutes
Total cooking time: 1 hour 30 minutes
Serves 4

2 tablespoons olive oil
one 6 cutlet rack of veal,
    trimmed to a neat shape
2 medium leeks, finely sliced
30 g (1 oz) butter
1 tablespoon plain (all-purpose)
    flour

1 tablespoon grated lemon zest
500 ml (17 fl oz/2 cups) chicken
    stock
375 ml (13 fl oz/1½ cups) white
    wine
2 tablespoons fresh lemon thyme
    leaves
125 ml (4 fl oz/½ cup) cream

1 Heat the oil in a deep heavy-based frying pan over medium heat and brown the veal well on all sides, then remove from the pan. Add the leeks and butter to the pan, reduce the heat and cover. Simmer for 10 minutes,

stirring occasionally. Be careful not to burn the leeks or they will be bitter.
2 Add the flour to the pan and stir continuously for 2 minutes. Add the zest and a little pepper, stir in the stock and wine and bring to the boil, stirring continuously. Reduce the heat.
3 Return the veal to the pan, with any juices. Cover and simmer for 1 hour, or until the veal is tender. Cut the veal into cutlets. Add the thyme, cream and salt to the sauce. Serve over the veal.

Remove the fat and trim the veal rack into a neat shape.

Add the grated lemon zest to the leeks in the pan.

Put the browned veal back in the pan once you have braised the leeks.

*Famous Irish Stew (top)
and Veal Braised with Lemon Thyme*

COQ AU VIN

Preparation time: 20 minutes
Total cooking time: 1 hour
Serves 6

plain (all-purpose) flour
2 kg (4 lb 8 oz) chicken pieces
3 tablespoons oil
4 thick bacon rashers, sliced
12 small pickling onions
2 garlic cloves, crushed
2 tablespoons brandy
375 ml (13 fl oz/1½ cups) good
    red wine
375 ml (13 fl oz/1½ cups)
    chicken stock
2 bay leaves
1 fresh bouquet garni
3 tablespoons tomato paste
    (concentrated purée)
250 g (9 oz) small button
    mushrooms

1 Season the flour with a little salt and pepper and coat the chicken; shake off any excess flour. Heat 2 tablespoons of the oil in a heavy-based pan and brown the chicken in small batches; drain on paper towels.

2 Heat the remaining oil in the cleaned pan. Add the bacon, onions and garlic and cook, stirring, until the onions are browned. Add the chicken, brandy, wine, stock, bay leaves, bouquet garni and tomato paste. Bring to the boil, reduce the heat and simmer, covered, for 30 minutes.

3 Add the mushrooms, stirring to combine, and simmer, uncovered, for 10 minutes, until the chicken is tender and the sauce has slightly thickened. Serve with crusty French bread.

Wrap some fresh herbs in muslin to make a bouquet garni.

Brown the chicken well and then drain on paper towels.

Add the chicken, brandy, wine, stock, bouquet garni and tomato paste.

BEEF STEW WITH PECANS

Preparation time: 15 minutes
Total cooking time: 2 hours
Serves 4

3 tablespoons olive oil
1 onion, sliced
120 g (4¼ oz) mushrooms, sliced
1–2 garlic cloves, crushed
1½ tablespoons plain (all-purpose) flour
1 teaspoon ground cinnamon
1½ teaspoons salt
½ teaspoon black pepper
½ teaspoon ground nutmeg
½ teaspoon ground coriander
pinch cayenne pepper
1 teaspoon grated ginger
750 g (1 lb 10 oz) lean stewing beef, cubed
185 ml (6 fl oz/¾ cup) beef stock
3 tablespoons red wine
1 tablespoon soy sauce
12 prunes, pitted, soaked in 125 ml (4 fl oz/½ cup) beef stock
1 tablespoon soft brown sugar
60 g (2¼ oz) pecan nuts

1 Heat half the oil in a large pan. Fry the onion for 3 minutes until soft, add the mushrooms and garlic and cook for 2 minutes. Remove from the pan.

Combine the flour, half the cinnamon, 1 teaspoon salt, spices and ginger, then coat the meat. Add the remaining oil to the pan and brown the meat in batches. Remove from the pan.

2 Add the stock, wine, soy sauce and extra stock (from the prunes) to the pan. Bring to the boil, return the onions, mushrooms, garlic and meat to the pan. Simmer for 2 hours. Add the sugar and cook for 10 minutes, or until the meat is tender.

3 Heat the remaining oil in a small pan and fry the pecans for 4 minutes, or until golden brown. Add the rest of the salt and cinnamon and toss to coat the pecans. Add these to the stew with the prunes 5 minutes before serving.

To coat the meat toss it in a plastic bag with the seasoned flour.

Return the onions, mushrooms, garlic and meat to the pan.

Make sure the pecans are well coated with the cinnamon and salt.

LAMB CHOP CASSEROLE

Preparation time: 15 minutes
Total cooking time: 1 hour 15 minutes
Serves 4

6–8 lamb chump chops
1 teaspoon oil
1 large onion, finely chopped
4 tablespoons redcurrant jelly
1 teaspoon grated lemon zest
1 tablespoon lemon juice
1 tablespoon barbecue sauce
1 tablespoon tomato sauce
  (ketchup)

125 ml (4 fl oz/½ cup) chicken stock

1 Trim any fat from the lamb. Preheat the oven to 170°C (325°F/Gas 3). Heat the oil in a large heavy-based frying pan; add the chops and cook over medium–high heat for 3 minutes, turning once, until well browned. Transfer to a casserole dish.

2 Add the onion to the frying pan and cook over medium heat, stirring frequently, for 5 minutes or until the onion is softened. Add the jelly, lemon zest and juice, barbecue and tomato sauces and stock. Stir for 2–3 minutes until heated through. Pour over the chops and stir well, cover and place in the oven. Cook for 1 hour, or until the meat is tender, turning 2–3 times. Lift out the chops onto a side plate and leave them to keep warm.

3 Pour the sauce into a pan and boil rapidly for 5 minutes, until the sauce has thickened and reduced. Return the chops to the sauce before serving.

COOK'S FILE

Storage time: Keep covered and refrigerated for up to 2 days. Suitable to freeze for up to 1 month.

Once the chops have been well browned put them in a casserole dish.

Pour the sauce over the chops in the dish and stir to combine.

Use a pair of tongs to turn the chops a couple of times during cooking.

VEGETARIAN CHILLI

Preparation time: 15 minutes
Total cooking time: 40 minutes
Serves 6–8

130 g (4½ oz/¾ cup) burghul
    (cracked wheat)
2 tablespoons olive oil
1 large onion, finely chopped
2 garlic cloves, crushed
1 teaspoon chilli powder
2 teaspoons ground cumin
1 teaspoon cayenne pepper
½ teaspoon ground cinnamon

2 x 400 g (14 oz) cans crushed
    tomatoes
750 ml (26 fl oz/3 cups)
    vegetable stock
440 g (15½ oz) can red kidney
    beans, rinsed and drained
2 x 300 g (10½ oz) cans
    chickpeas, rinsed and drained
310 g (10¾ oz) can corn
    kernels, drained
2 tablespoons tomato paste
    (concentrated purée)
corn chips and sour cream

1 Soak the burghul in 250 ml (9 fl oz/
1 cup) of hot water for 10 minutes.

Heat the oil in a large heavy-based pan
and cook the onion for 10 minutes,
stirring often, until soft and golden.
2 Add the garlic, chilli powder, cumin,
cayenne and cinnamon and cook,
stirring, for a further minute.
3 Add the tomatoes, stock and
burghul. Bring to the boil and simmer
for 10 minutes. Stir in the beans,
chickpeas, corn and tomato paste and
simmer for 20 minutes, stirring often.
Serve with corn chips and sour cream.

*Stir the garlic and spices into the pan with
the onion and cook for a minute.*

*Add the crushed tomatoes, stock and
burghul to the pan.*

*Stir in the beans, chickpeas, corn kernels
and tomato paste.*

KASHMIR LAMB WITH SPINACH

Preparation time: 20 minutes
Total cooking time: 1 hour 30 minutes
Serves 4

2 tablespoons oil
750 g (1 lb 10 oz) diced leg of lamb
2 large onions, chopped
3 garlic cloves, crushed
4 cm (1½ inch) fresh ginger, grated
2 teaspoons ground cumin
2 teaspoons ground coriander
2 teaspoons turmeric
¼ teaspoon ground cardamom
¼ teaspoon ground cloves
3 bay leaves
375 ml (13 fl oz/1½ cups) chicken stock
125 ml (4 fl oz/½ cup) cream
2 bunches English spinach leaves, washed and chopped

1 Heat the oil in a heavy-based pan and brown the lamb in batches, stirring regularly. Remove from the pan. Add the onions, garlic and ginger and cook for 3 minutes, stirring regularly. Add the spices and cook, stirring, for 1–2 minutes or until fragrant. Return the lamb to the pan with any juices. Add the bay leaves and stock.

2 Bring to the boil and then reduce the heat, stir well, cover and simmer for 35 minutes. Add the cream and cook, covered, for a further 20 minutes or until the lamb is very tender.

3 Add the spinach and cook until softened. Season and serve with rice.

COOK'S FILE

Storage time: Curry is best cooked a day in advance and refrigerated. Do not add the spinach until reheating.

Return the browned lamb to the pan and add the bay leaves.

Stir in the cream and simmer until the lamb is very tender.

It will only take a few minutes for the spinach to soften and reduce.

ROMAN CHICKEN

Preparation time: 10 minutes
Total cooking time: 45 minutes
Serves 2–4

1 tablespoon olive oil
1 small onion, sliced
4 thick rashers bacon, diced
4 large or 8 small chicken legs
1 garlic clove, crushed
4 tablespoons chopped parsley
250 ml (9 fl oz/1 cup) chicken stock
1 tablespoon chopped marjoram
440 g (15½ oz) can crushed tomatoes

1 Heat the oil in a large heavy-based pan and cook the onion and bacon over medium heat for 5 minutes. Increase the heat and add the chicken in batches. Brown the chicken on all sides, turning often and taking care not to overcook the onion and bacon, for about 5 minutes.

2 Reduce the heat, add the garlic and parsley and cook for 2–3 minutes. Add the stock and marjoram, stirring well. Add the tomatoes, stir well and season with salt and pepper to taste.

3 Bring to the boil, cover the pan and simmer gently for 30 minutes, turning the chicken legs occasionally, until they are cooked through.

Brown the chicken well, taking care not to burn the onion.

Add the stock and marjoram. Stir well to prevent anything sticking to the pan base.

Turn the chicken legs occasionally to ensure even cooking on all sides.

Kashmir Lamb with Spinach (top) and Roman Chicken

OXTAIL RAGOUT

Preparation time: 20 minutes +
  3 hours soaking
Total cooking time: 4 hours
Serves 4

1 kg (2 lb 4 oz) oxtail, cut into
  short pieces (ask your
  butcher to do this)
3 tablespoons plain (all-purpose)
  flour
1 tablespoon ghee or oil
2 rashers bacon, chopped
1 small onion, peeled and
  studded with 6 whole cloves
2 garlic cloves
2 carrots, quartered lengthways
375 ml (13 fl oz/1½ cups) beef
  or chicken stock
425 g (15 oz) can puréed tomato
1 parsnip, peeled and quartered
  lengthways
1 leek, thickly sliced

1 Trim any fat from the oxtail and
discard. Put the oxtail in a large bowl,
cover with water and set aside for
3 hours. Drain and transfer the meat
to a large heavy-based pan, cover with
fresh water and bring to the boil.
Reduce the heat and simmer for
10 minutes, skimming any froth from
the surface with a spoon or absorbent
paper towel. Drain the meat, allow to
cool and pat dry with paper towels.
2 Preheat the oven to 150°C
(300°F/Gas 2). Put the flour and a little
salt and pepper in a large plastic bag;
put the oxtail in the bag and shake to
coat with flour. Heat the ghee or oil in
a large frying pan, add the bacon and
cook over medium heat for 3 minutes,
stirring frequently. Remove the bacon
from the pan.
3 Add the oxtail and cook, stirring
continuously over medium–high heat
for 2–3 minutes, or until browned.
Transfer to a casserole dish.
4 Add the bacon, onion, garlic and
half the carrot to the dish. Stir in the
stock and tomato purée. Cover and
bake for 3 hours. Add the remaining
vegetables and cook for 30–40 minutes,
or until tender.

*Press the cloves firmly into the onion so
they don't fall out during cooking.*

*Put the oxtail in a plastic bag with the flour
and shake to coat evenly.*

*Cook the oxtail over medium–high heat
until browned.*

*Add the remaining carrot with the parsnip
and leek.*

Use a couple of wooden spoons to toss the lamb cubes in the marinade.

Remove the cardamom pods and cinnamon stick and discard.

Add the marinade and apricot nectar to the meat in the pan.

Add the apricots and prunes and stir through gently.

LAMB AND APRICOT STEW

Preparation time: 30 minutes +
   marinating
Total cooking time: 1 hour 30 minutes
Serves 4–6

2 kg (4 lb 8 oz) leg of lamb,
   boned (ask your butcher
   to do this)
1 onion, thickly sliced
125 ml (4 fl oz/½ cup) white
   wine
1 tablespoon grated lemon zest
3 tablespoons lemon juice
1 tablespoon ground coriander
4 cardamom pods
1 cinnamon stick
2 tablespoons oil
170 ml (5½ fl oz/⅔ cup) apricot
   nectar
90 g (3¼ oz/½ cup) dried
   apricots
110 g (3¾ oz/½ cup) pitted
   prunes
1 tablespoon cornflour
   (cornstarch)
80 g (2¾ oz/½ cup) roasted
   unsalted cashew nuts

3 tablespoons finely chopped
   fresh parsley

1 Trim away the skin and excess fat and cut the meat into 3 cm (1¼ inch) cubes. In a large ceramic or glass bowl, combine the onion, wine, lemon zest, juice, coriander, cardamom pods, cinnamon stick, salt and pepper. Toss the lamb in the marinade, cover and refrigerate for at least 8 hours, or overnight. Stir 2 or 3 times.

2 Drain the meat and onion mixture, reserving the marinade, and dry on paper towels. Discard the cardamom and cinnamon. Heat the oil in a large heavy-based frying pan and brown the meat and onion, in batches, over high heat for 2–3 minutes.

3 Return all the meat and onion to the pan; add the marinade and apricot nectar. Bring to the boil, then cover with a tight-fitting lid, reduce the heat to low and simmer for 30 minutes; stirring once. Stir through the apricots and prunes, cover and simmer for a further 30 minutes.

4 Mix the cornflour and 1 tablespoon water to a smooth paste. Add to the pan and stir until thickened; simmer for a further 15 minutes, or until the lamb is tender. Scatter with the cashews and parsley and serve with steamed rice.

145

POACHER'S RABBIT

Preparation time: 30 minutes
Total cooking time: 2 hours
  15 minutes
Serves 4

1 tablespoon vinegar
1 tablespoon salt
1 rabbit, about 1 kg (2 lb 4 oz),
  cut into 12 portions (ask your
  butcher to do this)
3 tablespoons plain (all-purpose)
  flour
4 tablespoons olive oil
2 rashers bacon, roughly
  chopped
8 bulb spring onions, trimmed
2 medium carrots, finely sliced
375 ml (13 fl oz/1½ cups) cider
2 teaspoons French mustard
½ teaspoon dried rosemary
½ teaspoon dried thyme
1 bay leaf
4 tablespoons finely chopped
  fresh parsley

1 Add the vinegar and salt to a bowl of water and leave the rabbit portions to soak overnight. Drain, rinse well and dry on paper towels. Combine the flour, salt and pepper in a large bowl and toss in the rabbit portions. Preheat the oven to 180°C (350°F/Gas 4).
2 Heat 3 tablespoons of the oil in a large heavy-based frying pan and brown the rabbit portions quickly in batches over medium heat. Transfer to a 2 litre (8 cup) casserole dish.
3 Add the remaining oil to the pan; add the bacon, bulb spring onions and carrot and fry over medium heat for 5 minutes, or until lightly browned. Add to the casserole dish.
4 Pour the cider into the frying pan and stir in the mustard, rosemary, thyme and bay leaf. Bring to the boil and then pour over the rabbit. Cover with a tight-fitting lid and bake for 2 hours, or until the rabbit is tender. Remove the bay leaf and stir in the parsley before serving.

COOK'S FILE

Storage time: Refrigerate for up to 2 days. Freeze for up to 1 month.

Use paper towels to dry the drained and rinsed rabbit portions.

Trim off the tops and tails from the bulb spring onions.

Fry the bacon, onions and carrot until lightly browned.

Add the mustard, herbs and bay leaf to the cider in the frying pan.

SAUSAGE CARBONADE

Preparation time: 15 minutes
Total cooking time: 45 minutes
Serves 4–6

750 g (1 lb 10 oz) good-quality
    beef sausages
1 tablespoon olive oil
1 large onion, chopped
2 garlic cloves, chopped
2 teaspoons soft brown sugar

2 tablespoons plain (all-purpose)
    flour
375 ml (13 fl oz/1½ cups) beer
500 ml (17 fl oz/2 cups) beef
    stock
2 bay leaves
2 tablespoons chopped fresh
    parsley

1 Put the sausages in a pan and cover with cold water. Bring to the boil, then reduce the heat and simmer for 5 minutes. Drain and cool.

2 Heat the oil in a large pan, cook the onion and garlic for 5 minutes, stirring regularly. Stir in the sugar and flour and cook for 5–8 minutes over low heat, until the flour is golden brown.

3 Gradually stir in the beer and stock. Add the sausages and bay leaves and bring to the boil, then reduce the heat, cover the pan and simmer for 20 minutes. Remove the bay leaves, stir in the parsley and season.

Put the sausages in a pan with enough cold water to cover them.

Cook the onion and garlic for 5 minutes, stirring regularly.

Lift the bay leaves out of the pan just before serving.

CAJUN SPICED FISH BRAISE

Preparation time: 15 minutes
Total cooking time: 25 minutes
Serves 4

750 g (1 lb 10 oz) ling fillets
2 tablespoons plain (all-purpose) flour
2 tablespoons Cajun spice mix
2 tablespoons olive oil
30 g (1 oz) butter
1 large onion, thickly sliced
1 red capsicum (pepper), sliced
125 ml (4 fl oz/½ cup) white wine
500 g (1 lb 2 oz/2 cups) bottled tomato pasta sauce
1 wide strip lemon zest
8 raw prawns (shrimp), peeled and deveined

1 Cut the fish into bite-sized, thick pieces. Mix the flour and Cajun spice mix together, then lightly coat the fish. Heat the oil and butter in a large heavy-based pan over medium heat. Cook the fish, turning occasionally, until browned on all sides. Remove from the pan.

2 Add the onion and capsicum to the pan and cook, stirring regularly, for 5 minutes. Add the wine and bring to the boil, stirring continuously. Add the tomato pasta sauce and the lemon zest. Bring to the boil, then reduce the heat and simmer for a further 10 minutes.

3 Add the fish and prawns; cook over low heat for 3 minutes, or until the prawns are pink and the fish is tender and easily flaked with a fork. Remove the lemon zest and season with salt and pepper. Serve immediately.

Coat the fish in flour and Cajun spice mix by putting in a bag and shaking.

Cook the fish in the oil and butter until browned on all sides.

When the fish is tender it should be easy to flake with a fork.

CLAY POT CHICKEN AND VEGETABLES

Preparation time: 20 minutes +
    30 minutes marinating
Total cooking time: 25 minutes
Serves 4

500 g (1 lb 2 oz) chicken thigh
    fillets
1 tablespoon soy sauce
1 tablespoon dry sherry
6 dried Chinese mushrooms
2 small leeks
250 g (9 oz) orange sweet
    potato
2 tablespoons peanut oil
5 cm (2 inch) piece ginger,
    shredded
125 ml (4 fl oz/½ cup) chicken
    stock
1 teaspoon sesame oil

3 teaspoons cornflour
    (cornstarch)

1 Wash the chicken under cold water. Pat dry with paper towels and then cut into small pieces. Place in a dish with the soy sauce and the sherry, cover and marinate for 30 minutes in the refrigerator.
2 Soak mushrooms in hot water to cover for 30 minutes. Drain, squeeze to remove excess liquid. Remove stems and chop caps into shreds. Wash leeks thoroughly to remove all grit; cut leeks and sweet potato into thin slices.
3 Drain the chicken, reserving the marinade. Heat half the oil in a wok or heavy-based frying pan, swirling it gently to coat base and side. Carefully add half the chicken pieces and stir-fry briefly until seared on all sides. Transfer to a flameproof clay pot or casserole and

then stir-fry the remaining chicken and add to the clay pot.
4 Heat remaining oil in wok, add leek and ginger and stir-fry 1 minute. Add the mushrooms, the remaining marinade, the stock and sesame oil. Transfer to the clay pot, add the sweet potato and cook, covered, on the top of the stove over a very low heat for about 20 minutes.
5 Dissolve cornflour with a little water and add to the pot. Cook, stirring, until the mixture boils and thickens. Serve the chicken and vegetables at once with steamed brown or white rice or with noodles.

COOK'S FILE

Storage time: This is an example of a slow-cooked dish that can be cooked 1 to 2 days ahead. Store, covered, in the refrigerator. Bring to room temperature and reheat.

CHICKEN AND ORANGE CASSEROLE

Preparation time: 50 minutes
Total cooking time: 1 hour 30 minutes
Serves 4–6

2 small chickens
1 tablespoon olive oil
2 thick rashers bacon, rind
    removed and thinly sliced
50 g (1¾ oz) butter
16 small pickling onions, peeled
    (ensure ends are intact)
2–3 garlic cloves, crushed
3 teaspoons grated fresh ginger
2 teaspoons grated orange zest
2 teaspoons ground cumin
2 teaspoons ground coriander
2 tablespoons honey
250 ml (9 fl oz/1 cup) fresh
    orange juice
250 ml (9 fl oz/1 cup) white wine
125 ml (4 fl oz/½ cup) chicken
    or vegetable stock
1 bunch baby carrots
1 large parsnip, peeled
fresh coriander (cilantro) and
    orange zest, to serve

1 Using a sharp knife or a pair of kitchen scissors, cut each chicken into 8 pieces discarding the backbone. Remove any excess fat and discard (remove the skin as well, if preferred).
2 Heat about a teaspoon of the oil in a large, deep heavy-based pan. Add the bacon and cook over medium heat for 2–3 minutes, or until just crisp. Remove from the pan and set aside to drain on paper towels. Add the remaining oil and half the butter to the pan. Cook the onions over medium heat until dark golden brown. Shake the pan occasionally to ensure even

cooking and browning. Remove from the pan and set aside.
3 Add the chicken pieces to the pan in small batches and brown over medium heat. Remove from the pan and drain on paper towels.
4 Add the remaining butter to the pan. Stir in the garlic, ginger, orange zest, cumin, coriander and honey and cook, stirring, for 1 minute. Add the orange juice, wine and stock to the pan. Bring to the boil and then reduce the heat and simmer for 1 minute. Return the chicken pieces to the pan, cover and leave to simmer over low heat for 40 minutes.
5 Return the onions and bacon to the pan and simmer, covered, for a further 15 minutes. Remove the lid and leave to simmer for a further 15 minutes.
6 Trim the carrots, leaving a little green stalk, and wash well or peel if necessary. Cut the parsnip into small batons. Add the carrots and parsnip to the pan. Cover and cook for 5–10 minutes or until the carrots and parsnip are just tender. Do not overcook the carrots or they will lose their bright colouring. When you are ready to serve, arrange 2–3 chicken pieces on each plate. Put a couple of carrots and a few parsnip batons on top and spoon over a little juice. Garnish with coriander leaves and orange zest.

COOK'S FILE

Storage time: Can be refrigerated for up to 1 day at the end of step 5. Reheat the casserole gently over low heat and add the carrots and parsnip just prior to serving.

Cut each chicken into 8 even-sized pieces using a knife or pair of scissors.

Cook the pickling onions until they are dark golden brown.

Brown the chicken pieces in batches and drain on paper towels.

Add the orange juice, white wine and stock to the pan.

Return the browned pickling onions and cooked bacon to the pan.

Cut the parsnip into batons and leave the stalks on the carrots to provide colour.

HAM, BEAN AND SWEDE CASSEROLE

Preparation time: 35 minutes
Total cooking time: 1 hour 45 minutes
Serves 4

200 g (7 oz/1 cup) black-eyed
  beans, soaked in cold water
  overnight
1 smoked ham hock
18 small pickling onions
30 g (1 oz) butter
2 tablespoons oil
2 garlic cloves, crushed

2 tablespoons golden syrup
3 teaspoons ground cumin
1 tablespoon German or French
  mustard
1 swede (rutabaga) or turnip,
  peeled, diced
2 tablespoons tomato paste
  (concentrated purée)

1 Drain the beans and place in a pan. Add the hock and 2 litres (8 cups) water, cover and bring to the boil. Reduce to low; simmer for 30 minutes. Drain, reserving 500 ml (17 fl oz/ 2 cups) of stock. Remove the skin from hock; chop meat into bite-sized pieces.

2 Peel the onions, leaving the bases intact. Heat the butter, oil, garlic and syrup in the cleaned pan. Add the onions and cook for 5–10 minutes, or until just starting to turn golden.

3 Stir in the ham, cumin, mustard and swede or turnip and cook for 2 minutes, until golden. Season and return the beans to the pan. Add the reserved stock and tomato paste, bring to the boil, reduce the heat and simmer, covered, for 1 hour. Uncover and simmer for 5–10 minutes longer, or until reduced and thickened.

Remove the skin and chop the cooked ham hock into bite-sized pieces.

Peel the onions, leaving the bases intact so that they hold their shape.

Stir in the ham, cumin, mustard and swede or turnip.

PEPPERED VEGETABLE HOTPOT

Preparation time: 30 minutes
Total cooking time: 1 hour 5 minutes
Serves 8–10

2 tablespoons olive oil
2 onions, chopped
2 leeks, washed and chopped
2 garlic cloves, crushed
1.5 litres (6 cups) chicken stock
2 tablespoons chopped fresh
    rosemary

1–2 teaspoons green
    peppercorns
4 large potatoes, cubed
2 large turnips, cubed
200 g (7 oz) broccoli, cut into
    small florets
200 g (7 oz) cauliflower, cut into
    small florets
155 g (5½ oz/1 cup) fresh or
    frozen peas

1 Heat the oil in a large heavy-based pan and cook the onion and leek over medium heat for 10 minutes, or until they are tender.

2 Add garlic and cook for 1 minute further, then add the stock, rosemary, peppercorns and potato to the pan. Bring to the boil and then reduce the heat, cover and leave to simmer for 30 minutes. Add the turnip and simmer for a further 15 minutes.

3 Add the broccoli, cauliflower and peas and simmer, uncovered, for a further 5 minutes. Season with salt and black pepper to taste.

COOK'S FILE

Hint: Serve as a main course with pesto and crusty bread.

Wash the turnips well and roughly chop into large cubes.

Add the stock, rosemary, peppercorns and potato to the pan.

Add the broccoli, cauliflower and peas for the last 5 minutes of cooking.

CHILLI CON CARNE

Preparation time: 10 minutes
Total cooking time: 50 minutes
Serves 4

1 tablespoon olive oil
1 medium onion, chopped
3 garlic cloves, crushed
1 stick celery, sliced
500 g (1 lb 2 oz) lean minced
　(ground) beef
2 teaspoons chilli powder
pinch cayenne pepper
1 teaspoon dried oregano
440 g (15½ oz) can crushed
　tomatoes
2 tablespoons tomato paste
　(concentrated purée)
1 teaspoon soft brown sugar
1 tablespoon cider or red wine
　vinegar
420 g (14½ oz) can red kidney
　beans, drained

1 Heat the oil in a large saucepan and add the onion, garlic and celery. Stir over medium heat for 5 minutes, until soft. Add the beef to the pan and stir over high heat for 5 minutes, or until well browned.
2 Add the chilli powder, cayenne and oregano, stir to combine and cook for 5 minutes. Add the tomatoes, 125 ml (4 fl oz/½ cup) of water and the tomato paste and stir well.
3 Simmer, uncovered, for 30 minutes, stirring occasionally. Add the sugar, cider or vinegar and beans. Season with salt and pepper and heat through for 5 minutes. Serve hot with white or brown rice.

COOK'S FILE

Storage time: Keep covered and refrigerated for up to 3 days.

Hint: For a spicier dish, add some chopped fresh red chillies when you are cooking the onions.

Use a fork to break up any lumps of meat as it browns.

Add the tomatoes, water and tomato paste and stir well.

Add the sugar, cider or vinegar, seasoning and kidney beans and heat through.

154

NAVARIN OF LAMB

Preparation time: 20 minutes
Total cooking time: 1 hour 45 minutes
Serves 4

1.25 kg (2 lb 12 oz) boned
    shoulder or leg of lamb (ask
    your butcher to do this)
30 g (1 oz) butter
1 tablespoon oil
1 small onion, quartered
1 garlic clove, crushed
2 rashers bacon, finely chopped
12 small bulb spring onions,
    stems removed
1 tablespoon plain (all-purpose)
    flour

250 ml (9 fl oz/1 cup) chicken
    stock
1 tablespoon tomato paste
    (concentrated purée)
1 turnip or swede (rutabaga),
    peeled and cubed
1 large carrot, thickly sliced
4–6 new potatoes, halved
80 g (2¾ oz/½ cup) frozen peas

1 Remove any excess fat from the
lamb and cut the meat into bite-sized
cubes. Preheat the oven to 150°C
(300°F/Gas 2). Heat the butter and oil
in a heavy-based frying pan. Cook the
onion, garlic, bacon and spring onions
over medium heat for 5 minutes, or
until the onion is soft. Transfer to a
large heatproof casserole dish.

2 Add the lamb to the frying pan and
brown quickly in batches; set aside.
When all the meat is browned return
it to the pan and sprinkle with the
flour. Stir for 1 minute to combine,
then pour on the stock and tomato
paste. Stir until thickened and smooth,
then pour into the casserole dish.

3 Stir in the turnip or swede, carrot
and potato. Cover with a tight-fitting
lid and bake for 1½ hours, or until the
lamb is tender. Stir 2–3 times during
cooking. Add the peas after 1¼ hours.

COOK'S FILE

Storage time: Keep covered and
refrigerated for up to 3 days.

*Transfer the onion, spring onion, garlic
and bacon to a casserole dish.*

*Return the browned meat to the pan and
sprinkle with flour.*

*Add the turnip, swede, carrot and potato to
the meat in the casserole dish.*

MINTY LAMB SHANKS

Preparation time: 20 minutes
Total cooking time: 2 hours
   10 minutes
Serves 6

6 lamb shanks
1 tablespoon olive oil
1 red onion, finely chopped
2 garlic cloves, crushed
35 g (1¼ oz/¾ cup) chopped
   mint leaves
1 sprig fresh thyme

2 bay leaves
425 g (15 oz) can crushed
   tomatoes
500 ml (17 fl oz/2 cups)
   vegetable stock
3 tablespoons white wine

1 Preheat the oven to 200°C (400°F/Gas 6). Put the shanks in a baking dish in a single layer, close together. Season with salt and pepper. Bake for 20 minutes, then turn the shanks, reduce the oven temperature to 180°C (350°F/Gas 4) and bake for a further 20 minutes.

2 Heat the oil in a frying pan. Cook the onion and garlic for 5–8 minutes, or until soft. Stir in 25 g (1 oz/½ cup) of the mint, the thyme and bay leaves. Scatter over the meat, return to the oven and cook for 15 minutes.

3 Combine the tomato, stock and wine and pour over the meat. Cover the dish tightly with foil or a lid and bake for 1¼ hours. Garnish with the remaining mint and serve with pasta. Best made a day or two in advance.

Put the shanks in one layer, close together and season with salt and pepper.

Once the onion is soft, stir in the thyme, bay leaves and mint.

Mix together the tomato, stock and wine and pour over the lamb shanks.

CHICKEN AND COCONUT CREAM CURRY

Preparation time: 20 minutes
Total cooking time: 50 minutes
Serves 4

1.5 kg (3 lb 5 oz) chicken thigh
   fillets, trimmed of fat
1 tablespoon vegetable oil
400 ml (14 fl oz) coconut cream
2 tablespoons fish sauce
1–2 small red chillies, finely
   chopped

4 coriander (cilantro) roots,
   chopped, leaves reserved
1 lemon grass, chopped finely
6 pieces dried galangal
6 dried makrut (kaffir lime)
   leaves
1 tablespoon red curry paste
2 teaspoons soft brown sugar
1 tablespoon lemon juice
2 small zucchini (courgettes),
   thickly sliced
80 g (2¾ oz/½ cup) green peas

1 Cut the chicken into bite-sized pieces and pat dry with paper towels.

Heat the oil in a frying pan and brown the chicken in batches. Set aside.

2 Combine the coconut cream, fish sauce, chilli, coriander root, lemon grass, galangal and lime leaves in a large pan. Bring to the boil, stirring, then reduce the heat; add the chicken. Simmer for 30 minutes, or until the chicken is tender, stirring often.

3 Add the curry paste, sugar and lemon juice and stir well. Stir in the zucchini and peas and simmer for a further 5 minutes, until the vegetables are just tender. Remove the galangal and lime leaves to serve.

Lemon grass, makrut (kaffir lime) leaves and galangal are available at Asian stores.

Reduce the heat and return the browned chicken to the pan.

Use a pair of tongs to lift out and discard the galangal and lime leaves.

*Minty Lamb Shanks (top) and Chicken and
Coconut Cream Curry*

CIOPPINO

Preparation time: 20 minutes
Total cooking time: 55 minutes
Serves 4

1 kg (2 lb 4 oz) firm white-fleshed fish fillets, skinned and boned
375 g (13 oz) raw king prawns (shrimp)
1 raw lobster tail, in shell
12 fresh mussels
2 dried mushrooms
3 tablespoons olive oil
1 large onion, finely chopped
1 green capsicum (pepper), chopped
2–3 garlic cloves, crushed
425 g (15 oz) can crushed tomatoes
250 ml (9 fl oz/1 cup) white wine
250 ml (9 fl oz/1 cup) tomato juice
250 ml (9 fl oz/1 cup) fish stock or water
bay leaf
2 sprigs parsley
6 basil leaves, chopped
60 g (2¼ oz/1 cup) chopped fresh parsley

1 Cut the fish into bite-sized pieces. Remove the heads and shells from the prawns, leaving tails intact, then devein. Remove lobster meat from the shell and cut into small pieces. (Make your own stock by simmering the fish, lobster and prawn trimmings in water for 5 minutes, then strain.) Scrub the mussels and remove their beards. Discard any open or damaged mussels, then soak the rest in cold water for 10 minutes. Soak the mushrooms in water for 20 minutes, then squeeze dry and chop finely.

2 Heat the oil in a pan; cook the onion, capsicum and garlic for 5 minutes, or until soft. Add the mushrooms, tomato, wine, tomato juice, stock, bay leaf and herbs. Bring to the boil, then simmer for 30 minutes.

3 Layer the fish and prawns in a large pan, add the sauce, cover and leave on a low heat for 10 minutes, until prawns are pink and fish is cooked. Add the lobster and mussels and simmer for 2–3 minutes. Discard any unopened mussels. Sprinkle with parsley.

Remove the heads and shells from the prawns but leave the tails intact.

To remove the lobster shell, cut the shell on the softer, white underside.

Scrub the mussels and remove their beards. Discard any open or damaged mussels.

Squeeze the mushrooms gently to get rid of the excess liquid.

MEXICAN BEEF STEW

Preparation time: 30 minutes
Total cooking time: 1 hour 30 minutes
Serves 6

500 g (1 lb 2 oz) Roma (plum) tomatoes, halved
6 flour tortillas
1–2 red chillies, finely chopped
1 tablespoon olive oil
1 kg (2 lb 4 oz) stewing beef, cubed
½ teaspoon black pepper

2 onions, thinly sliced
375 ml (13 fl oz/1½ cups) beef stock
3 tablespoons tomato paste (concentrated purée)
375 g (13 oz) can kidney beans, drained
1 teaspoon chilli powder
125 g (4½ oz/½ cup) sour cream

1 Preheat the oven to 180°C (350°F/Gas 4). Grill (broil) the tomatoes, skin side up, for 6–8 minutes, or until the skin is blackened and blistered. Cool, then peel away the skin and roughly chop the flesh.

2 Bake 2 of the tortillas for 4 minutes, or until crisp. Break into pieces, put in a food processor with the tomato and chilli and process until almost smooth.
3 Heat the oil in a pan. Brown the beef in batches, then remove. Add the onion to the pan; cook for 5 minutes. Return the meat to the pan. Stir in the tomato mixture, stock and tomato paste and bring to the boil. Reduce the heat, cover and simmer for 1¼ hours. Add the beans and chilli powder.
4 Grill the remaining tortillas for 3 minutes each side; cool and then cut into wedges. Serve with the stew and sour cream.

Grill the tomatoes until the skin is black and blistered and it will peel away easily.

Once the tortillas are crisp, break into pieces and put in the food processor.

Stir in the processed mixture, stock and tomato paste.

MEDITERRANEAN VEGETABLE POT

Preparation time: 20 minutes
Total cooking time: 40 minutes
Serves 4

3 tablespoons olive oil
1 onion, chopped
2 garlic cloves, crushed
1 red and 1 green capsicum
    (pepper), chopped
3 slender eggplants
    (aubergines), sliced

3 zucchini (courgettes),
    sliced
400 g (14 oz/2 cups) long-grain
    rice
100 g (3½ oz) button
    mushrooms, sliced
750 ml (26 fl oz/3 cups) chicken
    stock
250 ml (9 fl oz/1 cup) white
    wine
400 g (14 oz) can crushed
    tomatoes
2 tablespoons tomato paste
    (concentrated purée)
150 g (5½ oz) feta cheese

1 Heat the oil in a pan and cook the onion over medium heat for 10 minutes until very soft but not brown. Add the garlic and cook for a further minute.
2 Add the capsicum and stir for 3 minutes. Add the eggplant and zucchini and stir for 5 minutes, then add the rice, stirring for 2 minutes.
3 Stir in the mushrooms, stock, wine, tomatoes and tomato paste until combined. Bring to the boil, then reduce the heat, cover and simmer for 20 minutes—the rice should absorb most of the liquid. Serve topped with crumbled feta.

Cook the onion until it is very soft but not browned.

Add the eggplant and zucchini to the pan and stir a little longer.

Add the mushrooms, stock, wine, crushed tomatoes and tomato paste.

INDONESIAN CHICKEN IN COCONUT MILK

Preparation time: 15 minutes + 1 hour
 marinating time
Total cooking time: 50 minutes
Serves 4

8 large or 12 small chicken
 drumsticks
2 teaspoons crushed garlic
1 teaspoon salt
½ teaspoon ground black pepper
2 teaspoons ground cumin
2 teaspoons ground coriander
½ teaspoon ground fennel
½ teaspoon ground cinnamon
3 tablespoons oil
2 medium onions, finely sliced
185 ml (6 fl oz/¾ cup) coconut
 milk
250 ml (9 fl oz/1 cup) water
1 tablespoon lemon juice, malt
 vinegar or tamarind liquid

1 Wash chicken under cold water. Pat dry with paper towels. Combine the garlic, salt, pepper, cumin, coriander, fennel, cinnamon and 2 tablespoons oil. Rub the mixture thoroughly over the chicken and marinate, covered, for 1 hour in the refrigerator.

2 Heat the remaining oil in a large pan. Add the onion and cook, stirring, until soft and golden. Add the chicken and cook quickly over medium–high heat until well browned.

3 Combine the coconut milk, water and lemon juice. Pour over the chicken, cover and simmer until the chicken is tender and the sauce is well reduced; this will take about 40 minutes. Serve with steamed rice.

1

2

3

LANCASHIRE HOTPOT

Preparation time: 20 minutes
Total cooking time: 2 hours
Serves 8

8 forequarter chops, cut 2.5 cm
    (1 inch) thick
4 lamb kidneys, cut into
    quarters, cores removed
50 g (1¾ oz) dripping or butter
3 tablespoons plain (all-purpose)
    flour
4 medium potatoes, thinly
    sliced
2 large brown onions, sliced
2 sticks celery, chopped
1 large carrot, chopped
435 ml (15¼ fl oz/1¾ cups)
    chicken or beef stock
200 g (7 oz) button mushrooms,
    sliced
2 teaspoons chopped fresh
    thyme
1 tablespoon Worcestershire
    sauce

1 Preheat the oven to 160°C (315°F/ Gas 2–3). Grease a large casserole dish. Trim the meat of excess fat and sinew and toss the chops and kidneys in flour, shaking off the excess. Heat the dripping in a frying pan and brown the chops quickly on both sides. Remove from the pan and brown the kidneys. Layer half the potato slices in the base of the dish and place the chops and kidneys on top of them.

2 Add the onion, celery and carrot to the pan and cook until the carrot begins to brown. Layer on top of the meat. Sprinkle the remaining flour over the base of the pan and cook, stirring, until dark brown. Pour in the stock and bring to the boil, stirring.

Add the mushrooms, thyme and Worcestershire sauce, reduce the heat, season and simmer for 10 minutes. Pour into the casserole dish.

3 Layer the remaining potato over the top of the casserole, to cover the meat

and vegetables. Cover and bake for 1¼ hours. Remove the lid and cook for a further 30 minutes, or until the potatoes are tender and golden.

Brown the kidneys in the hot dripping or butter, stirring regularly.

Stir in the mushrooms, seasoning, herbs and Worcestershire sauce.

Layer the remaining potato over the top of the casserole.

162

GAME CASSEROLE

Preparation time: 30 minutes
Total cooking time: 2 hours
Serves 6

1 kg (2 lb 4 oz) venison shoulder
2 tablespoons oil
3 rashers bacon, chopped
3 medium onions, thickly sliced
2 tablespoons plain (all-purpose)
    flour
250 ml (9 fl oz/1 cup) red wine
125 ml (4 fl oz/½ cup) chicken
    stock

2 tablespoons port
2 medium carrots, chopped
1 stick celery, chopped
1 garlic clove, crushed
1 bay leaf
1 cinnamon stick
2 cloves
½ teaspoon ground nutmeg
½ teaspoon dried thyme
½ teaspoon chopped chilli
150 g (5½ oz) button
    mushrooms, cut in half

1 Preheat the oven to 180°C (350°F/
Gas 4). Trim the excess fat and sinew
from the venison and cut into cubes.

Heat half the oil in a large pan, add
the bacon and fry over medium heat
until brown. Remove. Add the onion
and cook until soft and golden. Remove
and set aside.

2 Add the remaining oil to the pan.
Brown the venison in small batches,
return all to the pan, sprinkle with the
flour and cook, stirring, for 1 minute.
Remove from the heat and stir in the
wine, stock, port, bacon, onion, carrot,
celery, garlic, bay leaf, cinnamon,
cloves, nutmeg, thyme and chilli.

3 Pour into a casserole dish, cover
and bake for 1½ hours. Add the
mushrooms, then cook for 30 minutes.

Cook the onion until soft and golden.

*Return all the browned venison to the pan
and sprinkle with flour.*

*Add the mushrooms to the casserole and
cook for a further 30 minutes.*

163

BEEF OLIVES

Beef olives can be filled with the traditional sage filling or the sun-dried tomato filling below. Each filling will serve 4 people.

Preparation time: 20 minutes
Total cooking time: 1 hour 30 minutes
Serves 4

1 kg (2 lb 4 oz) skirt steak, cut into thin slices lengthways
3 tablespoons plain (all-purpose) flour
1 tablespoon olive oil
1 carrot, finely chopped
250 ml (9 fl oz/1 cup) red wine
425 g (15 oz) can crushed tomatoes
2 bay leaves

Traditional sage filling
1 tablespoon olive oil
1 small onion, chopped
2 garlic cloves, chopped
2 large tomatoes, diced
40 g (1¼ oz/½ cup) fresh breadcrumbs
2 tablespoons chopped sage

Sun-dried tomato, mushroom and olive filling
1 tablespoon olive oil
4 spring onions (scallions), chopped
2 garlic cloves, crushed
100 g (3½ oz) mushrooms, chopped
8 sun-dried tomatoes, chopped
60 g (2¼ oz) black olives, chopped
40 g (1¼ oz/½ cup) fresh breadcrumbs
2 tablespoons chopped basil

1 Put the steak between sheets of plastic wrap and pound with a meat mallet until very thin, taking care not to tear the meat. Set aside.

2 To make the Sage Filling: Heat the oil in a deep heavy-based pan and cook the onion and garlic, stirring, for 3 minutes. Transfer the mixture to a bowl; mix in the tomato, breadcrumbs and sage, then season. Set aside.

To make the Sun-dried Tomato Filling: Heat the oil in a heavy-based pan, add the spring onion, garlic and mushrooms and cook for 3 minutes, stirring continuously, over medium heat. Transfer to a bowl and add the tomatoes, olives, breadcrumbs, basil and salt and pepper, to taste. Mix well and set aside.

Lay a slice of meat on a board and place about ⅓ cup of filling neatly along the short edge. Roll up firmly, folding in the sides a little as you roll, and tie with string to secure.

3 Repeat with the remaining meat and filling. Roll the beef olives lightly in flour, shaking off any excess.

4 Wipe out the pan with paper towels and add the oil. Brown the carrots and beef olives in batches over medium heat, turning regularly, and then return them all to the pan.

5 Add the wine, undrained tomatoes and bay leaves to the pan and turn the olives to coat them. Cover and simmer very gently over low heat for 1 hour, or until tender. Remove from the sauce, trim away the string and slice the olives. Remove the bay leaves and purée the sauce in a food processor or blender until smooth. Serve poured over the beef olives.

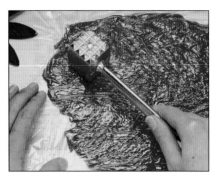

Pound the steak with a meat mallet between two sheets of plastic wrap.

For the sage filling, add the breadcrumbs with the other ingredients and mix well.

Roll the olives firmly, folding in the sides a little as you roll.

Once they are rolled up, secure the olives with string.

Brown the olives in batches and then return them all to the pan.

Use a pair of tongs to lift the beef olives from the sauce.

CHICKPEA AND VEGETABLE CURRY

Preparation time: 30 minutes
Total cooking time: 35 minutes
Serves 4

1 tablespoon oil
1 onion, chopped
1 tablespoon grated fresh ginger
3 garlic cloves, crushed
½ teaspoon fennel seeds
2 teaspoons curry powder
1 teaspoon finely chopped chilli, optional

400 ml (14 fl oz) coconut milk
425 g (15 oz) chickpeas, drained
3 zucchini (courgettes), chopped
200 g (7 oz) orange sweet potato, chopped
150 g (5½ oz) green beans, chopped
200 g (7 oz) broccoli, cut into small florets
4 tablespoons shredded coconut

1 Heat the oil in a large heavy-based pan and cook the onion over medium heat for about 10 minutes, or until soft and golden. Add the ginger, garlic, fennel seeds, curry powder and chilli (if using). Cook, stirring, for 2 minutes, or until fragrant.

2 Stir in the coconut milk, chickpeas, zucchini, orange sweet potato, beans and broccoli florets and bring to the boil. Reduce the heat, cover and leave to simmer for 20 minutes, or until the vegetables are tender.

3 Preheat the oven to 180°C (350°F/ Gas 4). Spread the coconut on a large baking tray and toast in the oven for a few minutes until lightly golden. Serve over the curry as a garnish.

Add the ginger, garlic and spices and cook until fragrant.

Add the drained chickpeas to the pan with the other vegetables.

Spread the coconut on a baking tray and toast until lightly golden.

The beans will soak up a lot of water so make sure they are well covered.

Brown the meat in batches, draining it on paper towels.

The large sprig of fresh rosemary will give a distinctive flavour.

Find the sprig of rosemary and lift it out before serving the casserole.

LAMB AND WHITE BEAN CASSEROLE

Preparation time: 20 minutes +
   overnight soaking
Total cooking time: 2 hours
   45 minutes
Serves 4

150 g (5½ oz/¾ cup) dried
   cannellini beans
1 kg (2 lb 4 oz) lamb neck chops
1 tablespoon oil
2 onions, chopped
3 garlic cloves, crushed
800 g (1 lb 12 oz) can crushed
   tomatoes
1 tablespoon sugar
½ teaspoon chopped chilli
125 ml (4 fl oz/½ cup) chicken
   stock
2 tablespoons white wine
   vinegar
large sprig fresh rosemary
1 tablespoon lemon juice
1 teaspoon finely grated lemon
   zest

1 Place the beans in a large bowl, cover them with plenty of water and leave to soak overnight.
2 Trim the meat of any excess fat and sinew. Heat the oil in a large heavy-based pan and brown the meat in batches. Remove all the meat from the pan and set aside. Add the onion to the pan and cook for 5 minutes until soft and lightly golden. Add the garlic and cook for a further minute.
3 Preheat the oven to 180°C (350°F/ Gas 4). Put the meat and onion in an ovenproof casserole dish, add the tomatoes, sugar, chilli, stock, vinegar, rosemary and drained beans. Cook, covered, for 2½ hours, until the meat is very tender.
4 Remove the rosemary sprig. Add the juice, zest and season to taste. Serve with thick crusty bread.

COOK'S FILE

Variation: Use a 310 g (11 oz) can of butterbeans (lima beans) instead. Add in the last 30 minutes of cooking.

CREAMY CHICKEN WITH MUSHROOMS

Preparation time: 20 minutes
Total cooking time: 40 minutes
Serves: 6

2 tablespoons olive oil
200 g (7 oz) button mushrooms, halved
200 g (7 oz) field mushrooms, chopped
1 small red capsicum (pepper), sliced
4 chicken breast fillets, cut into bite-sized pieces

2 tablespoons plain (all-purpose) flour
250 ml (9 fl oz/1 cup) chicken stock
125 ml (4 fl oz/½ cup) red wine
3 spring onions (scallions), finely chopped
300 ml (10½ fl oz/1¼ cups) cream
¼ teaspoon turmeric
1 tablespoon chopped chives
1 tablespoon finely chopped fresh parsley

1 Heat the oil in a large pan and add the mushrooms and capsicum. Cook over medium heat for 4 minutes or until soft. Remove and set aside.

2 Brown the chicken quickly in batches over a medium–high heat. Sprinkle the pan with flour and cook for 2 minutes, until golden. Add the stock and wine; bring to the boil. Cover and simmer for 10 minutes, or until the chicken is tender.

3 Add the spring onion and cream, return to the boil and simmer for 10–15 minutes, or until the cream has reduced and thickened. Return the mushrooms and capsicum to the pan; stir in the turmeric and herbs, season with salt and pepper, then simmer for 5 minutes to heat through.

Choose large field mushrooms and wipe them with a damp cloth before chopping.

Add the spring onions and cream and return to the boil.

Add the mushrooms, capsicum, chives, parsley and turmeric.

COUNTRY BEEF STEW

Preparation time: 40 minutes
Total cooking time: 2 hours
　10 minutes
Serves 8

1 small eggplant (aubergine),
　cubed
2–3 tablespoons olive oil
2 red onions, sliced
2 garlic cloves, crushed
1 kg (2 lb 4 oz) chuck steak,
　cubed
1 teaspoon ground coriander
½ teaspoon allspice
¾ teaspoon sweet paprika

6 ripe tomatoes, chopped
250 ml (9 fl oz/1 cup) red wine
750 ml (26 fl oz/3 cups) beef
　stock
2 tablespoons tomato paste
　(concentrated purée)
250 g (9 oz) baby new potatoes,
　halved
2 sticks celery, sliced
3 carrots, chopped
2 bay leaves
3 tablespoons chopped fresh
　parsley

1 Put the eggplant in a colander, sprinkle generously with salt and leave for 20 minutes. Rinse, pat dry with paper towels and set aside.

2 Heat the oil in a large pan and cook the onion for 5 minutes, until soft. Add the garlic and cook for 1 minute. Remove from the pan. Add the eggplant and cook for 5 minutes. Remove from the pan. Brown the meat in batches, sprinkle with spices, season and cook for 1–2 minutes. Add the tomato, onion mixture, wine, stock and tomato paste; bring to the boil. Reduce the heat and simmer, covered, for 25 minutes.

3 Add the potato, celery, carrot and bay leaves, bring to the boil, reduce the heat, cover and simmer for 1 hour. Add the eggplant and simmer for 30 minutes, uncovered. Remove the bay leaves and stir in the parsley.

Put the eggplant in a colander and sprinkle with salt to draw out any bitterness.

Add the tomato, onion, wine, stock and tomato paste to the pan.

Add the potato, celery, carrot and bay leaves to the pan.

169

RICH STEAK AND KIDNEY STEW

Preparation time: 35 minutes
Total cooking time: 2 hours
    30 minutes
Serves 4–6

1 kg (2 lb 4 oz) chuck steak
2–3 tablespoons oil
1 thick rasher bacon, rind
    removed and thinly sliced
40 g (1½ oz) butter
1 large onion, chopped
300 g (10½ oz) button
    mushrooms
250 ml (9 fl oz/1 cup) brown
    muscat
2–3 garlic cloves, crushed
¼ teaspoon ground allspice
½ teaspoon paprika
2 teaspoons coriander seeds,
    lightly crushed
8 lamb kidneys (425 g/15 oz),
    quartered, cores removed
1 tablespoon wholegrain
    mustard
250 ml (9 fl oz/1 cup) beef or
    vegetable stock
2–3 tablespoons soft brown
    sugar
1–2 teaspoons fresh thyme
1–2 teaspoons fresh rosemary

1 Trim the steak of excess fat and sinew; cut into 2–3 cm (¾–1½ inch) cubes. Heat 1 teaspoon of the oil in a large heavy-based pan. Add the bacon and cook for 2–3 minutes until just crisp; remove. Add 2 tablespoons oil and 30 g (1 oz) butter to the pan. Brown the steak in batches, then remove from the pan and set aside.
2 Add the onion to the pan and cook for 2–3 minutes, until soft and golden.

Add the mushrooms and cook, stirring, for 3 minutes, until just brown. Stir in half the muscat and simmer for 3–4 minutes. Remove from the pan.
3 Add the remaining oil and butter to the pan. Stir in the garlic, allspice, paprika and coriander seeds and cook for 1 minute. Add the kidneys and cook, stirring, over medium heat until just beginning to brown. Stir in the remaining muscat and mustard and simmer for 2 minutes. Return the

mushroom and onion mixture to the pan, with the steak and bacon. Stir until combined. Stir in the stock. Bring to the boil, reduce the heat, cover and simmer for 1 hour. Stir in the sugar (the amount depends on the sweetness of the muscat), cover and simmer for 40 minutes. Uncover and simmer for 20 minutes. Stir in the thyme and rosemary during the last 10 minutes.

Cut under and up to remove the attached inner cores from the kidneys.

When the mushrooms start to brown stir in half the muscat.

Return the browned steak and bacon to the pan and stir in the stock.

HOT AND SOUR PORK CURRY

Preparation time: 20 minutes +
  overnight marinating
Total cooking time: 2 hours
Serves 6

1.5 kg (3 lb 5 oz) pork (shoulder
  or forequarter)
6 teaspoons crushed garlic
1 tablespoon finely grated ginger
1 tablespoon ground cumin
1 teaspoon ground black pepper
1½ teaspoons ground cinnamon

1 teaspoon ground nutmeg
¾ teaspoon ground cloves
250 ml (9 fl oz/1 cup) white
  vinegar
3 tablespoons ghee or oil
3 medium onions, finely chopped
125 ml (4 fl oz/½ cup) tomato
  juice
3 red chillies, seeded and finely
  chopped
1 teaspoon salt
1 tablespoon soft brown sugar

1 Remove skin from pork and cut meat into 3 cm (1¼ inch) cubes. Place in a large glass or ceramic bowl.

Combine the garlic, ginger, cumin, pepper, cinnamon, nutmeg, cloves and half the vinegar; add to bowl. Turn meat to coat with marinade, cover and refrigerate overnight. Drain pork and reserve marinade.

2 Heat the ghee or oil in a large pan and cook the onion until it is softened and slightly golden. Add the pork to the pan and cook over a high heat until it changes colour.

3 Add the tomato juice, remaining vinegar, chilli and salt. Simmer on low heat, covered, for 1½ hours or until liquid has reduced and thickened and the meat is tender. Stir in the sugar.

COUSCOUS

PASTA WITH SEEDS

MASHED POTATOES

Accompaniments for Stews

Some stews, such as Lancashire Hotpot and Irish Stew, contain potatoes and are a complete meal in themselves, but most are best served with an accompaniment to 'sop up' their delicious sauce. 'Soppers' should not be bland, but should not rival the stew in richness and tastiness. Mashed and baked potatoes remain enduringly popular for family meals on wintry evenings, but we also have a few ideas for more interesting and exciting accompaniments. Lighter and often flavoured with herbs or spices, these are ideal for serving to guests or to accompany the more cosmopolitan stews. All of the following recipes serve 4 people.

PASTA WITH SEEDS

Cook 500 g (1 lb 2 oz) pasta in a large saucepan of rapidly boiling water until just tender. Drain, then return to the pan and toss through a little olive oil and 2–3 tablespoons sesame seeds. Season to taste with a little salt and freshly ground pepper and serve immediately, perhaps with some chopped fresh herbs tossed through.

COUSCOUS

Place 185 g (6½ oz/1 cup) of instant couscous in a large heatproof bowl and add 185 ml (6 fl oz/¾ cup) of boiling water. Leave to stand for 3–5 minutes. Stir through 30 g (1 oz) butter with a fork, until the butter has melted and the grains have been fluffed up. Serve to accompany your favourite stew. As a variation, try stirring through 1–2 tablespoons of your favourite chopped fresh herbs or a clove of crushed garlic.

MASHED POTATOES

Peel 4 medium-sized potatoes, cut into even-sized pieces and cook in a large pan of boiling salted water until very tender. Drain thoroughly, then return to the pan while still hot and mash quickly using a potato masher or fork. Add 20–30 g (½–1 oz) butter and 2–3 tablespoons milk or cream. Season to taste with salt and freshly ground pepper and beat until smooth and creamy. As a variation, try sprinkling with chopped fresh herbs. Do not mash potatoes in a food processor or they will become gluey.

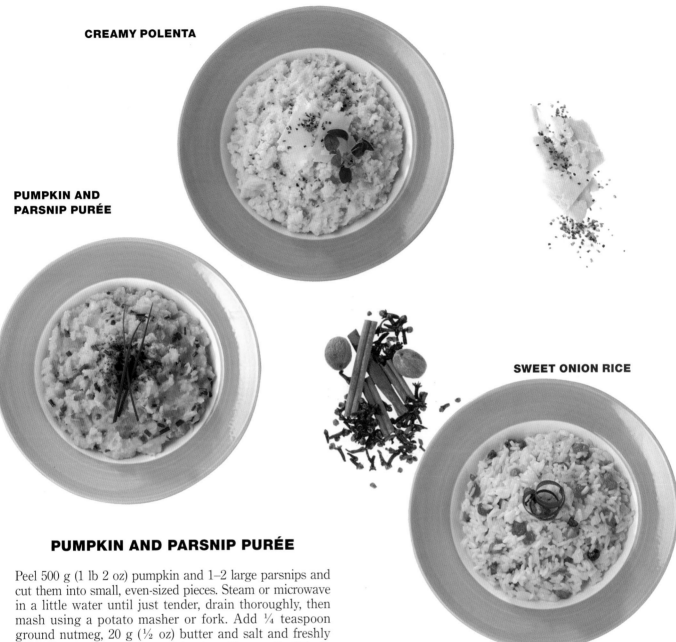

CREAMY POLENTA

PUMPKIN AND PARSNIP PURÉE

SWEET ONION RICE

PUMPKIN AND PARSNIP PURÉE

Peel 500 g (1 lb 2 oz) pumpkin and 1–2 large parsnips and cut them into small, even-sized pieces. Steam or microwave in a little water until just tender, drain thoroughly, then mash using a potato masher or fork. Add ¼ teaspoon ground nutmeg, 20 g (½ oz) butter and salt and freshly ground pepper to taste and beat until smooth. Stir in 1 tablespoon chopped fresh chives. As an alternative, omit the nutmeg and chives and instead add 1–2 teaspoons ground cumin and 1–2 teaspoons soft brown sugar.

CREAMY POLENTA

Put 330 ml (11¼ fl oz/1⅓ cups) of chicken or vegetable stock and 250 ml (9 fl oz/1 cup) of water in a heavy-based pan and bring to the boil. Stir in 150 g (5½ oz/1 cup) of polenta (cornmeal) and stir continuously over medium heat for 10 minutes, or until the polenta is very thick. Remove from the heat and stir in 3–4 tablespoons of cream and 30 g (1 oz) butter. Stir until smooth. Alternatively, omit the butter and stir in 3 tablespoons of cream and 50 g (1¾ oz/½ cup) of grated Parmesan cheese. Polenta is a delicious accompaniment to any stew.

SWEET ONION RICE

Heat 1 tablespoon olive or mustard seed oil in a large heavy-based pan. Add 1 large finely chopped onion and ½ teaspoon turmeric and stir over medium heat until the onion has softened. Stir in 4 tablespoons of sultanas, 2 cloves, 1 cinnamon stick and 200 g (7 oz/1 cup) of long-grain rice. Cook for 1 minute, then pour in enough water or stock to cover the rice by 2 cm (¾ inch). Bring to the boil, then reduce the heat, cover and cook for 10–15 minutes, or until all the liquid has been absorbed. Remove from the heat and leave to stand, covered, for 3–5 minutes. Fluff up the rice with a fork before serving. For a plainer dish, omit the spices and sultanas.

173

RICH PORK AND COCONUT CURRY

Preparation time: 10 minutes
Total cooking time: 1 hour 15 minutes
Serves 4

750 g (1 lb 10 oz) pork leg or
    shoulder
1 tablespoon oil
5 curry leaves
1 large onion, finely chopped
3 teaspoons finely chopped
    garlic
1 teaspoon grated ginger
½ teaspoon chilli powder
½ teaspoon salt
½ teaspoon ground cinnamon
¼ teaspoon ground cloves
½ teaspoon fennel seeds
1 teaspoon ground cumin
3 teaspoons ground coriander
2 tablespoons lemon juice, malt
    vinegar or tamarind liquid
125 ml (4 fl oz/½ cup) hot
    water
125 ml (4 fl oz/½ cup) coconut
    milk

1 Trim rind from pork. Cut pork into 3 cm (1¼ inch) cubes.
2 Heat the oil in a large pan; add the curry leaves, onion and garlic and cook until the onion is soft. Add the ginger, chilli, salt and spices and cook for 1 minute.
3 Add the pork and coat with the spice mixture. Add the juice and cook for 45 minutes, stirring occasionally, or until the moisture has evaporated and meat is cooking in its own juices.
4 Cook, stirring, for 5 minutes. Add the water and coconut milk; simmer for 10 minutes, until gravy thickens.

COOK'S FILE

Storage time: Cook 3 days ahead and refrigerate. Can also be frozen for up to 1 month.

LAMB KORMA

Preparation time: 15 minutes
Total cooking time: 1 hour
Serves 4

1 kg (2 lb 4 oz) leg of lamb,
   boned
2 large onions, chopped
2 teaspoons grated ginger
3 teaspoons chopped garlic
3 large dried chillies, or to taste
3 tablespoons ghee or oil
¾ teaspoon turmeric
2 teaspoons ground cumin
3 teaspoons ground coriander
100 g (3½ oz/½ cup) tomatoes,
   peeled and chopped
¼ teaspoon ground cloves
½ teaspoon ground cinnamon
¼ teaspoon ground cardamom
¼ teaspoon ground black pepper

4 tablespoons water
125 ml (4 fl oz/½ cup) cream

Onion and mint in yoghurt
1 medium white onion, very
   finely sliced
2 tablespoons white vinegar
¼ teaspoon salt
1 tablespoon coarsely chopped
   fresh mint
2 tablespoons plain yoghurt

1 Trim fat and sinew from lamb. Cut lamb into 3 cm (1¼ inch) cubes and set aside. Place the onion, ginger, garlic and chillies in a food processor bowl or blender and process until smooth. Add a little water to make blending easier, if necessary.
2 Heat the ghee or oil in a pan and add the onion mixture. Add the turmeric, cumin and coriander and cook, stirring, until the moisture has evaporated and the mixture has a rich appearance. Add the meat and stir over high heat until browned all over.
3 Reduce heat, add the remaining ingredients and simmer gently, covered, for 30–40 minutes. Stir occasionally to prevent the mixture sticking to the base of the pan. Serve with steamed long-grain rice and onion and mint in yoghurt.
4 To make onion and mint in yoghurt, place the onion in a small glass or ceramic bowl. Pour on the vinegar and leave for 30 minutes. Drain off the vinegar and rinse the onion twice in cold water. Drain well; stir in the salt, mint and yoghurt. Refrigerate. Serve well chilled.

COOK'S FILE

Storage time: Cook 3 days ahead and refrigerate. This dish can also be frozen for up to 1 month.

1

2

3

BEEF AND PORK WITH RED WINE

Preparation time: 10 minutes
Total cooking time: 2 hours
  30 minutes
Serves 4–6

1.2 kg (2 lb 10 oz) rump steak
400 g (14 oz) pork belly
60 g (2¼ oz/½ cup) plain
  (all-purpose) flour
200 g (7 oz) speck
1 large carrot
2 medium onions, thickly
  sliced
2 tablespoons olive oil
2 garlic cloves, crushed
2 teaspoons finely grated
  orange zest

1 tablespoon chopped fresh
  thyme
500 ml (17 fl oz/2 cups)
  good-quality red wine
2 bay leaves
60 g (2¼ oz/½ cup) pitted black
  olives, sliced

1 Trim meat of excess fat and sinew. Cut rump steak and pork belly into 3 cm (1¼ inch) cubes. Toss lightly in seasoned flour, shake off excess. Cut speck into 1 cm (½ inch) cubes.
Cut the carrot into 1 cm (½ inch) thick slices. Heat the oil in a large heavy-based pan. Add the speck and cook for 3 minutes, until brown. Remove from pan. Add the rump and pork belly and cook quickly over medium–high heat until well browned. Drain on paper towels. Add the carrot

and onion and cook over medium heat for 15 minutes or until softened. Stir in the garlic and orange zest.
2 Return the speck, rump and pork belly to the pan and sprinkle with the thyme. Stir to combine.
3 Add the red wine and bay leaves. Increase the heat and bring to the boil, then reduce heat to low and simmer, covered, for 2 hours or until meat is tender. Stir in olives and heat through. May be served with pasta tossed in extra chopped fresh herbs.

COOK'S FILE

Storage time: This dish can be made up to two days ahead. Store, covered, in refrigerator. Reheat just before serving. May also be frozen in an airtight container up to one month.

1

2

3

CURRIED LAMB CASSEROLE

Preparation time: 20 minutes
Total cooking time: 2 hours
  20 minutes
Serves 4

1 kg (2 lb 4 oz) lamb neck chops
3 tablespoons oil
1 garlic clove, crushed
1 tablespoon grated fresh ginger
1 large onion, chopped
1 teaspoon garam masala
1 teaspoon ground chilli powder
2 tablespoons Madras curry
  powder
500 ml (17 fl oz/2 cups) chicken
  or lamb stock

1 tablespoon soft brown sugar
1 tablespoon tomato paste
  (concentrated purée)
3 whole cloves
1 large apple, peeled, chopped
3 tablespoons sultanas

1 Trim meat of excess fat and sinew. Heat 2 tablespoons oil in a heavy-based pan. Cook meat quickly in small batches over medium heat until well browned. Drain on paper towels.

2 Heat remaining oil in pan. Add garlic, ginger and onion, stir over medium heat for 3 minutes or until soft. Add garam masala, chilli and curry powder. Cook, stirring, over medium heat for 2 minutes.

3 Return meat to pan, add stock, sugar, tomato paste and cloves. Bring to the boil, then reduce the heat and simmer, covered, for 1½ hours or until meat is tender, stirring occasionally. Add the apple and sultanas. Cook, covered, for a further 30 minutes. Serve with pilaf rice.

COOK'S FILE

Storage time: Curry paste may be made ahead of time and kept in an airtight container in the refrigerator. Suitable for freezing.

Hints: Lamb stock (bouillon) cubes are available from the supermarket. Alternatively, make your own stock using browned lamb bones. For an accompaniment, buy poppadoms from the supermarket and prepare just before serving.

177

CHICKEN, LEEK AND WHITE WINE CASSEROLE

Preparation time: 30 minutes
Total cooking time: 1 hour
Serves 6

2 kg (4 lb 8 oz) chicken thigh
  cutlets
60 g (2¼ oz/½ cup) plain
  (all-purpose) flour
2 tablespoons oil
30 g (1 oz) butter
4 bacon rashers, roughly
  chopped
2 medium leeks

2 celery sticks
2 garlic cloves, crushed
2 medium carrots, cut into thin
  strips
1 bay leaf
375 ml (13 fl oz/1½ cups)
  chicken stock
250 ml (9 fl oz/1 cup)
  good-quality white wine

1 Trim the chicken of any excess fat and sinew. Toss the chicken pieces lightly in seasoned flour; shake off excess. Heat the oil and butter in a heavy-based pan. Cook the chicken pieces quickly, in batches, until well browned. Drain on paper towels. Cook

the bacon for 3 minutes, until brown. Drain on paper towels. Drain the excess fat from the frying pan, leaving approximately 2 tablespoons.
2 Cut the leek and celery into 5 cm (2 inch) long strips, 1 cm (½ inch) thick. Add to the pan with the garlic. Cook, stirring, until the leek is soft.
3 Add the chicken, bacon, carrots, bay leaf, stock and wine. Bring to the boil, then reduce the heat and simmer, covered, for 30 minutes. Remove the lid and simmer for 15 minutes, until thickened slightly.

1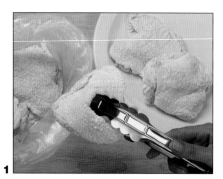

2

3

BEEF WITH GUINNESS

Preparation time: 20 minutes
Total cooking time: 1 hour 45 minutes
Serves 4–6

1 kg (2 lb 4 oz) round steak
30 g (1 oz) butter
1 tablespoon olive oil
2 large onions, chopped
2 tablespoons plain (all-purpose)
   flour
250 ml (9 fl oz/1 cup) Guinness
250 ml (9 fl oz/1 cup) beef
   stock
3 large carrots, peeled and cut
   into 3 cm (1¼ inch) pieces
2 large parsnips, peeled and
   cut into 3 cm (1¼ inch)
   pieces
2 bay leaves
30 g (1 oz/½ cup) chopped fresh
   parsley

1 Preheat oven to 160°C (315°F/ Gas Mark 2–3). Trim meat of fat and sinew. Cut into 3 cm (1¼ inch) cubes.
2 Heat butter and oil in a large frying pan; add cubes of meat in small batches and cook for 4–5 minutes or until browned on all sides. Remove meat from the pan with slotted spoon or tongs and place in a casserole dish.
3 Add onions to pan and cook gently 3–4 minutes or until brown. Add flour and stir over low heat 2 minutes or until flour is lightly golden.
4 Add combined Guinness and stock gradually to pan, stirring until mixture is smooth. Stir constantly over medium heat for 2 minutes or until mixture boils and thickens; boil for another minute. Place carrots, parsnips and bay leaves in the casserole dish and pour sauce over. Cover and cook for 1½ hours or until meat and vegetables are tender. Sprinkle parsley on top just before serving.

COOK'S FILE

Storage time: Recipe may be made up to three days ahead. Store, covered, in refrigerator. May be frozen.
Variation: Replace round steak with chuck steak. A boned leg of lamb, cut into cubes, may be used as a substitute for beef steak.
Hints: Serve with mashed potatoes or boiled new potatoes and steamed beans or broccoli.
Guinness is a traditional Irish draught stout. It has a strong, bitter taste and is dark in colour. When added to beef dishes, it gives the meat a very distinctive taste. You may find the taste of Guinness too strong. If this is the case, a lighter ale may be used as a substitute in this recipe.

CHICKEN AND APPLE CURRY

Preparation time: 20 minutes
Total cooking time: 1 hour 5 minutes
Serves 4–6

1 kg (2 lb 4 oz) chicken wings
3 tablespoons oil
1 large onion, sliced
1 tablespoon curry powder
1 large carrot, chopped
1 stick celery, sliced
400 ml (14 fl oz) coconut cream
250 ml (9 fl oz/1 cup) chicken
   stock
2 medium green apples, chopped
1 tablespoon finely chopped
   fresh coriander (cilantro)
3 tablespoons sultanas
80 g (2¾ oz/½ cup) roasted
   peanuts

1 Wash chicken wings and pat dry.
Tuck wing tips to underside.
2 Heat 2 tablespoons oil in a large
heavy-based pan. Cook the chicken in
small batches over medium heat for
5 minutes or until well browned on
both sides. Drain on paper towels.
3 Heat the remaining oil in the pan.
Add the onion and curry powder and
stir over medium heat for 3 minutes or
until the onion is soft.
4 Return the chicken to the pan. Add
the carrot, celery, coconut cream and
stock. Bring to the boil, then reduce
the heat and simmer, covered, for
30 minutes. Add the apples, coriander
and sultanas and cook for a further
20 minutes or until the chicken is
tender, stirring occasionally. Serve
sprinkled with roasted peanuts.

COOK'S FILE

Storage time: Cook this dish up to
two days in advance.
Hints: Coconut cream is available in
cans or tetra packs from supermarkets
and delicatessens.
Serve curry with steamed or boiled
rice. Sliced bananas can be served with
a sprinkling of lemon juice and rolled
in desiccated coconut. For refreshing
the palate, mix a peeled, chopped
cucumber into 125 g (4½ oz/½ cup)
plain yoghurt and serve.

GREEK LAMB AND MACARONI

Preparation time: 25 minutes
Total cooking time: 50 minutes
Serves 4–6

750 g (1 lb 10 oz) boneless lamb
3 tablespoons olive oil
2 large onions, chopped
2 garlic cloves, crushed
410 g (14½ oz) can tomatoes
3 tablespoons tomato paste
  (concentrated purée)
250 ml (9 fl oz/1 cup) beef stock
2 tablespoons red wine vinegar

1 tablespoon soft brown sugar
1 teaspoon dried oregano
200 g (7 oz) macaroni
125 g (4½ oz) pecorino cheese,
  coarsely grated

1 Trim the meat of excess fat and sinew. Cut the meat into 1 cm (½ inch) cubes. Heat the oil in a heavy-based pan. Cook the meat quickly, in small batches, over medium–high heat until well browned; drain on paper towels.
2 Remove the excess oil from the pan. Add the onions and garlic. Cook over low heat until the onions are soft. Add the tomatoes, tomato paste, stock, vinegar, sugar and oregano.

3 Return the meat to the pan and bring to the boil. Reduce the heat and simmer, covered, for 20 minutes, stirring occasionally.
4 Add the pasta and stir to combine. Bring to the boil, then reduce the heat and simmer, covered, for 15 minutes or until the meat and pasta are tender. Serve, topped with the cheese, in individual bowls or a large bowl.

SPICY BRAISED PORK

Preparation time: 10 minutes
Total cooking time: 35–40 minutes
Serves 4

4 tablespoons plain (all-purpose)
　　flour
1 tablespoon ground
　　coriander
2 teaspoons turmeric
2 teaspoons ground cumin
1 teaspoon paprika

1 teaspoon cayenne pepper
750 g (1 lb 10 oz) diced pork
2 tablespoons oil
2 onions, thinly sliced
4 dried curry leaves
1 teaspoon grated fresh ginger
625 ml (21½ fl oz/2½ cups)
　　chicken stock
4 tablespoons fruit chutney

1 Combine the flour, coriander, turmeric, cumin, paprika and cayenne pepper in a bowl. Add the pork and stir until it is well coated with spices.

Heat the oil in a large pan, add the onion, curry leaves and ginger and stir over medium heat for 3 minutes or until tender. Remove from pan.

2 Add the pork to the pan and cook over medium–high heat for 3 minutes or until browned, turning occasionally. Return the onion mixture to the pan with the stock and chutney. Bring to the boil, then reduce the heat to low, cover and simmer for 30–40 minutes or until the pork is tender. Serve with rice or noodles.

1

2

3

TENDER BEEF CASSEROLE WITH TOMATO AND SPICE

Preparation time: 20 minutes
Total cooking time: 1 hour 35 minutes
Serves 4

750 g (1 lb 10 oz) chuck steak
2 tablespoons oil
2 onions, thinly sliced
4 garlic cloves, crushed
2 teaspoons cumin seeds
2 teaspoons ground
   coriander

1 teaspoon garam masala
1 teaspoon dried chilli flakes
425 g (15 oz) can tomatoes,
   undrained, crushed
125 ml (4 fl oz/½ cup) water
125 ml (4 fl oz/½ cup) beef
   stock
2 tablespoons chopped parsley,
   optional

1 Trim the steak of excess fat and sinew and cut into 2.5 cm (1 inch) cubes. Heat the oil in a heavy-based pan and cook the steak in small batches over high heat for 2 minutes or until browned. Remove, set aside.

2 Add the onion and garlic to the pan, stir over heat for 2 minutes or until onion is tender. Add cumin, coriander, garam masala and chilli; stir over heat for 1 minute. Return meat to pan.

3 Add the tomatoes, water and stock, bring to the boil, then reduce heat to low, cover and simmer for 1½ hours or until steak is very tender. Stir in the parsley just before serving.

COOK'S FILE

Storage time: Casserole can be stored in refrigerator for up to 2 days.

1

2

3

CHICKEN IN MUSHROOM AND PAPRIKA SAUCE

Preparation time: 25 minutes
Total cooking time: 20 minutes
Serves 4

4 chicken breast fillets
3 tablespoons plain (all-purpose)
    flour
30 g (1 oz) butter
1 tablespoon oil
1 onion, finely chopped
2 garlic cloves, crushed
250 g (9 oz) button mushrooms,
    thinly sliced
1 tablespoon sweet paprika

1 tablespoon tomato paste
    (concentrated purée)
125 ml (4 fl oz/½ cup) chicken
    stock
4 tablespoons sour cream
2 tablespoons finely chopped
    fresh parsley

1 Trim the chicken of excess fat and sinew and cut into bite-sized pieces. Coat the chicken pieces with flour by shaking together in a plastic bag. Heat half the butter and oil in a large frying pan, add the chicken in small batches and cook over medium heat for 5 minutes or until the chicken is browned. Drain on paper towels.
2 Heat the remaining butter and oil in

the same pan. Add the onion and garlic and cook over medium heat for 2 minutes or until the onion has softened. Add the mushrooms and cook for 1–2 minutes, or until tender. Remove from heat. Add the paprika and cooked chicken; stir to combine.
3 Combine the tomato paste with the stock in a small bowl; add to the pan and stir until well combined with the chicken mixture. Season to taste. Return to the heat; bring to the boil, then reduce the heat and simmer, covered, for 5 minutes or until the chicken is cooked through. Stir in the sour cream and warm through—do not boil. Serve sprinkled with parsley.

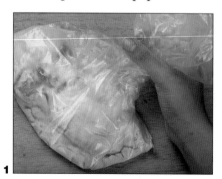

LAMB WITH BORLOTTI BEANS

Preparation time: 20 minutes +
  overnight soaking
Total cooking time: 2 hours
Serves 6

200 g (6½ oz/1 cup) dried
  borlotti beans
1 tablespoon olive oil
12 lamb loin chops
1 onion, finely chopped
1 stick celery, chopped
1 carrot, chopped
3 garlic cloves, finely chopped
½ teaspoon dried chilli flakes
1 teaspoon cumin seeds
500 ml (17 fl oz/2 cups) lamb or
  chicken stock
2 bay leaves
3 tablespoons lemon juice
4 tablespoons chopped fresh
  parsley
1 tablespoon shredded fresh
  mint

1 Soak the beans overnight in cold water. Drain, rinse well and set aside.
2 Preheat oven to 180°C (350°F/Gas 4). Heat oil in a large heavy-based pan. Cook the lamb over high heat in batches until browned and transfer to a casserole dish.
3 Add the onion, celery and carrot to the pan and cook over low heat for about 10 minutes, or until soft and golden. Add the garlic, chilli and cumin seeds and cook for 1 minute, then transfer to the casserole dish.
4 Add the stock, beans and bay leaves. Cover tightly and bake for 1½–1¾ hours, or until the lamb is very tender and the beans are cooked. Season with salt and freshly cracked black pepper. Stir in the lemon juice, parsley and mint just before serving.

When the oil is hot, brown the lamb over high heat in batches.

Add the onion, celery and carrot to the pan and cook until soft and golden.

Add the stock, drained borlotti beans and bay leaves to the casserole.

185

MEDITERRANEAN CHICKEN

Preparation time: 30 minutes
Total cooking time: 1 hour 10 minutes
Serves 4

8 chicken thigh cutlets
2 tablespoons olive oil
150 g (5 oz) French shallots
4 garlic cloves
125 ml (4 fl oz/½ cup) white
  wine
425 g (14 oz) can chopped
  tomatoes
12 Kalamata olives

1 tablespoon red wine vinegar
2 teaspoons tomato paste
  (concentrated purée)
1 tablespoon oregano leaves
1 tablespoon chopped basil
  leaves
1 teaspoon sugar
4 slices prosciutto
1 teaspoon grated lemon zest
30 g (1 oz/½ cup) chopped fresh
  parsley
1 tablespoon capers, rinsed

1 Preheat the oven to 180°C (350°C/ Gas 4). Remove the skin and fat from the chicken thighs. Heat half the oil in a large pan and brown the chicken over high heat for 3–4 minutes on each side, then arrange in a large flameproof casserole dish.

2 Heat the remaining oil in the same pan. Add the shallots and garlic and cook over medium heat for 4 minutes, or until soft but not brown. Add the wine and bring to the boil.

3 Add the tomatoes, olives, vinegar, tomato paste, herbs and sugar. Season with salt and cracked black pepper. Boil, stirring, for 2 minutes, then pour over the chicken and cover with a tight-fitting lid. Bake for 45 minutes, or until the chicken is tender.

4 Meanwhile, place the prosciutto slices in a single layer in a frying pan, without any oil. Dry-fry for 3 minutes, or until crispy, turning once. Break into large chunks and set aside.

5 Arrange the chicken on a serving dish; cover and keep warm. Transfer the casserole to the stovetop and boil the pan juices for 5 minutes, or until thickened, stirring occasionally. Spoon the juices over the chicken, sprinkle with lemon zest, parsley and capers and top with the prosciutto to serve.

When the shallots and garlic are soft, add the wine.

Place the prosciutto slices in a single layer in a dry frying pan and fry until crisp.

Peel two strips of orange zest. Remove the pith and slice the orange into rounds.

Combine the chicken stock and wine and add to the softened onion mixture.

Grill (broil) the capsicum, skin-side-up, until the skin is blistered and black.

Stir the capsicum strips, orange slices, olives and parsley into the sauce.

MAJORCAN CHICKEN

Preparation time: 30 minutes
Total cooking time: 1 hour 30 minutes
Serves 4

2 tablespoons olive oil
30 g (1 oz) butter
1.5 kg (3 lb) chicken pieces
1 orange
1 red onion, thinly sliced
2 garlic cloves, chopped
185 ml (6 fl oz/¾ cup) chicken
    stock
125 ml (4 fl oz/½ cup) white
    wine
1 tablespoon plain (all-purpose)
    flour
1 red capsicum (pepper),
    quartered
12 stuffed green olives
3 tablespoons chopped fresh
    parsley

1 Preheat the oven to 180°C (350°F/ Gas 4). Heat the oil and butter in a large pan. Brown the chicken in batches over high heat and transfer to a flameproof casserole dish.

2 Cut two large strips of zest from the orange and set aside. Remove the pith from the orange, then slice the orange into thin rounds. Set aside.

3 Cook the onion and garlic in the pan for 3 minutes over medium heat, or until softened. Combine the stock and wine. Stir the flour into the pan, then slowly add the stock and wine and stir until the mixture comes to the boil. Add the orange zest, then pour over the chicken. Cover and bake for 1 hour.

4 Meanwhile, grill (broil) the capsicum, skin-side-up, for 8 minutes, or until black and blistered. Place in a plastic bag to cool. Peel away the skin and cut the flesh into strips.

5 Remove the chicken from the dish; cover and keep warm. Bring the sauce to the boil on the stovetop, skimming off the fat. Boil for 5 minutes to thicken slightly. Add the capsicum strips, orange slices, olives and parsley. To serve, remove the orange zest, season to taste and spoon the sauce over the chicken.

SPICED PORK WITH BUTTERBEANS

Preparation time: 25 minutes +
  30 minutes soaking
Total cooking time: 1 hour 50 minutes
Serves 4–6

200 g (6½ oz) dried butterbeans
  (lima beans)
1 large dried chilli
2 tablespoons oil
750 g (1½ lb) pork neck, cut
  into bite-sized pieces
2 teaspoons ground cumin
1 teaspoon ground coriander
2 onions, chopped
2 large potatoes, chopped
200 g (6½ oz) butternut
  pumpkin (squash), peeled
  and cut into bite-sized pieces
1 large red apple, grated
750 ml (24 fl oz/3 cups) chicken
  stock
125 ml (4 fl oz/½ cup) cream

1 Soak the beans in boiling water for 30 minutes. In a separate bowl, soak the chilli in boiling water for 20 minutes. Drain the beans well and set aside. Chop the chilli and set aside.
2 Heat the oil in a large heavy-based saucepan. Brown the meat in batches over medium–high heat. Remove from the pan with any juices and set aside.
3 Cook the spices, chopped chilli and onion in the pan for 5 minutes over medium heat, stirring often. Return the meat and any juices to the pan. Add the potato, pumpkin, apple and stock and season well with salt and freshly ground pepper. Cover and simmer over very low heat for 1 hour. Add the drained beans and simmer for 25 minutes, or until tender.

4 Stir through the cream and simmer, uncovered, for 10 minutes, or until the sauce is thick, stirring occasionally.

COOK'S FILE

Notes: Pork neck, also called pork scotch fillet, is a succulent cut that is perfect for stews.

During cooking, the vegetables will dissolve to thicken the stew. If you prefer to keep them chunky, add them 15 minutes after adding the stock.

Using separate bowls, cover the dried beans and dried chilli with boiling water.

Cook the spices, chopped chilli and onions over medium heat for about 5 minutes.

Add the drained beans to the casserole mixture. Simmer until tender.

In a bowl, combine the leeks, shallots, garlic, parsley, mint and zucchini.

Brush the veal with browned butter, then overlap a layer of veal over the vegetables.

Cut the bacon in half crossways and arrange over the top layer of vegetables.

Evenly pour the cream in around the edge of the dish.

SPRING VEAL WITH BACON AND ZUCCHINI

Preparation time: 20 minutes
Total cooking time: 1 hour 50 minutes
Serves 4–6

3 medium leeks, thinly sliced
6 French shallots, chopped
2 garlic cloves, crushed
2 tablespoons chopped fresh
    parsley
2 tablespoons chopped fresh mint
200 g (6½ oz) small zucchini
    (courgettes), thickly sliced
85 g (3 oz) butter
1 kg (2 lb 4 oz) thin leg veal
    slices
4 rashers lean bacon
4 tablespoons cream
4 baby zucchini (courgettes),
    with flowers

1 Combine the leeks, shallots, garlic, parsley, mint and sliced zucchini. Spread a thin layer in a deep, oiled ovenproof dish; season well. Preheat the oven to 170°C (325°F/Gas 3).
2 Gently melt the butter in a pan until golden brown with a nutty aroma. Remove from the heat.
3 Cut the veal into 9 cm (3½ inch) pieces, brush with the browned butter and season well. Overlap a veal layer over the vegetables. Repeat the layers, finishing with a layer of vegetables.
4 Remove the rind from the bacon. Cut the bacon in half crossways and arrange over the vegetables. Cover and bake for 40 minutes. Pour the cream in around the edge, then bake, partially covered, for 40 minutes more.
5 Arrange the baby zucchini over the bacon rashers. Cover and bake for 15–20 minutes: the vegetables and veal will shrink in from the sides of the dish to form a mould. If the sauce is thin, simmer in a pan until thick. Cut the mould into portions and drizzle with the sauce to serve.

BOSTON BAKED BEANS

Preparation time: 25 minutes +
  6–8 hours soaking
Total cooking time: 1 hour 35 minutes
Serves 4–6

350 g (11 oz/1¾ cups) dried
  cannellini beans
1 whole ham hock
2 onions, chopped
2 tablespoons tomato paste
  (concentrated purée)
1 tablespoon Worcestershire
  sauce
1 tablespoon molasses
1 teaspoon French mustard
3 tablespoons brown sugar
125 ml (4 fl oz/½ cup) tomato
  juice

1 Cover the beans with cold water and soak for 6–8 hours, or overnight.
2 Drain the beans, rinse them well and place in a large pan. Add the ham hock and cover with cold water. Bring to the boil, then reduce the heat and simmer, covered, for 25 minutes, or until the beans are tender. Preheat the oven to 160°C (315°F/Gas 2–3).
3 Remove the ham hock from the pan and set aside to cool. Drain the beans, reserving 250 ml (9 fl oz/1 cup) of the cooking liquid. Trim the ham of all skin, fat and sinew, then roughly chop the meat and discard the bone.
4 Transfer the meat and beans to a 2 litre (8 cup) casserole dish. Add the reserved liquid and all remaining ingredients. Mix gently, then cover and bake for 1 hour. Serve with hot toast.

COOK'S FILE

Notes: Any type of dried bean can be used in this recipe.

To quick-soak beans, place them in a pan, add hot water to cover, bring slowly to the boil, then remove from the heat. Leave to soak for 1 hour before draining and using.
Cooked beans can be frozen in 1 cup quantities and thawed as required.

Place the drained beans in a large pan. Add the ham hock and cover with cold water.

Trim the ham of all fat, skin and sinew, then roughly chop the meat.

Add the reserved liquid and remaining ingredients to the meat and beans.

SPICY BEEF, POTATO AND CAPSICUM STEW

Preparation time: 35 minutes
Total cooking time: 2 hours
    20 minutes
Serves 4–6

300 g (10 oz) French shallots
2 tablespoons olive oil
1 kg (2 lb 4 oz) gravy beef, cut
    into 4 cm (1¼ inch) cubes
4 garlic cloves, crushed
3 teaspoons paprika
1 teaspoon fennel seeds
½ teaspoon ground cumin
1 tablespoon plain (all-purpose)
    flour
125 ml (4 fl oz/½ cup) red wine

2 tablespoons brandy
½ teaspoon dried thyme
½ teaspoon dried oregano
1 bay leaf
375 ml (12 fl oz/1½ cups) beef
    stock
1 tablespoon honey
400 g (13 oz) potatoes, cut into
    large chunks
2 red capsicums (peppers),
    chopped
125 g (4 oz/½ cup) sour cream
chopped chives, for serving

1 Preheat the oven to 180°C (350°F/ Gas 4). Place the shallots in a bowl, cover with boiling water and leave for 30 seconds. Drain and peel.
2 Heat the oil in a large heavy-based pan, then brown the meat in batches over medium–high heat and transfer to a large casserole dish.
3 Add the shallots to the pan and cook over medium heat until soft and golden. Add the garlic, paprika, fennel seeds and cumin; cook until fragrant.
4 Add the flour, cook for 30 seconds, then remove from the heat. Stir in the red wine and brandy. Return to the heat and add the thyme, oregano, bay leaf and stock. Stir until the mixture bubbles, then add to the meat.
5 Cover and bake for 1½ hours, then add the honey, potato and capsicum. Cook, uncovered, for 30 minutes, or until the potato is tender. Season to taste. Serve with a dollop of sour cream and a sprinkling of chives.

Remove the skin from the blanched and drained shallots.

Brown the meat in batches in the hot oil over medium–high heat.

Add the red wine and brandy to the spice mixture and stir well.

191

TAGINE OF LAMB WITH QUINCE AND LEMON

Preparation time: 25 minutes
Total cooking time: 2 hours
    10 minutes
Serves 4

1.5 kg (3 lb) boned shoulder of
    lamb, cut into 12 even pieces
1 onion, finely chopped
2 garlic cloves, crushed
1 cinnamon stick
1 teaspoon ground ginger
½ teaspoon saffron threads
1 large quince, peeled, seeded
    and cut into 12 pieces

3 tablespoons honey
1 teaspoon ground cinnamon
½ preserved lemon
chopped fresh parsley, for
    serving

1 Trim the lamb of excess fat and
place in a large pan. Add the onion,
garlic, cinnamon stick, ginger and
saffron and enough cold water to
cover. Slowly bring to the boil, stirring
occasionally. Reduce the heat, cover
and simmer for 45 minutes. Transfer
the meat to a large casserole dish and
set aside.
2 Add the quince, honey and ground
cinnamon to the cooking liquid and
simmer for 15 minutes, or until the

quince is tender. Discard the cinnamon
stick; remove the quince and add to
the meat, reserving the liquid.
3 Preheat an oven to 180°C (350°F/
Gas 4). Boil the cooking liquid for
30 minutes, or until reduced by half,
then pour over the meat and quince.
Remove and discard the flesh from the
lemon. Slice the rind thinly, then add
to the meat. Cover and bake for 40
minutes, or until the meat is tender.
Sprinkle with parsley to serve.

COOK'S FILE

Hint: As you work, place the peeled
quince in water with a little lemon
juice to prevent discolouring.

Add the onion, garlic, cinnamon stick, ginger, saffron and cold water to the lamb.

Add the quince, honey and ground cinnamon to the cooking liquid.

Remove and discard the flesh from the preserved lemon and slice the rind thinly.

VEAL, LEMON AND CAPER STEW

Preparation time: 30 minutes
Total cooking time: about 2 hours
Serves 4–6

1 tablespoon olive oil
50 g (1¾ oz) butter
1 kg (2 lb 4 oz) stewing veal, cut into 4 cm (1¼ inch) chunks
300 g (10 oz) French shallots
3 leeks, cut into large chunks
2 garlic cloves, crushed
1 tablespoon plain (all-purpose) flour
500 ml (17 fl oz/2 cups) chicken stock
1 teaspoon grated lemon zest
4 tablespoons lemon juice
2 bay leaves
2 tablespoons capers, drained and well rinsed
chopped fresh parsley, for serving
caperberries, to garnish

1 Preheat the oven to 180°C (350°F/ Gas 4). Heat the oil and half the butter in a large heavy-based pan. Brown the veal in batches over medium–high heat. Transfer to a casserole dish.
2 Blanch the shallots in boiling water for 30 seconds, then peel and add to the pan with the leeks. Gently cook for 5 minutes, or until soft and golden. Add the garlic and cook for 1 minute, then transfer to the casserole dish.
3 Melt the remaining butter in the pan, add the flour and cook for 30 seconds. Remove from the heat, add the stock and stir until well combined. Return to the heat and cook, stirring, until it begins to bubble.
4 Pour the sauce into the casserole dish and stir in the lemon zest, lemon juice and bay leaves. Cover and bake for 1–1½ hours, or until the veal is tender. During the last 20 minutes of cooking, remove the lid to allow the sauces to reduce a little.
5 To serve, stir in the capers and season with salt and freshly cracked black pepper. Sprinkle with the parsley and garnish with a few caperberries.

COOK'S FILE

Notes: Caperberries are sold in jars of brine or vinegar in speciality stores and some supermarkets.

If possible, use tiny capers in this dish as they have a superb flavour. Regular capers can be used instead.

Add the leeks and peeled shallots to the pan and gently fry until soft and golden.

Remove the pan from the heat and stir in the stock, scraping up the brown bits.

BEEF AND GLOBE ARTICHOKE STEW

Preparation time: 30 minutes
Total cooking time: 2 hours
    15 minutes
Serves 4–6

2 tablespoons olive oil
1 kg (2 lb 4 oz) stewing beef,
    cut into large cubes
2 red onions, sliced
4 garlic cloves, crushed
1 teaspoon cumin seeds
2 teaspoons ground cumin
1 teaspoon ground coriander
2 teaspoons sweet paprika
1 tablespoon plain (all-purpose)
    flour
500 ml (17 fl oz/2 cups) beef
    stock
1 teaspoon grated lemon zest
1 tablespoon soft brown sugar
1 tablespoon tomato paste
    (concentrated purée)
3 tablespoons lemon juice
4 fresh globe artichokes
3 tablespoons small black olives

1 Preheat the oven to 180°C (350°F/ Gas 4). Heat half the oil in a large heavy-based pan. Brown the meat in batches over medium–high heat and transfer to a large casserole dish.

2 Add the remaining oil to the pan and cook the onion over medium heat for 5 minutes, or until soft. Add the garlic, cumin seeds, cumin, coriander and paprika and cook for 1 minute.

3 Add the flour, cook for 30 seconds and remove from the heat. Add the stock, return to the heat and stir until the mixture bubbles. Add to the meat with the zest, sugar and tomato paste. Cover tightly and bake for 1½ hours.

4 Meanwhile, add the lemon juice to a bowl of water. Cut the top third from each artichoke, trim the stem to 5 cm (2 inches) and cut away the dark outer leaves. Cut the artichokes lengthways in half. Remove the prickly lavender-topped leaves in the centre and scoop out the hairy choke. Drop into the lemon-water until ready to use.

5 Drain the artichokes and add to the casserole, covering them in the liquid.

Cover and cook for 30 minutes, or until tender. For a thicker gravy, cook uncovered for 15 minutes more. Season and stir in the olives to serve.

COOK'S FILE

Note: Tiny black olives have a great flavour and are sold in delicatessens.

Add the garlic and spices to the fried onion and cook for 1 minute.

Cut the trimmed artichokes lengthways in half and place them in the lemon-water.

Drain the artichokes and add them to the casserole, covering them with the liquid.

STUFFED PORK CHOPS WITH WILD RICE

Preparation time: 15 minutes
Total cooking time: 2 hours
 30 minutes
Serves 6

Stuffing
90 g (3 oz) butter
40 g (1¼ oz/½ cup) fresh
 breadcrumbs
1 small onion, finely chopped
5 button mushrooms, finely
 chopped
2 tablespoons pine nuts
½ teaspoon chopped fresh thyme
2 tablespoons chopped fresh
 parsley

6 pork loin chops, trimmed
plain (all-purpose) flour,
 seasoned with salt and
 freshly ground pepper
2 tablespoons olive oil
60 g (2 oz) butter
1 large tomato, sliced into
 rounds
1 onion, sliced into rounds
190 g (6½ oz/1 cup) wild rice
125 ml (4 fl oz/½ cup) cider
250 ml (9 fl oz/1 cup) chicken
 stock
1 garlic clove, crushed
¼ teaspoon paprika

1 Preheat the oven to 170°C (325°F/ Gas 3). To make the stuffing, heat a third of the butter in a pan. Add the breadcrumbs and stir over medium heat until golden; remove and set aside. Heat the remaining butter and fry the onion for 5 minutes, or until soft. Add the remaining stuffing ingredients and fry for 3 minutes. Remove from the heat, add the breadcrumbs and season well.
2 Cut a pocket in the meaty part of each pork chop, then fill with the stuffing. Secure with a toothpick and coat in the seasoned flour.
3 Heat the oil and half the butter in the pan. Brown the chops over high heat; transfer to an oiled ovenproof dish wide enough to fit them in a single layer. Place a slice of tomato and onion on each; secure with a toothpick. Scatter the rice around and pour on the cider.

4 Add the stock, garlic and paprika to the same pan the pork was browned in. Cook over high heat for 1 minute, scraping the base and side of the pan. Pour the sauce over the chops, adding water if needed to cover the rice. Dot with the remaining butter; cover

tightly and bake for 1½ hours. Check the liquid: you may need to add more water to cover the rice. Cover tightly and bake for 30 minutes more, or until the pork is very tender. Remove the toothpicks before serving.

Fill each pork chop with the prepared stuffing and secure with a toothpick.

Scatter the rice around the pork and pour the cider over the top.

CREAMY TOMATO AND CHICKEN STEW

Preparation time: 35 minutes
Total cooking time: 50 minutes
Serves 4–6

4 rashers bacon, roughly chopped
2 tablespoons oil
50 g (1¾ oz) butter
300 g (10 oz) small button
    mushrooms, halved
1.5 kg (3 lb) chicken pieces
2 onions, chopped
2 garlic cloves, crushed
400 g (13 oz) can tomatoes
250 ml (9 fl oz/1 cup) chicken
    stock
250 ml (9 fl oz/1 cup) cream
2 tablespoons chopped fresh
    parsley
2 tablespoons fresh lemon thyme

1 Place a large, heavy-based pan over medium heat. Brown the bacon, then remove and set aside on paper towels.
2 Heat half the oil and a third of the butter in the pan until foaming, then stir in the mushrooms and cook until softened and golden brown. Remove from the pan with a slotted spoon.
3 Heat the remaining oil in the pan with a little more butter. Brown the chicken in batches over high heat until the skin is golden all over and a little crisp. Remove from the pan.
Heat the remaining butter in the pan. Add the onion and garlic and cook over medium–high heat for about 3 minutes, or until softened. Pour in the tomatoes, stock and cream. Return the bacon, mushrooms and chicken to the pan and simmer over low–medium heat for 25 minutes. Stir in the herbs, season and simmer for 5 minutes.

When the oil and butter are foaming, add the mushrooms and cook until soft.

Brown the chicken pieces in batches over high heat until the skin is golden and crisp.

Add the tomatoes, stock and cream to the softened onion and garlic.

BRAISED CHICKEN WITH CHICKPEAS

Preparation time: 35 minutes
Total cooking time: 1 hour 35 minutes
Serves 4

50 g (1¾ oz) butter
1 onion, roughly chopped
3 garlic cloves, crushed
1 carrot, finely chopped
½ stick celery, finely
    chopped
1.5 kg (2 lb) chicken pieces
    (about 8 portions)
4 tablespoons Marsala
250 ml (9 fl oz/1 cup) chicken
    stock

2 tablespoons lemon juice
40 g (1¼ oz/½ cup) fresh
    breadcrumbs
300 g (10 oz) can chickpeas,
    rinsed and drained
200 g (6½ oz) button
    mushrooms, sliced
2 tablespoons shredded fresh
    mint
2 tablespoons chopped fresh
    parsley

1 Heat half the butter in a large, heavy-based pan and cook the onion over medium heat until soft and golden. Add the garlic, carrot and celery to the pan and cook over gentle heat for 5 minutes. Remove from the pan and set aside.

2 Melt the remaining butter in the pan and brown the chicken in batches over high heat. Return all the chicken to the pan with the carrot and celery mixture. Quickly add the Marsala and stir well, scraping the sides and base of the pan. Add the stock and lemon juice, bring to the boil, then reduce the heat and simmer gently for 1 hour, stirring occasionally.

3 Remove the chicken; keep warm. In a food processor, purée the contents of the pan, then add the breadcrumbs and blend for another 15 seconds.

4 Return the chicken to the pan, pour in the purée, add the chickpeas and mushrooms and simmer, covered, for 15 minutes. Season to taste, and scatter with mint and parsley to serve.

Gently fry the garlic, carrot and celery in the butter for 5 minutes.

Pour the Marsala over the vegetables and chicken, stirring well.

Add the fresh breadcrumbs to the puréed pan mixture and process until smooth.

BEEF AND PEPPERCORN STEW

Preparation time: 15 minutes
Total cooking time: 2 hours
Serves 4

1 kg (2 lb 4 oz) chuck steak, cut
    into 3 cm (1¼ inch) cubes
2 teaspoons cracked black
    peppercorns
40 g (1¼ oz) butter
2 tablespoons oil
1 large onion, thinly sliced
2 garlic cloves, sliced
1½ tablespoons plain
    (all-purpose) flour

2 tablespoons brandy
750 ml (24 fl oz/3 cups) beef
    stock
1 tablespoon Worcestershire
    sauce
2 teaspoons Dijon mustard
500 g (1 lb 2 oz) baby new
    potatoes
3 tablespoons cream
2 tablespoons chopped fresh
    parsley

1 Toss the steak in the peppercorns. Heat half the butter with half the oil in a large heavy-based pan. Brown half the steak over high heat; remove and set aside. Heat the remaining butter and oil and brown the remaining steak. Remove and set aside.

2 Add the onion and garlic to the pan and cook, stirring, until the onion is golden. Add the flour and stir until browned. Remove from the heat.

3 Combine the brandy, beef stock, Worcestershire sauce and mustard, and gradually stir into the onion mixture. Return to the heat, add the steak and any juices, then simmer, covered, for 1¼ hours.

4 Add the potatoes and simmer, uncovered, for a further 30 minutes, or until the meat and potatoes are tender. Stir in the cream and parsley and season to taste with salt and freshly ground pepper.

Cut the steak into 3 cm (1¼ inch) cubes, using a sharp knife.

Add the brandy, stock, Worcestershire sauce and mustard to the onion mixture.

Add the potatoes and simmer, uncovered, for a further 30 minutes, or until tender.

VEAL AND FENNEL CASSEROLE

Preparation time: 20 minutes
Total cooking time: 2 hours
  15 minutes
Serves 4–6

1 tablespoon oil
30 g (1 oz) butter
4 veal shanks, cut into 4 cm
  (1½ inch) pieces
1 large onion, sliced
1 garlic clove, crushed
2 sticks celery, thickly sliced
3 carrots, thickly sliced

2 small fennel bulbs, quartered
3 tablespoons plain (all-purpose)
  flour
425 g (14 oz) can crushed
  tomatoes
4 tablespoons white wine
250 ml (9 fl oz/1 cup) chicken
  stock
1 tablespoon chopped thyme
12 black olives

1 Preheat the oven to 180°C (350°F/ Gas 4). Heat the oil and butter in a large heavy-based pan and brown the meat quickly in batches on both sides over high heat. Transfer to a large, shallow casserole dish.

2 Add the onion and garlic to the pan and cook over medium heat until soft. Add the celery, carrot and fennel and cook for 2 minutes. Add the flour, stir until golden, then add the tomatoes, wine, stock and thyme. Bring to the boil, reduce the heat and simmer for 5 minutes, or until thickened. Season with salt and freshly ground pepper.
3 Add the sauce to the veal; cover and bake for 1½–2 hours, or until tender. Scatter with olives to serve.

COOK'S FILE

Note: Many butchers sell veal shanks already cut into pieces. You will need 12 medium pieces for this recipe.

Trim the leaves and base from the celery sticks and then thickly slice.

Heat the oil and butter, then brown the meat in batches over high heat.

Add the celery, carrots and fennel to the onion and garlic and cook for 2 minutes.

CASSEROLE OF CURRIED VEGETABLES

Preparation time: 25 minutes
Total cooking time: 1 hour 25 minutes
Serves 4–6

1 tablespoon vegetable oil
1 leek, thickly sliced
2–3 garlic cloves, crushed
1 stick celery, thickly sliced
1 large carrot
1 large parsnip
1 large potato
1 medium swede (rutabaga) or
    turnip
500 g (1 lb 2 oz) sweet potato
500 g (1 lb 2 oz) pumpkin
280 g (9 oz) can curried cooking
    sauce (see Notes)
400 ml (13 fl oz) coconut milk
155 g (5 oz/1 cup) shelled fresh
    green peas
15 g (½ oz/½ cup) chopped
    coriander (cilantro) leaves

1 Preheat the oven to 180°C (350°F/ Gas 4). Heat the oil in a large flameproof casserole dish. Cook the leek, garlic and celery over medium heat for 2–3 minutes, or until tender. Remove the pan from the heat.

2 Peel the root vegetables and cut into 5 cm (2 inch) pieces. Add them to the dish, place over medium heat and stir well to combine. Stir in the curry sauce and coconut milk and cook, stirring, for 2–3 minutes.

3 Cover and bake for about 1¼ hours, or until the vegetables are tender, stirring gently once or twice.

4 Meanwhile, cook the peas in boiling water until just tender. Drain, refresh under cold water and stir into the casserole with the coriander leaves. Serve immediately.

COOK'S FILE

Notes: Curried cooking sauces are not to be confused with concentrated curry pastes. They are available in many brands and flavours, ranging from mild to hot. Choose one to suit your taste.
If fresh peas are not available, frozen peas can be substituted.

In a flameproof casserole dish, fry the leek, garlic and celery until tender.

Peel the root vegetables and cut them into 5 cm (2 inch) pieces.

POLENTA WITH SPICY VEGETABLES

Preparation time: 30 minutes
Total cooking time: 1 hour 10 minutes
Serves 4

1 tablespoon olive oil
1 large onion, sliced
4 garlic cloves, finely chopped
¼ teaspoon chilli powder
2 teaspoons ground cumin
2 teaspoons ground coriander
½ teaspoon ground turmeric
½ teaspoon ground cinnamon
2 potatoes, cubed
3 carrots, thickly sliced
375 ml (12 fl oz/1½ cups)
    vegetable stock
300 g (10 oz) baby yellow
    squash, halved
3 zucchini (courgettes), cut into
    chunks
300 g (10 oz) pumpkin, cut into
    chunks
2 tablespoons chopped fresh
    parsley

Polenta
1 litre (4 cups) vegetable stock
    or water
250 g (9 oz/1⅔ cups) fine
    polenta (cornmeal)
100 g (3½ oz) butter, chopped
4 tablespoons finely grated
    Parmesan cheese

1 Heat the oil in a large saucepan. Fry the onion over low heat for 5 minutes, or until soft and translucent. Add the garlic and spices and cook over medium heat for 3 minutes.
2 Add the potato, carrot and stock. Bring to the boil, reduce the heat, then cover and simmer for 10 minutes.

3 Add the squash and zucchini. Cover partially and simmer for 15 minutes. Add the pumpkin; cook for 10 minutes more, or until the vegetables are soft and the mixture is thick. Season with salt and freshly ground pepper. Remove from heat, cover and keep warm.
4 To make the polenta, bring the stock to the boil. Add the polenta in a thin stream, stirring constantly with a

wooden spoon. Simmer gently for 20 minutes, stirring constantly so it doesn't stick. When thick, add the butter and Parmesan and mix until melted. Season well and serve at once.
5 Stir the parsley into the vegetables. Spoon the polenta onto serving plates, swirling it into nests with a hole in the centre. Spoon in the spicy vegetables and serve immediately.

Add the pumpkin to the partially cooked vegetable mixture.

Simmer the polenta gently for 20 minutes, stirring constantly until thick.

When the polenta has thickened, add the butter and Parmesan. Stir until melted.

TURKEY OSSO BUCO

Preparation time: 25 minutes + thawing
Total cooking time: 1 hour 30 minutes
Serves 4–6

3 red capsicums (peppers)
2.1 kg (4 lb 3 oz) frozen turkey hindquarters (legs with thighs), chopped (see Notes)
plain (all-purpose) flour, seasoned with salt and freshly ground pepper
3 tablespoons olive oil
60 g (2 oz) butter
185 ml (6 fl oz/¾ cup) chicken stock
¼ teaspoon chilli flakes
4 fresh sage leaves, chopped, or ½ teaspoon dried sage
2 garlic cloves, crushed
1 teaspoon finely grated lemon zest
150 g (5 oz) sliced pancetta or thinly sliced bacon
1 sprig of rosemary
2 tablespoons chopped fresh flat-leaf (Italian) parsley

1 Preheat the grill (broiler) to high. Cut the capsicums in half, then remove the seeds and membranes. Place the capsicum skin-side-up under the grill and cook for 5–8 minutes, or until the skin blackens and blisters. Transfer to a plastic bag, seal and allow to cool, then peel away the skin. Cut the flesh into thick slices.
2 Thaw the turkey pieces in a single layer in the refrigerator. When they have thawed, pat with paper towels to remove all the excess moisture, then coat them well in the seasoned flour, dusting off any excess.

3 Heat the oil and butter in a large pan. Brown the turkey pieces in batches over medium–high heat, then drain the pan of excess oil.
4 Pour the chicken stock into the pan and stir well, scraping the base and side of the pan to mix in all the pan juices. Add the chilli flakes, sage, garlic and lemon zest and cook, stirring, for 1 minute.
5 Return all the turkey pieces to the pan. Cover with the capsicum slices, then layer the pancetta over the top to completely cover. Add the rosemary sprig, cover the pan and cook over low heat for 1 hour, or until the turkey is succulent, yet not falling off the bone.
6 Discard the rosemary sprig and transfer the pancetta, capsicum slices and turkey pieces to a serving plate. Cover and keep warm. If the sauce is a little thin, place it over high heat and simmer for 3–4 minutes to thicken. Stir in the chopped parsley, adjust the seasoning if necessary, then spoon the sauce around the turkey to serve.

COOK'S FILE

Notes: Ask your butcher or poulterer to saw the frozen turkey into 1½–2 cm (¾ inch) pieces for you.
Pancetta is an Italian unsmoked bacon, rolled and cured with salt and spices, that is sold in many delicatessens. As an alternative, you could use prosciutto in this recipe.
Serving suggestion: This dish is delicious with creamy mashed potatoes or polenta.

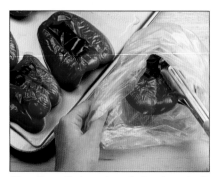

Place the grilled capsicum halves in a plastic bag, seal and allow to cool.

Coat the thawed turkey pieces lightly in the seasoned flour.

In batches, brown the turkey in the hot oil and butter over medium–high heat.

Pour the chicken stock into the pan and stir well to mix in all the pan juices.

Cover the turkey with the capsicum slices, then cover with the pancetta.

Stir the chopped parsley into the simmering pan juices.

DUCK WITH JUNIPER BERRIES

Preparation time: 35 minutes
Cooking time: 1 hour 50 minutes
Serves 4

1.8 kg (3 lb 10 oz) duck
1 Granny Smith apple, peeled
    and thinly sliced
1 leek, cut into large chunks
½ small red cabbage, shredded
2 bay leaves
2 sprigs of thyme
6 juniper berries, lightly crushed
¼ teaspoon whole black
    peppercorns
375 ml (12 fl oz/1½ cups)
    chicken stock
250 ml (9 fl oz/1 cup) orange
    juice
50 g (1¾ oz) butter, chopped
2 tablespoons soft brown sugar
4 tablespoons cider vinegar
1½ teaspoons cornflour
    (cornstarch)
sprigs of chervil, to serve

1 Preheat the oven to 180°C (350°F/ Gas 4). Cut the duck in half by cutting down both sides of the backbone and through the breastbone. Discard the backbone. Cut each duck half into 4 portions, removing any fat. Brown the duck portions in a lightly oiled, heavy-based pan over medium heat; remove and set aside.

2 Drain pan of all but 1 tablespoon of oil, reserving the excess. Cook the apple until golden all over; remove and set aside. Add 1 tablespoon of the fat to the pan and lightly brown the leek.

3 Add cabbage, bay leaves, thyme, juniper berries and peppercorns and cook, stirring, for 10 minutes, or until

the cabbage softens. Transfer to a large flameproof casserole dish. Add the stock and orange juice and bring to the boil. Add the duck, pressing gently into the liquid, then cover and bake for 1½ hours.

4 Remove the duck and keep warm. Drain the liquid into a pan; simmer for 5 minutes, or until reduced to 250 ml (9 fl oz/1 cup). Stir in the butter, sugar

and vinegar. Blend the cornflour with 1 tablespoon water and stir into the mixture until it boils and thickens.

5 Stir the apple and half the sauce into the cabbage mixture and season to taste. Spoon onto a serving plate, top with the duck, drizzle with sauce and garnish with chervil to serve.

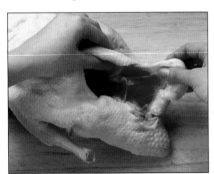

Remove the excess fat from the inside of the duck.

Add the duck portions to the cabbage mixture, pressing them into the liquid.

Stir the sugar, vinegar and butter into the reduced sauce.

SPICY VENISON AND VEGETABLE HOTPOT

Preparation time: 45 minutes
Total cooking time: 2 hours
Serves 6

1 tablespoon olive oil
25 g (¾ oz) butter
100 g (3½ oz) pancetta, chopped
1 kg (2 lb 4 oz) trimmed
    shoulder of venison, cut into
    4 cm (1½ inch) cubes
2 onions, each cut into 8 wedges
2 garlic cloves, crushed
1 tablespoon chopped fresh
    ginger

1 teaspoon ground cinnamon
½ teaspoon allspice
1 teaspoon dried thyme
1 bay leaf
500 g (1 lb 2 oz) tomatoes,
    peeled, seeded and diced
250 ml (9 fl oz/1 cup) beef stock
4 tablespoons orange juice
4 tablespoons port
200 g (6½ oz) turnip
200 g (6½ oz) parsnip
200 g (6½ oz) carrot
chopped chives, to garnish

1 Heat the oil and butter in a large heavy-based pan. Cook the pancetta over medium heat until lightly golden. Remove and set aside.

2 Brown the venison in batches and set aside. Cook the onion until golden; add the garlic and ginger and cook for 1 minute. Add the pancetta and venison and all ingredients except the root vegetables. Bring to the boil, then reduce the heat, cover tightly and very gently simmer for 1 hour.
3 Peel the turnip, parsnip and carrot, cut into even-sized wedges and add to the pan. Cook, covered, for 40 minutes, or until tender, then uncover to reduce the sauce. Season to taste, scatter with the chives and serve.

Brown the venison in batches in the hot oil and butter.

Add the pancetta and venison with all the ingredients except the root vegetables.

Peel and cut the turnip, parsnip and carrot into wedges about the same size.

LEMON GRASS, CORIANDER AND FISH STEW

Preparation time: 15 minutes
Total cooking time: 40 minutes
Serves 4

4 fish cutlets (200 g/6½ oz each)
plain (all-purpose) flour,
    seasoned with salt and
    freshly ground pepper
2–3 tablespoons peanut oil
2 stems lemon grass
4 makrut (kaffir lime) leaves
2 onions, sliced
1 teaspoon ground cumin
1 teaspoon ground coriander
1 teaspoon finely chopped red
    chilli
180 ml (6 fl oz/¾ cup) chicken
    stock
375 ml (12 fl oz/1½ cups)
    coconut milk
3 tablespoons chopped coriander
    (cilantro) leaves
2 teaspoons fish sauce

1 Preheat the oven to 180°C (350°F/ Gas 4). Toss the fish lightly in the flour. Heat half the oil in a large heavy-based frying pan and cook the fish over medium heat until lightly browned on both sides. Transfer to a shallow ovenproof dish.
2 Finely chop the white part of the lemon grass stems, and finely shred the lime leaves.
3 Heat the remaining oil in the pan. Add the onion and lemon grass and cook, stirring, for 5 minutes, or until the onion softens. Add the lime leaves, ground spices and chilli and stir for about 2 minutes, or until fragrant.
4 Add the stock and coconut milk and bring to the boil. Pour over the fish, then cover and bake for 30 minutes, or until the fish is tender.
5 Transfer the fish to a serving plate. Stir the coriander and fish sauce into the remaining sauce, and season to taste with salt and pepper. Pour the sauce over the fish to serve.

COOK'S FILE

Note: Makrut (kaffir lime) leaves are glossy and dark green, with double leaves and a floral citrus smell. They can be frozen.

Heat half the peanut oil and brown the lightly floured fish over medium heat.

Finely chop the white part of the lemon grass stems; shred the makrut leaves.

Add the makrut leaves, ground spices and chilli to the fried onions.

SEAFOOD STEW WITH FETA AND OLIVES

Preparation time: 20 minutes
Total cooking time: 35 minutes
Serves 4

500 g (1 lb 2 oz) fresh mussels
12 raw king prawns (shrimp)
750 g (1½ lb) firm white fish
    fillets
2 tablespoons olive oil
1 large onion, sliced
2 x 400 g (13 oz) cans tomatoes,
    chopped
1 tablespoon chopped fresh
    lemon thyme

2 strips lemon zest
4 tablespoons dry vermouth or
    white wine
1 teaspoon sugar
12 black olives
125 g (4 oz) feta cheese, cubed

1 Discard any open or damaged mussels; scrub the rest and remove the beards. Place the mussels in a pan of simmering water: as soon as the shells open, place the mussels in a bowl of cold water, discarding any unopened ones. Open them up and leave on their half shells, discarding the other half.
2 Peel and devein the prawns, leaving the tails intact. Cut the fish into bite-sized pieces, removing any bones.

Cover and refrigerate. Preheat the oven to 180°C (350°F/Gas 4).
3 Heat the oil in a large, heavy-based pan and cook the onion over low heat for 5 minutes, or until soft but not brown. Add the tomatoes, lemon thyme, lemon zest, vermouth and sugar. Bring to the boil and season to taste. Reduce the heat, cover and simmer for 10 minutes.
4 Place the seafood in a shallow ovenproof dish and cover with the hot sauce. Bake, covered, for 10 minutes. Add the remaining ingredients, covering the seafood with the sauce. Bake for 10 minutes, or until heated through. Serve immediately.

Scrub the mussels, remove the beards, then place in a pan of simmering water.

Peel and devein the prawns and cut the fish into bite-sized pieces.

Add the tomatoes, thyme, lemon zest, vermouth and sugar to the softened onion.

SMOKED SAUSAGE AND KIDNEY BEAN STEW

Preparation time: 20 minutes
Total cooking time: 2 hours 30
    minutes
Serves 4–6

1 small red capsicum (pepper),
    halved
2 tablespoons olive oil
2–3 garlic cloves, crushed
1 large onion, thinly sliced
1 carrot, cut into cubes
420 g (14 oz) can kidney beans,
    rinsed and drained
500 ml (17 fl oz/2 cups) beef
    stock
1 tablespoon treacle
600 g (1¼ lb) piece speck or
    bacon
425 g (14 oz) can chopped
    tomatoes, juice reserved
2 tablespoons tomato paste
    (concentrated purée)
150 g (5 oz) smoked sausages

1 Grill (broil) the capsicum halves, skin-side-up, under a hot grill until the skin is black and blistered. Cool, then peel off the skin and dice the flesh.
2 Heat the oil in a large, heavy-based pan. Add the garlic, onion and carrot and cook, stirring, over low heat for 4–5 minutes without browning.
3 Add the beans, stock, treacle and freshly ground black pepper to taste. Slowly bring to the boil, then add the speck or bacon. Reduce the heat; cover and simmer for 1 hour. Stir through the undrained tomatoes and tomato paste and simmer for 30 minutes.
4 Place the sausages in a pan of cold water. Slowly bring to the boil, then drain and add to the stew. Simmer,

uncovered, for 45 minutes, or until the sauce is thick and rich.
5 Remove the speck or bacon and sausages, using tongs. Slice them, removing any fat and skin, and return to the stew for serving. Serve hot.

COOK'S FILE

Note: Speck is a kind of smoked bacon, often sold in delicatessens.
Serving suggestion: This stew is lovely with a Pumpkin and parsnip purée. For the recipe, see page 173.

Add the beans, stock, treacle and pepper to the onion mixture.

Simmer the stew until rich and thick, then remove the speck and sausages.

Remove the skin and excess fat from the speck. Slice the sausages and speck.

LAMB STEW WITH ROSEMARY DUMPLINGS

Preparation time: 25 minutes
Total cooking time: 2 hours
Serves 4

8 lamb neck chops
plain (all-purpose) flour,
    seasoned with salt and
    freshly ground pepper
2 tablespoons oil
2 rashers bacon, finely chopped
1 large onion, sliced
500 ml (17 fl oz/2 cups) beef
    stock
1 tablespoon chopped fresh
    thyme
2 carrots, thickly sliced
2 potatoes, chopped

Rosemary dumplings
125 g (4 oz/1 cup) self-raising
    flour
20 g (¾ oz) butter, chopped
1 tablespoon chopped fresh
    rosemary
4 tablespoons milk

1 Trim the lamb of fat and sinew and toss in flour, shaking off excess. Heat the oil in a large, heavy-based pan and brown lamb over medium–high heat in batches. Remove and set aside.
2 Add the bacon to the pan and cook over medium heat for 2 minutes, or until brown. Add the onion and cook for about 5 minutes, or until soft.
3 Return lamb to the pan. Add stock, thyme and 125 ml (4 fl oz/½ cup) of water. Simmer, covered, over low heat for 30 minutes. Add the carrot and potato and simmer for 1 hour more.
4 To make the rosemary dumplings, sift the flour into a bowl, then rub in the butter with your fingertips until the mixture is fine and crumbly. Mix in the rosemary. Add most of the milk and mix to a soft dough with a knife, adding more milk if needed. Turn out onto a lightly floured surface and gently knead until smooth. Divide the dough into 12 portions and form into rough balls. Place the dumplings on top of the stew, then cover and cook for 15 minutes. Serve immediately.

COOK'S FILE

Storage time: The stew may be made a day ahead, but the dumplings should be made just before serving. Simply reheat the stew to simmering point, then add the fresh dumplings.

Lightly toss the trimmed lamb in the seasoned flour, shaking off any excess.

Sift the flour into a bowl. Rub in the butter with your fingertips until fine and crumbly.

Divide the dough into 12 portions, then form into rough balls.

HEARTY PORK AND RED LENTILS

Preparation time: 35 minutes
Total cooking time: 2 hours
Serves 4–6

1 kg (2 lb 4 oz) lean pork neck, sliced 2 cm (¾ inch) thick
plain (all-purpose) flour, seasoned with salt and freshly ground pepper
50 g (1¾ oz) butter
1 tablespoon olive oil
1 large onion, finely chopped
3 garlic cloves, finely chopped
2 tablespoons chopped sage
310 ml (10 fl oz/1¼ cups) vegetable stock
310 ml (10 fl oz/1¼ cups) red wine
250 g (9 oz/1 cup) red lentils, rinsed
2 carrots, chopped
2 potatoes, chopped
3 sticks celery, chopped
1 bay leaf, torn in three
2 teaspoons finely grated lemon zest
2 tablespoons chopped fresh parsley

1 Coat the pork in the flour, shaking off any excess. In a large, deep heavy-based pan, heat the butter and oil over medium heat until foamy. Brown the pork well, in batches if necessary.
2 Return all the pork to the pan. Add the onion, garlic, sage, stock and wine; season well. Bring to the boil, turning the pork to coat in the liquid. Reduce the heat, cover and simmer for 1 hour, turning the pork during cooking. If the sauce becomes too thick, add about 250 ml (9 fl oz/1 cup) of water.

3 Add the lentils, carrots, potatoes, celery and bay leaf to the stew with 500 ml (17 fl oz/2 cups) of water, and plenty of salt and pepper. Bring to the boil, then reduce the heat to low. Simmer, covered, for 40 minutes.
4 Add the zest and cook, uncovered, for 30 minutes, or until the sauce is thick and mash-like. If the pork is falling apart, remove and keep warm. To serve, pile the sauce onto the plates, rest some pork on top and sprinkle with parsley. Serve with mashed potatoes and steamed green beans.

Brown the pork well in the foamy butter and oil mixture.

When the wine mixture boils, turn the pork over to coat in the cooking liquid.

Add the lemon rind to the stew and cook, covered, for 30 minutes.

VEAL WITH SWEET VEGETABLES

Preparation time: 30 minutes
Total cooking time: 2 hours
  30 minutes
Serves 4

olive oil, for cooking
8 veal shank pieces, each 2 cm
  (¾ inch) thick
2 garlic cloves, finely chopped
2 onions, chopped
2 carrots, chopped
1 stick celery, chopped
2 bay leaves, torn
750 ml (24 fl oz/3 cups) beef
  stock

50 g (1¾ oz) butter
200 g (6½ oz) white sweet
  potato
200 g (6½ oz) parsnips
150 g (5 oz) baby turnips
150 g (5 oz) new potatoes
2 teaspoons soft brown sugar
2 tablespoons balsamic vinegar

1 Preheat the oven to warm 160°C (315°F/Gas 2–3). Heat 3 tablespoons of oil in a roasting pan over medium heat and brown the veal all over. Remove and set aside. Add the garlic, onion, carrot and celery and brown lightly for 10 minutes. Add the veal, bay leaves and stock and stir well. Bring to the boil, cover tightly with foil, then bake for 1½ hours.

2 Towards the end of baking, cut the sweet potato and parsnips into large chunks; trim the turnips and cut in half. Heat the butter and a little oil in a deep frying pan until foamy. Toss all the root vegetables over medium heat for 5–6 minutes, or until the edges are golden. Sprinkle with sugar and vinegar and toss well. Cook gently for 10 minutes, or until the vegetables soften and the juices caramelise.

3 Turn the veal in the stock, add the vegetables and toss well. If the meat is drying out, stir in 250 ml (9 fl oz/1 cup) water. Season well, then cover and cook for 20 minutes. This dish is delicious served with steamed rice or creamy polenta.

Heat the oil in a roasting pan, add the veal shanks and brown all over.

Add the root vegetables to the foaming butter. Cook until the edges are golden.

Add the caramelised vegetables to the veal mixture and toss well.

PORK AND EGGPLANT POT

Preparation time: 20 minutes
Total cooking time: 1 hour 40 minutes
Serves 4

olive oil, for cooking
375 g (12 oz) slender eggplants
    (aubergines), cut into 3 cm
    (1¼ inch) slices
8 bulb spring onions
400 g (13 oz) can tomatoes,
    chopped
2 garlic cloves, crushed
2 teaspoons ground cumin
500 g (1 lb 2 oz) pork fillet,
    sliced 3 cm (1¼ inches) thick

plain (all-purpose) flour,
    seasoned with salt and
    freshly ground pepper
170 ml (5½ fl oz/⅔ cup)
    cider
1 sprig of rosemary
2 tablespoons finely chopped
    toasted almonds

1 Heat 3 tablespoons of oil in a large, heavy-based pan. Brown the eggplant in batches over high heat, adding oil as needed. Remove and set aside.
2 Quarter the spring onions along their length. Add some oil to the pan and fry over medium heat for 5 minutes. Add the tomatoes, garlic and cumin; cook for 2 minutes. Remove and set aside.

3 Coat the pork in the flour, shaking off any excess. Brown in batches over medium–high heat until golden, adding oil as needed. Remove.
4 Add the cider to the pan and stir well, scraping down the side and base. Allow to boil for 1–2 minutes, then add 125 ml (4 fl oz/½ cup) water. Reduce the heat and stir in the spring onions and tomatoes. Add the pork, season to taste and poke the rosemary sprig into the stew. Partially cover and simmer gently for 20 minutes.
5 Layer the eggplant on top, partially cover and cook for 25 minutes, or until the pork is tender. Just before serving, gently toss the almonds through.

Fry the eggplant in batches over high heat until browned on both sides.

Add the cider to the frying pan, scraping the brown bits from the side and base.

Layer the eggplant over the top of the pork and tomato mixture.

BEEF SAUSAGE AND MUSHROOM STEW

Preparation time: 20 minutes +
 30 minutes standing
Total cooking time: 1 hour
Serves 4–6

15 g (½ oz) packet dried porcini
 mushrooms
12 thick beef sausages
300 g (10 oz) piece speck or
 bacon
2 teaspoons oil
2 onions, cut into eighths
8 garlic cloves
1 sprig of thyme
3 bay leaves
375 ml (12 fl oz/1½ cups) red
 wine

250 ml (9 fl oz/1 cup) beef stock
1 teaspoon Dijon mustard
350 g (12 oz) baby carrots
100 g (3½ oz) Swiss brown
 mushrooms, halved
100 g (3½ oz) button
 mushrooms, halved
1 tablespoon cornflour
 (cornstarch)
chopped fresh parsley, for
 serving

1 Soak the mushrooms for 30 minutes in enough boiling water to cover.
2 Brown the sausages well all over in a lightly oiled pan over medium heat. Drain on paper towels and place in a large, flameproof casserole dish.
3 Remove the rind from the speck or bacon; cut the meat into small strips. Heat the oil in a pan and add the speck, onions and garlic. Cook, stirring, until the onions are golden, then place in the casserole dish with the thyme, bay leaves, wine, stock and mustard. Cover, bring to the boil, then reduce the heat and simmer for 20 minutes.
4 Reserving 3 tablespoons of liquid, drain the mushrooms. Add the carrots and all mushrooms to the stew. Cover and simmer for 20 minutes. Mix the cornflour into the reserved liquid; stir into the stew until it boils and thickens. Sprinkle with parsley to serve.

COOK'S FILE

Note: Speck is a type of smoked bacon sold in delicatessens.

Cover the porcini mushrooms with boiling water and soak for 30 minutes.

Remove the rind from the speck and cut the meat into small strips.

Add the carrots and all the mushrooms to the sausages. Simmer for 20 minutes.

CHICKEN WITH SHERRY, RAISINS AND PINE NUTS

Preparation time: 30 minutes
Total cooking time: 50 minutes
Serves 4

1.5 kg (3 lb) chicken pieces
    (about 8 portions)
plain (all-purpose) flour,
    seasoned with salt and
    freshly ground pepper
3 tablespoons olive oil
2 onions, thinly sliced
2 red capsicums (peppers), sliced

4 garlic cloves, finely sliced
250 ml (9 fl oz/1 cup) chicken
    stock
125 ml (4 fl oz/½ cup) dry
    sherry
125 ml (4 fl oz/½ cup) orange
    juice
125 g (4 oz) raisins
125 g (4 oz) pine nuts, toasted

1 Toss the chicken in the seasoned flour to coat. Heat the oil in a large heavy-based pan. Brown the chicken in batches over medium heat until crisp and golden all over. Remove from the pan and set aside.

2 Drain the pan of excess oil and add the onion, capsicum and garlic. Cover the pan tightly and cook for about 3 minutes.
3 Add the chicken, chicken stock, sherry, orange juice and raisins and season to taste with salt and freshly ground pepper. Cover and simmer for about 35 minutes, turning the chicken now and then in the sauce.
4 Remove the chicken, keep warm and simmer the sauce for 5 minutes to thicken. Pour over the chicken and scatter with pine nuts to serve.

Toss the chicken in the seasoned flour to coat evenly all over.

Add the onion, capsicum and garlic to the pan. Cover and cook for 3 minutes.

Add the chicken, stock, sherry, orange juice and raisins to the capsicum mixture.

CHICKEN CACCIATORE

Preparation time: 20 minutes
Total cooking time: 1 hour 15 minutes
Serves 4

1.25 kg (2 lb 8 oz) chicken pieces
2 tablespoons plain (all-purpose)
    flour
1 tablespoon olive oil
1 large onion, finely chopped
2 garlic cloves, chopped
2 x 425 g (14 oz) cans tomatoes,
    roughly chopped

500 ml (17 fl oz/2 cups) chicken
    stock
125 ml (4 fl oz/½ cup) white wine
2 tablespoons tomato paste
    (concentrated purée)
1 teaspoon caster (superfine)
    sugar
2 tablespoons chopped fresh
    basil
2 tablespoons chopped fresh
    parsley
90 g (3 oz/½ cup) black olives

1 Toss the chicken in the flour to coat. Heat the oil in a large, heavy-based

pan and brown the chicken in batches over medium heat. Remove from the pan and drain on paper towels.
2 Cook the onion and garlic in the pan for 10 minutes over low heat, stirring. Add the tomatoes, stock and wine. Bring to the boil, reduce the heat and simmer for 15 minutes. Stir in the tomato paste, sugar and chicken.
3 Cover and simmer for 30 minutes, then add the herbs and olives and season to taste. Simmer for another 15 minutes, stirring occasionally.

Brown the chicken in batches in the hot oil and drain on paper towels.

Add the tomatoes, stock and wine to the softened onion and garlic mixture.

Stir in the herbs, olives and salt and pepper to taste.

Chicken with Sherry, Raisins and Pine Nuts (top) and Chicken Cacciatore

RED WINE AND PORK STEW

Preparation time: 30 minutes +
  overnight marinating
Total cooking time: 1 hour 30 minutes
Serves 4–6

750 g (1½ lb) pork
3 tablespoons oil
plain (all-purpose) flour,
  seasoned with salt and
  freshly ground pepper
12 bulb spring onions, trimmed
3 rashers bacon, cut into strips
2 carrots, chopped
200 g (6½ oz) button mushrooms

2 sticks celery, sliced
375 ml (12 fl oz/1½ cups)
  chicken stock
1 teaspoon thyme leaves
1 tablespoon chopped fresh
  parsley

Marinade
250 ml (9 fl oz/1 cup) red wine
1 tablespoon olive oil
4 garlic cloves, crushed
1 tablespoon thyme leaves
2 teaspoons rosemary leaves
2 tablespoons chopped fresh
  parsley

1 Combine the marinade ingredients in a large bowl. Cut the pork into cubes, add to the marinade and mix well. Cover and refrigerate overnight.
2 Reserving the marinade, drain the pork. Heat 2 tablespoons of the oil in a large, deep saucepan. Coat the pork in the flour and brown in batches over high heat. Remove and set aside.
3 Heat the remaining oil. Cook the onions and bacon over medium–high heat for 5 minutes. Add the carrots, mushrooms and celery and cook for 5 minutes, stirring constantly.
4 Add the pork, stock and reserved marinade. Bring to the boil, reduce the heat and simmer for 1¼ to 1½ hours, or until the pork is very tender, stirring often. Season with salt and pepper. Stir in the herbs and serve.

Combine the marinade ingredients and the pork in a large bowl.

Lightly coat the drained pork in the seasoned flour.

Add the reserved marinade to the meat and vegetables.

ROSEMARY-INFUSED LAMB AND LENTIL CASSEROLE

Preparation time: 20 minutes
Total cooking time: 2 hours
  30 minutes
Serves 6

25 g (¾ oz) butter
2 tablespoons olive oil
1 onion, finely sliced
2 garlic cloves, crushed
1 small carrot, finely chopped
2 teaspoons cumin seeds
¼ teaspoon chilli flakes
2 teaspoons finely chopped fresh
    ginger
1 kg (2 lb 4 oz) boned leg of
    lamb, cut into 4 cm (1½ inch)
    cubes
2 teaspoons rosemary leaves
750 ml (24 fl oz/3 cups) lamb or
    chicken stock
185 g (6 oz/1 cup) green or
    brown lentils
3 teaspoons soft brown sugar
2 teaspoons balsamic vinegar
sprigs of rosemary, to garnish

1 Preheat the oven to 180°C (350°F/ Gas 4). Heat the butter and half the oil in a large heavy-based pan. Add the onion, garlic and carrot and cook over medium heat for about 5 minutes, or until soft and golden. Add the cumin seeds, chilli flakes and ginger, cook for 1 minute, then transfer to a large casserole dish.
2 Heat the remaining oil in the pan and brown the lamb in batches over high heat. Transfer to the casserole.
3 Add the rosemary to the pan and stir in 625 ml (20 fl oz/2½ cups) of the stock, scraping up all the brown bits

from the base and side of the pan. Heat until the stock is bubbling, then pour into the casserole dish. Cover and bake for 1 hour.
4 Add the lentils, sugar and vinegar and cook for 1 hour more, or until the

lentils are cooked. If the mixture is too thick, stir in the remaining stock. Season with salt and freshly ground pepper and garnish with rosemary sprigs to serve.

When the oil is hot, add the onion, garlic and carrot and cook until soft and golden.

After browning the lamb, add the rosemary and stock, scraping up the brown bits.

Bake the casserole for 1 hour, then add the lentils, sugar and vinegar.

PORK WITH SOUR CHERRIES

Preparation time: 15 minutes
Total cooking time: 1 hour 35 minutes
Serves 4

1.5 kg (3 lb) pork neck (pork
   scotch fillet)
plain (all-purpose) flour,
   seasoned with salt and
   freshly ground pepper
3 tablespoons olive oil
30 g (1 oz) butter
2 onions, sliced
125 ml (4 fl oz/½ cup) chicken
   stock
125 ml (4 fl oz/½ cup) red wine
2 tablespoons chopped tarragon
   leaves
700 g (1 lb 7 oz) jar pitted
   cherries, syrup reserved

1 Preheat the oven to 160°C (315°F/
Gas 2–3). Cut the pork into 4 cm
(1½ inch) cubes and toss lightly in the
seasoned flour, shaking off any excess.
Heat the oil in a large heavy-based
pan. In batches, quickly brown the
pork over medium heat and transfer to
a large, shallow casserole dish.
2 Melt the butter in the pan. Cook the
onion over low heat for 10 minutes, or
until soft but not brown.
3 Add the stock, wine, tarragon and
250 ml (9 fl oz/1 cup) of the reserved
cherry syrup. Stirring, bring to the
boil and season to taste. Pour the
mixture over the pork, then cover and
bake for 1 hour. Drain the cherries, stir
them through the mixture and bake
for 15 minutes to heat through.

*Add the pork to the hot oil and cook over
medium heat until well browned.*

*Add the onions to the melted butter and
cook until soft but not brown.*

*Add the stock, wine, tarragon and the
cherry syrup to the softened onions.*

KIDNEYS IN CREAMY MUSTARD SAUCE

Preparation time: 15 minutes
Total cooking time: 25 minutes
Serves 4

8 lamb kidneys
50 g (1¾ oz) butter
6 French shallots, finely sliced
250 ml (9 fl oz/1 cup) cream
2 teaspoons wholegrain mustard
2 teaspoons Dijon mustard
4 tablespoons chopped fresh
  parsley

1 To prepare the kidneys, slice them in half lengthways. Using a pair of small sharp scissors, carefully snip out the core of each kidney and remove any membrane.
2 Melt half the butter in a small pan. Add the shallots and gently cook for 5 minutes, or until soft and golden. Add the cream and simmer for 10 minutes, or until reduced by a quarter. Remove from heat and stir in both mustards; mix well and set aside.
3 Melt the remaining butter in a frying pan over medium heat. When the butter foams, cook the kidney halves for 2 minutes on each side.

4 Pour the creamy mustard sauce over the kidneys and simmer, stirring, for 2 minutes. Stir in the chopped parsley and serve.

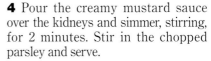

Note: When buying kidneys, select those that are firm and have a rich, even colour.
Serving suggestion: This dish is delicious served with mashed potatoes and steamed green beans.

Cut the kidneys in half lengthways and remove the core and membrane.

Add the two mustards to the cream and stir until well combined.

Pour the cream and mustard sauce over the kidneys.

CHICKEN MARSALA

Preparation time: 20 minutes
Total cooking time: 1 hour 10 minutes
Serves 4

3 tablespoons olive oil
3 leeks, finely sliced
1 teaspoon finely chopped
    rosemary
3 bay leaves, torn
1 kg (2 lb 4 oz) chicken pieces
plain (all-purpose) flour,
    seasoned with salt and
    freshly ground pepper
1 large eggplant (aubergine),
    cut into cubes
2 zucchini (courgettes), roughly
    chopped

125 ml (4 fl oz/½ cup) Marsala
300 ml (10 fl oz) chicken stock
500 ml (17 fl oz/2 cups) tomato
    purée
200 g (6½ oz) button
    mushrooms, halved

1 Heat the oil in a large, heavy-based pan. Fry the leek, rosemary and bay leaves over low heat for 5 minutes, or until soft, stirring occasionally. Remove with a slotted spoon, leaving as much oil in the pan as possible.
2 Toss the chicken pieces in the seasoned flour. Add the chicken to the pan and brown well in batches over medium heat. Return all the chicken to the pan with the leek mixture.
3 Add the eggplant and zucchini and cook, stirring, for 2–3 minutes, or until

softened, turning the chicken pieces over. Add the Marsala and stock and cook for about 15 minutes over medium–high heat.
4 Add the tomato purée and season well with salt and pepper. Bring to the boil, turning the chicken pieces in the sauce. Reduce the heat to a very gentle simmer, then cover and cook for 35 minutes. Add the mushrooms and cook, uncovered, for 5 minutes more.

COOK'S FILE

Note: Marsala is a famous Italian fortified wine. It has a smoky, rich flavour and ranges from dry to sweet.

Remove the softened leek and herbs from the pan with a slotted spoon.

Add the chopped eggplant and zucchini to the chicken and leek mixture.

Stir in the tomato purée and season well with salt and pepper.

CHICKEN CALVADOS WITH GLAZED APPLES

Preparation time: 15 minutes
Total cooking time: 1 hour 10 minutes
Serves 4

1.25 kg (2 lb 8 oz) chicken
    pieces
plain (all-purpose) flour,
    seasoned with salt and
    freshly ground pepper
2 tablespoons light olive oil
30 g (1 oz) butter
1 large onion, roughly chopped
1 tablespoon chopped marjoram
1 chicken stock (bouillon) cube
185 ml (6 fl oz/¾ cup) apple
    juice

4 tablespoons Calvados
185 ml (6 fl oz/¾ cup) cream

Glazed apples
2 red apples
40 g (1¼ oz) butter
2 teaspoons sugar

1 Preheat the oven to 180°C (350°F/ Gas 4). Trim the chicken of excess fat and sinew, then toss in the flour to coat, shaking off any excess. In a large, heavy-based pan, heat the oil and butter and brown the chicken all over, in batches if necessary. Transfer to a large casserole dish.
2 Add the onion to the pan and cook over low heat until soft but not brown. Add the marjoram, crumbled stock cube, apple juice and Calvados and

bring to the boil, stirring. Season well and simmer for 5 minutes.
3 Pour the sauce over the chicken and bake, covered, for 45 minutes or until the chicken is tender. Stir in the cream and bake for 5 minutes—the sauce will be thin but delicious.
4 Meanwhile, core (but do not peel) the apples, then cut into wedges. Melt the butter in a pan, add the apples and sugar and cook over very low heat, turning occasionally, until tender and glazed. Serve with the casserole.

COOK'S FILE

Note: Calvados is a French apple brandy. Cognac may be used instead.

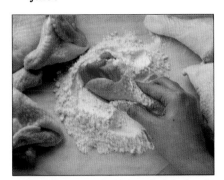

Toss the trimmed chicken lightly in the flour to coat, shaking off any excess.

Add the marjoram, stock cube, apple juice and Calvados to the fried onions.

Glaze the apple wedges in the sugar and butter and cook on both sides until tender.

BEEF BOURGUIGNON

Preparation time: 10 minutes
Total cooking time: 2 hours
Serves 4–6

1 kg (2 lb 4 oz) topside or round
    steak
plain (all-purpose) flour,
    seasoned with salt and
    freshly ground pepper
3 rashers bacon, rind removed
oil, for cooking
12 pickling onions
500 ml (17 fl oz/2 cups) beef
    stock

250 ml (9 fl oz/1 cup) red wine
1 teaspoon dried thyme
200 g (6½ oz) button mushrooms
2 bay leaves

1 Trim the steak of fat and sinew and
cut into 2 cm (¾ inch) cubes. Lightly
toss in the seasoned flour to coat,
shaking off the excess.
2 Cut the bacon into 2 cm (¾ inch)
squares. Heat some oil in a large pan
and quickly cook the bacon over
medium heat. Remove the bacon from
the pan, then add the meat and brown
well in batches. Remove and set aside.
Add the onions to the pan and cook
until golden.

3 Return the bacon and meat to the
pan with the remaining ingredients.
Bring to the boil, reduce the heat and
simmer, covered, for 1½ hours, or
until the meat is very tender, stirring
now and then. Remove the bay leaves
and serve with mashed potatoes and
steamed green beans.

COOK'S FILE

Storage time: Refrigerate in an
airtight container for up to 3 days.

*Trim the meat of fat and sinew and cut
into cubes.*

*Fry the bacon in the hot oil over medium
heat until lightly browned.*

*Return the bacon and meat to the pan and
add the remaining ingredients.*

PORK AND
MUSTARD STEW

Preparation time: 15 minutes
Total cooking time: 1 hour 10 minutes
Serves 4–6

2 tablespoons oil
1 kg (2 lb 4 oz) pork neck,
    cut into 3 cm (1¼ inch)
    cubes
20 g (¾ oz) butter

1 large onion, sliced
1 garlic clove, crushed
250 g (9 oz) button mushrooms,
    halved
1 tablespoon plain (all-purpose)
    flour
4 tablespoons lemon juice
250 ml (9 fl oz/1 cup) chicken
    stock
2 tablespoons wholegrain
    mustard
2 teaspoons honey
½ teaspoon ground cumin

1 Preheat the oven to 170°C (325°F/
Gas 3). Heat the oil in a large heavy-
based pan and brown the pork in
batches over high heat. Transfer to a
large casserole dish.
2 Add the butter to the pan and cook
the onion and garlic until soft but not
brown. Add the mushrooms and cook
for 1 minute. Stir in the flour, then the
remaining ingredients. Stirring, bring
to the boil. Season to taste and spoon
the mixture over the pork. Cover and
bake for 45 minutes, or until tender.

*Using a sharp knife, cut the pork neck into
large cubes.*

*In the same pan, melt the butter, add the
onion and garlic and cook until soft.*

*Stir the flour into the onion and garlic
mixture. Add the remaining ingredients.*

*Beef Bourguignon (top)
with Pork and Mustard Stew*

TRADITIONAL LAMB SHANKS

Preparation time: 30 minutes
Total cooking time: 2 hours
  25 minutes
Serves 4–6

8 lamb shanks
1 tablespoon olive oil
1 orange
1 large onion, sliced
4 garlic cloves
1 large carrot, cut into
    chunks
1 parsnip, cut into chunks
1 stick celery, cut into chunks
2 bay leaves
750 ml (24 fl oz/3 cups) chicken
    stock
500 ml (17 fl oz/2 cups) red
    wine
1 tablespoon redcurrant jelly
3 teaspoons cornflour
    (cornstarch)
sprigs of thyme, to garnish

1 Preheat the oven to 160°C (315°F/ Gas 2–3). Pat the shanks dry with paper towels. Heat the oil in a flameproof casserole or baking dish large enough to fit the shanks in a single layer, then brown the shanks over high heat for 3 minutes, turning frequently. Remove and set aside.
2 Peel three 5 cm (2 inch) strips of zest from the orange, avoiding the bitter white pith. Set aside.
3 Add the onion and garlic cloves to the dish and cook over medium heat for 2 minutes, stirring. Add the carrot, parsnip and celery and place the shanks snugly on top. Add the zest strips and bay leaves, then pour in the stock and red wine. Cover and bake for 2 hours, or until the meat is very tender and comes away from the bone.
4 Using tongs, carefully remove the shanks from the dish; cover with foil to keep warm. Remove the zest and bay leaves and strain the juices into a pan. Set the vegetables aside.
5 Add the redcurrant jelly to the dish and stir to dissolve. Boil rapidly for 20 minutes, or until the sauce is reduced to 375 ml (12 fl oz/1½ cups). Combine the cornflour with a little water and whisk into the sauce, stirring until thickened and glossy.

6 To serve, place the lamb shanks on serving plates, arrange the vegetables on top, drizzle with the sauce and garnish with thyme.

Note: This recipe can be made 2 days ahead, or frozen for up to 2 months.

Heat the oil in a baking dish and brown the shanks over high heat.

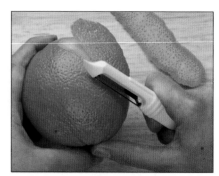

Peel strips of zest from the orange, avoiding the bitter white pith.

VEAL WITH ALMONDS AND MUSHROOMS

Preparation time: 20 minutes
Total cooking time: 1 hour 50 minutes
Serves 4–6

75 g (2½ oz) blanched almonds
olive oil, for cooking
2 onions, chopped
1 kg (2 lb 4 oz) diced veal
plain (all-purpose) flour,
    seasoned with salt and
    freshly ground pepper
125 ml (4 fl oz/½ cup) red wine
500 g (1 lb 2 oz) very ripe
    tomatoes, chopped
2 tablespoons chopped fresh
    oregano
50 g (1¾ oz) butter
400 g (13 oz) mushrooms (such
    as button, shiitake or porcini)

1 Preheat the oven to slow 150°C (300°F/Gas 2). Scatter the almonds on a baking tray and bake for 10 minutes, or until golden. Cool and roughly chop.
2 Heat 2 tablespoons of oil in a deep heavy-based pan. Cook the onion over low heat for 15 minutes, stirring often. Remove and set aside, leaving as much oil as possible in the pan.
3 Toss the veal in the flour, shaking off any excess. Reheat the pan and brown the veal over medium heat in batches, adding more oil if necessary.
4 Return all the veal to the pan with any juices; add the onion and wine. Bring to the boil and stir well. Reduce the heat to very low, cover with foil and a tightly fitting lid, then simmer very gently for 1 hour.
5 Stir well, then mix in the tomatoes and oregano. Cover and simmer for another 20 minutes. Season to taste.

6 Melt the butter until foamy in a frying pan over medium heat. Cut any large mushrooms and cook until just wilted, tossing well.

7 To serve, dish the stew onto serving plates, top with the mushrooms, drizzle over any juices and sprinkle with the chopped toasted almonds.

Gently cook the onion for 15 minutes, or until golden. Remove and set aside.

Return the browned veal to the pan with any juices. Add the onions and red wine.

When the butter is foaming, add all the mushrooms and cook until just wilted.

VIETNAMESE CHICKEN AND NOODLE CASSEROLE

Preparation time: 40 minutes
Total cooking time: 25 minutes
Serves 4

1 stem lemon grass
4 makrut (kaffir lime) leaves
1 litre (4 cups) chicken stock
400 ml (13 fl oz) coconut cream
3 tablespoons coconut milk
  powder
2 tablespoons peanut oil
400 g (13 oz) chicken breast
  fillet, cut into strips
12 raw king prawns (shrimp),
  peeled and deveined, tails
  intact
8 spring onions (scallions),
  sliced
2 teaspoons finely chopped fresh
  ginger
4 garlic cloves, finely chopped
2 small red chillies, seeded and
  finely chopped
500 g (1 lb 2 oz) Hokkien
  noodles
1 teaspoon dried shrimp paste
2 tablespoons lime juice
90 g (3 oz/1 cup) bean sprouts
mint leaves, to garnish
coriander (cilantro) leaves,
  to garnish

1 Finely chop the white stem of the lemon grass. Remove the centre stem from the makrut leaves, then finely shred the leaves.
2 Place the lemon grass and lime leaves in a large heavy-based pan with the stock, coconut cream and coconut milk powder. Bring to the boil, stirring constantly to dissolve the coconut milk powder. Reduce the heat and simmer, covered, for 15 minutes.
3 Heat a wok over high heat and add the peanut oil. Toss in the chicken, prawns, spring onion, ginger, garlic and chillies. Stir-fry for 5–10 minutes, or until the chicken and prawns are cooked through.
4 Place the noodles in the simmering coconut cream, then add the chicken and prawn mixture from the wok. Add the shrimp paste and lime juice. Allow the noodles to heat through.
5 Divide the sprouts among warmed deep bowls and place the noodles, chicken and prawns on top. Ladle the sauce over, scatter with mint and coriander and serve at once.

Using a sharp knife, finely chop the white stem of the lemon grass.

Stir-fry the chicken, prawns, spring onions, ginger, garlic and chilli.

Add the noodles to the simmering coconut cream mixture.

RABBIT, CHORIZO AND OLIVE CASSEROLE

Preparation time: 35 minutes
Total cooking time: 2 hours
  30 minutes
Serves 4–6

150 g (5 oz) French shallots
2 tablespoons olive oil
2 kg (4 lb) rabbit pieces
2 chorizo sausages, sliced
12 pickling onions
2 garlic cloves, crushed
1 teaspoon dried thyme
1 teaspoon paprika
1 tablespoon plain (all-purpose)
  flour
125 ml (4 fl oz/½ cup) white wine

375 ml (12 fl oz/1½ cups)
  chicken stock
1 tablespoon tomato paste
  (concentrated purée)
½ teaspoon grated orange zest
4 tablespoons orange juice
12 Kalamata olives
2 tablespoons chopped fresh
  parsley
2 tablespoons chopped fresh
  chives

1 Soak the shallots in boiling water for 30 seconds; drain and peel. Preheat the oven to 180°C (350°F/Gas 4).
2 In a large heavy-based pan, heat half the oil and brown the rabbit in batches over high heat, then transfer to a large casserole dish. Heat the remaining oil; fry the chorizo, shallots

and onions over medium heat until soft and golden.
3 Add the garlic, thyme and paprika and cook for 1 minute. Add the flour and cook for 30 seconds.
4 Remove from the heat, pour in the wine and stir well, scraping up any bits in the pan. Return to the heat, add the stock and stir until bubbling. Add the tomato paste, zest and orange juice, then add to the rabbit and mix well. Cover and cook for 2–2¼ hours, or until the rabbit is tender. Season to taste, stir in the olives and parsley and scatter with chives to serve.

COOK'S FILE

Note: Chorizo is a spicy Spanish pork sausage flavoured with cayenne.

Place the shallots in a bowl and cover with boiling water, then drain and peel.

Heat half the oil in a large pan. Brown the rabbit in batches over high heat.

Heat the remaining oil in the pan and add the chorizo, shallots and onions.

Mashed Potato Magic!

Mashed potato is a widely loved comfort food, and there are probably as many versions of this fluffy favourite as there are cooks. What follows is a simple recipe for a classic potato mash, and a handful of ways to stir in a dash of gourmet flavour and bring your meal to life. Bon appetit!

CREAMY MASHED POTATO

Peel 800 g (1 lb 10 oz) potatoes, cut into evenly sized pieces and place in a large pan of lightly salted cold water. Bring to the boil, reduce the heat and simmer until just tender. Drain well, return to the pan and stir over low heat until the liquid evaporates. Mash until smooth, or push through a sieve to remove any lumps. Heat 4 tablespoons milk and 45 g (1½ oz) chopped butter in a pan until the butter melts, then beat into the potato with a wooden spoon. Stir in salt and freshly ground pepper to taste, any other flavourings (see below) and serve at once. Serves 4.

GOUDA & CARAWAY MASH

Mix together ¼ teaspoon caraway seeds, 100 g (3½ oz) grated Gouda cheese, 1 tablespoon chopped fresh parsley and 2 tablespoons milk. Stir into the creamy mashed potato and sprinkle with extra caraway seeds. Serves 4.

PANCETTA & GARLIC POTATO

Thinly slice 2 garlic cloves and lightly brown in 30 g (1 oz) butter. Stir into the creamy mashed potato with 2 tablespoons chopped fresh garlic chives and 2 tablespoons sour cream. Top with crisp strips of pancetta. Serves 4.

PESTO POTATO

Swirl 2–3 tablespoons of pesto (bought or homemade) through the creamy mashed potato. Top with toasted pine nuts and flakes of Parmesan. Serves 4.

SWEET POTATO & ROASTED CORN

GOUDA & CARAWAY

LEEK & BACON

LEEK & BACON MASH

Finely chop a small leek and a bacon rasher and gently fry in 30 g (1 oz) butter until the leek is soft. Fold into the creamy mashed potato with 2 tablespoons plain yoghurt and a finely chopped spring onion (scallion) and sprinkle with sliced spring onion. Serves 4.

ROASTED CAPSICUM & CUMIN POTATO

Quarter a red capsicum (pepper), remove the seeds and membrane and grill (broil) until the skin blisters and blackens. Peel away the skin, cut the capsicum into thin strips, then fold through the creamy mashed potato with 1–2 tablespoons ricotta cheese and ¼–½ teaspoon ground cumin. Sprinkle with cumin seeds. Serves 4.

MUSHROOM MASH

Gently fry 150 g (5 oz) finely sliced button mushrooms in 45 g (1½ oz) butter until soft and lightly browned. Stir 2 teaspoons wholegrain mustard into the creamy mashed potato, fold in the mushrooms and add a little extra milk if the mixture is too thick. Garnish with sage. Serves 4.

SWEET POTATO & ROASTED CORN MASH

Instead of the potato, cook and mash 800 g (1 lb 10 oz) orange sweet potato in the creamy mashed potato recipe. Cook a cob of corn in boiling water for 5 minutes, drain and refresh in cold water, then chargrill in a lightly oiled pan until well browned all over. Slice the kernels off the cob and mix into the orange sweet potato with 4 finely chopped spring onions (scallions). Sprinkle with diced crispy bacon. Serves 4.

PANCETTA & GARLIC

MUSHROOM MASH

PESTO POTATO

ROASTED CAPSICUM & CUMIN POTATO

CREAMY MASHED POTATO

229

LEMON LAMB WITH JUNIPER BERRIES

Preparation time: 30 minutes
Total cooking time: 2 hours
Serves 4

3 tablespoons olive oil
2 large onions, chopped
2 garlic cloves, chopped
1 kg (2 lb 4 oz) diced lamb
500 ml (17 fl oz/2 cups) chicken
 stock
4 large carrots
3 sticks celery
15 juniper berries
185 ml (7 fl oz/¾ cup) dry white
 wine
1 wedge preserved lemon

1 Heat 1 tablespoon of the oil in a large, heavy-based pan. Add the onion and garlic, cover and cook gently, shaking the pan to prevent sticking, for 12 minutes or until the onion is very soft, sweet and starting to colour. Remove and set aside.
2 Heat some more oil in the pan. In batches, brown the lamb over high heat, adding oil as needed; remove and set aside. Return the onion to the pan with any juices from the lamb.
3 Over high heat, stir in 125 ml (4 fl oz/½ cup) of the stock and allow it to reduce by half. Repeat this process twice, until the liquid is rich and dark: do not rush this step, as it produces a superb flavour.
4 Chop the carrots and celery to an even size, and bruise the juniper berries with the flat side of a large knife. Add them to the pan with the lamb, wine and remaining stock. Season well. Cover and simmer for 1 hour, or until the lamb is tender.

5 Rinse the preserved lemon. Discard the salty flesh and cut the rind into strips. Add to the pan, then cover and simmer for 20 minutes, or until the stew has thickened. Season to taste with salt and freshly ground pepper and serve.

COOK'S FILE

Note: Juniper berries are sold in the spice section of good supermarkets.

Add the onion and garlic to the oil. Cover and gently cook until very soft.

Chop the carrots and celery into evenly sized pieces.

Using the flat side of a large knife, bruise the juniper berries.

CASSEROLE OF AUTUMN VEGETABLES

Preparation time: 25 minutes
Total cooking time: 30 minutes
Serves 4–6

185 g (6 oz) frozen broad (fava)
  beans, thawed
150 g (5 oz) pickling onions
50 g (1¾ oz) butter
2 teaspoons olive oil
400 g (13 oz) small parsnips
150 g (5 oz) Jerusalem
  artichokes

2 tablespoons plain (all-purpose)
  flour
600 ml (20 fl oz/2⅓ cups)
  chicken stock
300 ml (10 fl oz) cream
2 teaspoons grated lemon
  zest
1 teaspoon grated orange zest
400 g (13 oz) baby carrots,
  trimmed
500 g (1 lb 2 oz) baby turnips,
  trimmed

1 Peel and discard the tough outer skin of the broad beans. Carefully peel the onions, leaving the flat root end attached, then cut a cross through the root end of each onion.

2 Heat the butter and oil in a large, heavy-based pan until foamy. Add the onions and cook for 7 minutes over low–medium heat, turning often to colour evenly.

3 While the onions are browning, peel the parsnips and artichokes and cut into bite-sized pieces. Add to the pan and toss well. Scatter with the flour, toss to coat and cook for 2 minutes.

4 Stir in the stock, cream and rinds. Bring to the boil, stirring, then reduce the heat and simmer for 7 minutes, or until the vegetables are half-cooked.

5 Add the carrots and turnips; toss well. Cover and cook for 4–5 minutes, or until the vegetables are just tender. Season well with salt and freshly ground pepper, stir in the broad beans to heat through, and serve.

COOK'S FILE

Notes: Baby vegetables have a sweet, delicate flavour. If unavailable, choose the smallest vegetables and cook them for a few minutes longer.
Fresh broad beans can be used. Add them with the carrots and turnips.

Skin the broad beans and cut a cross through the root end of the peeled onions.

Peel the small parsnips and Jerusalem artichokes and cut into bite-sized pieces.

231

TOMATO AND POTATO STEW

Preparation time: 30 minutes
Total cooking time: 1 hour 15 minutes
Serves 6

3 tablespoons olive oil
2 red capsicums (pepper),
    chopped
2 green capsicums (pepper),
    chopped
3 onions, thinly sliced
4 garlic cloves, crushed
2 x 400 g (13 oz) cans chopped
    tomatoes
3–4 sprigs of thyme, and extra
    to garnish
2 bay leaves
2 teaspoons caster (superfine)
    sugar
1.2 kg (2 lb 7 oz) potatoes, cut
    into chunks
125 g (4 oz/1 cup) black olives,
    pitted
small block of Parmesan cheese,
    for shaving

1 Heat the oil in a large, heavy-based pan. When the oil is hot, cook the capsicum, onion and garlic over medium heat for 10 minutes, or until softened. Add the chopped tomatoes, 125 ml (4 fl oz/½ cup) of water, thyme sprigs, bay leaves and sugar. Season to taste and leave to simmer gently for 15 minutes.
2 Add the potato chunks, cover and cook very gently for 50–60 minutes, or until tender. Stir in the olives.
3 Using a vegetable peeler, carefully shave thin slivers from the Parmesan block, arrange over the stew and garnish with a sprig of thyme.

When the oil in the pan is hot, fry the capsicum, onion and garlic until soft.

Add the potato chunks to the tomato sauce mixture in the pan.

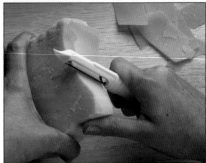

Using a vegetable peeler, carefully shave thin slivers from the Parmesan block.

LENTIL BHUJIA STEW

Preparation time: 30 minutes +
    overnight soaking + 30 minutes
    refrigeration
Total cooking time: 1 hour 10 minutes
Serves 4–6

370 g (12 oz/2 cups) green or
    brown lentils
1 large onion, grated
1 large potato, grated
1 teaspoon ground cumin
1 teaspoon ground coriander
1 teaspoon ground turmeric
90 g (3 oz/¾ cup) plain
    (all-purpose) flour
oil, for shallow-frying
2 garlic cloves, crushed
1 tablespoon grated fresh ginger
250 ml (9 fl oz/1 cup) tomato
    purée
500 ml (17 fl oz/2 cups)
    vegetable stock
250 ml (9 fl oz/1 cup) cream
200 g (6½ oz) green beans,
    topped, tailed and cut in half
2 carrots, sliced
2 hard-boiled eggs, chopped
sprig of rosemary, to garnish

1 Soak the lentils overnight in cold water. Drain well. Squeeze the excess moisture from the lentils, onion and potato using a tea towel. Place them in a bowl with the ground spices and flour; mix well and leave for 10 minutes. With floured hands, shape the mixture into walnut-sized balls and place on a foil-lined tray. Cover and refrigerate for 30 minutes.
2 Heat 2 cm (¾ inch) of oil in a heavy-based pan. Cook the balls in batches over high heat until golden brown. Drain on paper towels.

3 Heat 2 tablespoons of oil in a pan; gently fry the garlic and ginger for 2 minutes. Stir in the purée, stock and cream. Bring to the boil, reduce the heat and simmer for 10 minutes. Add the beans, lentil balls and carrots. Cook, covered, for 30 minutes, stirring twice. Add the egg; cook for

10 minutes. Garnish with rosemary sprigs to serve.

COOK'S FILE

Variation: Split peas can be used in this recipe in place of the lentils. Soak them in cold water overnight, then drain well before using.

Shape the lentil mixture into walnut-sized balls. Place on a foil-lined tray.

Fry the lentil balls in oil in batches over high heat, until golden brown.

Add the beans, lentil balls and carrots to the simmering sauce.

APRICOT CHICKEN

Preparation time: 15 minutes
Total cooking time: 30 minutes
Serves 6

1.5 kg (3 lb 5 oz) chicken thigh
    fillets
1 tablespoon oil
120 g (4¼ oz) dried apricots
375 ml (13 fl oz/1½ cups)
    apricot nectar
125 ml (4 fl oz/½ cup) chicken
    stock
40 g (1¼ oz) packet French
    onion soup mix
1 tablespoon finely chopped
    fresh parsley

1 Trim the chicken of excess fat and
sinew and cut into 3 cm (1¼ inch)
squares. Heat the oil in a large heavy-
based pan. Cook the chicken in batches
over medium–high heat until browned;
then remove from the heat and drain
on paper towels.

2 Slice the apricots into strips. Return
chicken to pan with apricots, apricot
nectar, stock and soup mix; season to
taste, mix well. Bring to boil, reduce
heat and simmer, covered, 20 minutes,
stirring occasionally until chicken is
tender and cooked through and sauce
is slightly thickened.

3 Remove pan from heat. Stir in
parsley. Serve hot with steamed green
vegetables and crusty bread.

COOK'S FILE

Variations: Replace dried apricots
and apricot nectar with a large can of
apricots in heavy syrup, if liked.
Any cut of chicken can be used in this
recipe. Increase cooking times for
larger pieces.

1

2

3

CHICKEN AND VEGETABLE HOT POT

Preparation time: 20 minutes
Total cooking time: 35 minutes
Serves 4

8 (1.5 kg/3 lb 5 oz) chicken thigh cutlets
60 g (2¼ oz/½ cup) plain (all-purpose) flour
2 tablespoons oil
1 medium onion, sliced
1 garlic clove, crushed
4 bacon rashers, chopped
2 medium potatoes, peeled and cut into 1.5 cm (⅝ inch) cubes
1 large carrot, chopped
1 celery stick, cut into wide slices
2 medium zucchini (courgettes), sliced
300 g (10½ oz) cauliflower, cut into small florets
425 g (15 oz) can tomatoes
2 tablespoons tomato paste (concentrated purée)
170 ml (5½ fl oz/⅔ cup) red wine
170 ml (5½ fl oz/⅔ cup) chicken stock

1 Trim chicken of excess fat and sinew. Combine flour and pepper on a sheet of greaseproof paper. Toss chicken lightly in seasoned flour; shake off excess. Heat oil in a large heavy-based pan. Cook chicken over medium heat, turning occasionally, until browned and cooked through. Drain on paper towels; keep warm.

2 Add onion, garlic and bacon to pan. Cook, stirring, until onion is soft. Add potatoes, carrot and celery and cook, stirring, 2 minutes. Add vegetables, undrained crushed tomatoes, tomato paste, wine and stock. Season to taste. Bring to boil; reduce heat. Simmer, covered, 10 minutes, stirring occasionally, or until the sauce is slightly thickened and vegetables are tender. Do not overcook vegetables.

3 Add chicken to sauce mixture, gently stir until heated through.

235

MOROCCAN VEGETABLE STEW

Preparation time: 30 minutes
Total cooking time: 45 minutes
Serves 4

2 tablespoons olive oil
1 onion, sliced
2 teaspoons yellow mustard
   seeds
2 teaspoons ground cumin
1 teaspoon paprika
1 garlic clove, crushed
2 teaspoons grated fresh ginger
2 sticks celery, chopped
2 carrots, peeled and chopped

2 small parsnips, peeled and
   cubed
300 g (10 oz) pumpkin, diced
2 zucchini (courgettes), halved
   and thickly sliced
375 ml (12 fl oz/1½ cups)
   vegetable stock
185 g (6 oz/1 cup) instant
   couscous
30 g (1 oz) butter, diced
harissa, to taste (see Note)

1 Heat the oil in a large, heavy-based pan. Add the onion and cook over medium heat for 10 minutes, or until very soft, stirring occasionally.
2 Add the mustard seeds, cumin, paprika, garlic and ginger and stir for 1 minute. Add all the vegetables and stir to coat. Add the stock, bring to the boil, then reduce the heat and simmer, partially covered, for about 30 minutes, or until tender.
3 Place the couscous in a heatproof bowl. Add 185 ml (6 fl oz/¾ cup) of boiling water and leave to stand for 2 minutes. Add the butter, then fluff up the grains with a fork, stirring through the butter. Serve with the vegetables and a little harissa.

COOK'S FILE

Note: Harissa is a fiery relish made of ground chillies and spices. You will find it in speciality stores.

Chop the celery and peeled carrots into evenly sized pieces.

Fry the onions in the oil over medium heat until soft and golden.

Add the butter to the couscous and fluff up the grains using a fork.

CHILLI BEANS

Preparation time: 45 minutes +
 overnight soaking
Total cooking time: 1 hour 35 minutes
Serves 4–6

110 g (3½ oz/½ cup) dried black
 beans
110 g (3½ oz/½ cup) dried pinto
 beans
110 g (3½ oz/½ cup) dried
 chickpeas
2 small red chillies
1 small green chilli
1 tablespoon olive oil
1 onion, sliced
4 garlic cloves, finely chopped

4 cm (1½ inch) piece fresh
 ginger, finely chopped
¼ teaspoon chilli powder
2 teaspoons ground cumin
2 teaspoons ground coriander
1 litre (4 cups) vegetable stock
440 g (14 oz) can chopped
 tomatoes
1 small red capsicum (pepper),
 diced
1 small yellow capsicum
 (pepper), diced
3 tablespoons chopped coriander
 (cilantro) leaves
3 tablespoons lime juice

1 Cover the beans and chickpeas in
boiling water and soak overnight.
Drain and rinse well.

2 Discard the seeds and membranes
from the chillies. Chop finely; set aside.
3 Heat the oil in a large pan. Cook the
onion over low heat for 5 minutes, or
until soft and translucent. Add the
garlic, ginger, chillies, ground spices,
stock, beans and chickpeas. Bring to
the boil, reduce the heat, cover and
simmer for 1 hour. (There should be
just enough liquid to coat the beans.)
4 Add the tomatoes and the red and
yellow capsicums and simmer gently
for 30 minutes, or until the capsicum
and beans are tender. Stir in the
coriander leaves and lime juice. Season
to taste with salt and freshly cracked
pepper and serve.

*Cover the dried beans and chickpeas with
boiling water and leave to soak overnight.*

*Remove the seeds and membranes from the
red and green chillies.*

*Add the drained beans and chickpeas to the
spiced stock mixture.*

MOROCCAN LAMB SHANKS

Preparation time: 25 minutes
Total cooking time: 3 hours
  15 minutes
Serves 4

Spicy paste
30 g (1 oz) bunch coriander
  (cilantro), roots intact
1 teaspoon ground turmeric
2 teaspoons ground cumin
1 teaspoon paprika
1 teaspoon ground coriander
½ teaspoon ground cinnamon
1 dried red chilli
2 garlic cloves, crushed
2 tablespoons honey
3 tablespoons olive oil

light olive oil, for cooking
8 lamb shanks
3 onions, sliced into thick rings
sugar, for sprinkling
250 ml (9 fl oz/1 cup) white
  wine
500 ml (17 fl oz/2 cups) chicken
  stock
4 lime quarters, to garnish
coriander (cilantro) leaves,
  to garnish

1 In a food processor, blend the spicy paste ingredients (including coriander roots) to a smooth paste. Set aside.
2 Heat 3 tablespoons of oil in a large, heavy-based pan. Brown the shanks in batches over high heat and transfer to a large, ovenproof dish. Preheat the oven to 180°C (350°F/Gas 4).
3 Heat a tablespoon of oil in the pan. Add the onion rings, sprinkle with sugar and saute over medium heat for 10–15 minutes, or until golden.

4 Add the spicy paste and saute for 2 minutes. Season well, add the wine and stock and simmer for 15 minutes.
5 Pour the wine sauce over the lamb shanks. Cover and bake for 1 hour, then turn the shanks over and bake for another 1½ hours, or until the meat is tender. Spoon any fat from the surface,

transfer to plates and garnish with lime quarters and coriander leaves. Serve with couscous.

Blend all the spicy paste ingredients in a food processor until smooth.

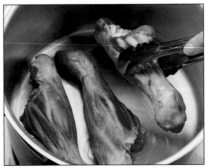

Heat the oil in a large pan. Brown the shanks over high heat.

Add the spicy paste to the fried onion and saute for 2 minutes.

238

BEEF IN BEER WITH CAPERS AND ANCHOVIES

Preparation time: 25 minutes
Total cooking time: 3 hours
    20 minutes
Serves 4–6

1 kg (2 lb 4 oz) gravy beef
plain (all-purpose) flour,
    seasoned with salt and
    freshly ground pepper
olive oil, for cooking
4 garlic cloves, finely chopped
500 ml (17 fl oz/2 cups) beef
    stock
375 ml (12 fl oz/1½ cups) beer

2 onions, chopped
3 bay leaves
4 tablespoons stuffed or pitted
    green olives, sliced
6 anchovies
2 tablespoons capers, drained

1 Cut the beef into 4 cm (1½ inch) chunks, following the sinew and separation of the meat. Lightly coat in the flour. Heat 3 tablespoons of oil in a deep heavy-based pan, add the garlic, then brown the beef over high heat.
2 Add the stock, beer, onions and bay leaves, season well and bring to the boil. Reduce the heat; cover and gently simmer for 2½ hours, stirring about three times during cooking. Remove

the lid and simmer for 30 minutes more. Stir, then mix in the olives.
3 Heat 2 teaspoons of oil in a small pan. Add the anchovies and capers, gently breaking up the anchovies. Cook over medium heat for 4 minutes, or until brown and crisp. To serve, place the meat on serving plates, drizzle with the sauce, sprinkle with anchovies and capers, and season with salt and freshly cracked pepper.

COOK'S FILE

Note: The capers should be squeezed very dry before being added to the pan, or they will spit in the hot oil.

Cut the beef into large chunks, following the sinew and separation of the meat.

Add the stock, beer, onions and bay leaves to the browned beef.

Fry the anchovies and capers in a little hot oil until brown and crisp.

COUNTRY-STYLE CHICKEN WITH BABY VEGETABLES

Preparation time: 45 minutes
Total cooking time: 2 hours
Serves 4

1.5 kg (3 lb) chicken pieces
    (about 8 portions)
60 g (2 oz) clarified butter
12 baby pickling onions
250 ml (9 fl oz/1 cup) dry white
    wine
250 ml (9 fl oz/1 cup) chicken
    stock
250 ml (9 fl oz/1 cup) cream
12 baby carrots
16 snow peas (mangetout)
16 asparagus spears
12 button mushrooms
1 tablespoon chopped chives

1 Season the chicken portions with a little salt and pepper. Heat half the butter in a frying pan, then brown the chicken in batches for 2–3 minutes on each side to seal. Place in a casserole dish and add the onions. Preheat the oven to 200°C (400°F/Gas 6).

2 Pour the wine into the frying pan and stir over medium heat, scraping down the side and base of the pan. Add the stock and whisk in the cream. Bring to the boil, then reduce the heat and simmer for 20 minutes. Pour the sauce over the chicken; cover and bake for 1 hour 10 minutes.

3 Meanwhile, bring a pan of salted water to the boil. In separate batches, boil or steam the carrots, snowpeas and asparagus until just cooked, but still slightly crunchy. Plunge in iced water, then drain and set aside.

4 Heat the remaining butter in a frying pan. Saute the mushrooms for 2–3 minutes, stirring constantly.

5 Place the mushrooms on top of the stew with the blanched vegetables and cook for another 20 minutes, or until the chicken is tender. Skim off any fat, stir carefully to mix all the vegetables through and sprinkle with the chives to serve.

Lightly brown the seasoned chicken in half the melted butter.

Plunge the blanched vegetables into a bowl of iced water to stop them cooking.

Place the drained blanched vegetables on top of the stew and cook for 20 minutes.

240

GINGERED DUCK CURRY

Preparation time: 30 minutes +
  30 minutes refrigeration + soaking
Total cooking time: 1 hour 30 minutes
Serves 4

1.8 kg (3 lb 10 oz) duck
1 garlic clove, crushed
1 teaspoon grated fresh ginger
1 tablespoon dark soy sauce
½ teaspoon sesame oil
8 dried Chinese mushrooms
5 cm (2 inch) piece fresh ginger,
  peeled and thinly sliced
2 tablespoons yellow curry paste
2 tablespoons chopped lemon
  grass, white part only
400 ml (13 fl oz) can coconut
  milk

4 makrut (kaffir lime) leaves,
  shredded
100 g (3½ oz) Thai pea
  eggplants (aubergines)
2 teaspoons soft brown sugar
2 teaspoons fish sauce
1 tablespoon lime juice

1 Cut the duck in half by cutting down both sides of the backbone, through the breastbone. Discard the backbone. Cut each duck half into 4 portions, removing any fat. Rub the duck with the combined garlic, ginger, soy sauce and oil. Refrigerate for 30 minutes.

2 Soak the mushrooms in boiling water for 20 minutes. Drain, remove the stalks and cut in half.

3 Heat a lightly oiled pan. Brown the duck over medium heat. Leaving only

1 tablespoon of fat in the pan, stir-fry the ginger, curry paste and lemon grass for 3 minutes. Stir in the coconut milk, makrut leaves and 125 ml (4 fl oz/½ cup) water. Add the duck; cover and simmer gently for 45 minutes. Skim well.

4 Remove the eggplant stems; add the eggplants to the pan with the sugar, fish sauce and mushrooms. Simmer, partly covered, for 30 minutes, or until tender. Stir in lime juice to taste.

COOK'S FILE

Note: To reduce the fat in this dish, use light coconut milk and remove the skin from the duck.

Cut the duck down the middle. Cut the legs and breasts in half to give 8 portions.

Stir the coconut milk, water and makrut leaves into the stir-fried spice mixture.

Remove the stems from the pea eggplants and add the eggplants to the pan.

ZARZUELA

Preparation time: 40 minutes
Total cooking time: 1 hour 10 minutes
Serves 4

Sofrito sauce
1 tablespoon olive oil
2 onions, finely chopped
2 large tomatoes, peeled, seeded
   and chopped
1 tablespoon tomato paste
   (concentrated purée)

Picada sauce
3 slices white bread, crusts
   removed
10 blanched almonds, toasted
3 garlic cloves
1 tablespoon olive oil

1 raw lobster tail
750 g (1½ lb) white boneless
   fish, cut into bite-sized pieces
plain (all-purpose) flour,
   seasoned with salt and
   freshly ground pepper
1 tablespoon olive oil
125 g (4 oz) calamari rings
12 raw king prawns (shrimp)
125 ml (4 fl oz/½ cup) white
   wine
12 mussels, scrubbed and
   beards removed
125 ml (4 fl oz/½ cup) brandy
3 tablespoons chopped fresh
   parsley

1 To make the sofrito sauce, heat the oil in a pan over medium heat. Add the onion and cook, stirring, for 5 minutes without browning. Add the tomato, tomato paste and 125 ml (4 fl oz/ ½ cup) water and cook, stirring, over medium heat for a further 10 minutes.

Stir in another 125 ml (4 fl oz/½ cup) water, season with salt and freshly ground pepper and set aside.

2 To make the picada sauce, finely chop the bread, almonds and garlic in a food processor. With the motor running, gradually add the oil to form a paste, adding another ½ tablespoon of oil if necessary.

3 Preheat the oven to 180°C (350°F/ Gas 4). Cut the lobster tail into rounds through the membrane that separates the shell segments. Set aside.

4 Lightly coat the fish in the flour. Heat the oil in a large pan and fry the fish over medium heat for 2–3 minutes, or until cooked and golden all over. Transfer to a large casserole dish.

5 Add the calamari to the pan and cook, stirring, for 1–2 minutes, then remove and add to the fish. Cook the lobster rounds and unshelled prawns for 2–3 minutes, or until just pink, then add to the casserole.

6 Add the wine to the pan and, when hot, add the mussels, discarding any which are already open. Cover and steam the mussels for 2–3 minutes. Discard any that do not open and add the rest to the casserole.

7 Ensuring nothing flammable is nearby, pour the brandy into one side of the pan and, when it has warmed, carefully ignite the brandy. Gently shake the pan until the flames have died down. Pour this mixture over the seafood in the casserole.

8 Pour over the sofrito sauce. Cover the casserole and bake for 20 minutes. Stir in the picada sauce and cook for a further 10 minutes, or until warmed through—do not overcook, or the seafood will toughen. Sprinkle with parsley to serve.

Add the tomatoes, tomato paste and water to the softened onions.

Finely chop the bread, almonds and garlic in a food processor. Gradually add the oil.

Cut the lobster tail into rounds through the membrane, separating the shell segments.

Transfer the lightly fried seafood to the casserole dish.

Add the mussels to the hot wine. Cover and steam for 2–3 minutes.

Remove the mussels and carefully pour the brandy into one side of the pan.

243

Trim the ends from the fennel and slice the bulb thinly.

Add the Pernod and wine to the softened fennel, leek and garlic mixture.

When the mussels are cool, remove them from their shells.

Cut off the octopus heads. Grasp the body firmly and push out the beak.

SEAFOOD, FENNEL AND POTATO STEW

Preparation time: 10 minutes
Total cooking time: 30 minutes
Serves 6

1 large fennel bulb
2 tablespoons olive oil
2 leeks, thinly sliced
2 garlic cloves, crushed
½ teaspoon paprika
2 tablespoons Pernod or Ricard
200 ml (6½ fl oz) dry white wine
18 mussels, scrubbed and
    beards removed
¼ teaspoon saffron threads
¼ teaspoon thyme leaves
6 baby octopus
16 raw prawns (shrimp), peeled
    and deveined
500 g (1 lb 2 oz) swordfish
    steaks, cut into large chunks
400 g (13 oz) baby new potatoes
fennel greens, to garnish

1 Trim and thinly slice the fennel. Heat the oil in a large pan over medium heat. Add the fennel, leek and garlic. Stir in the paprika, season lightly and cook for 8 minutes, or until softened. Add the Pernod and wine and stir for 1 minute, or until reduced by a third.
2 Add the mussels, discarding any open ones. Cover and cook for 1 minute or until opened, discarding any which do not. Remove from the pan to cool; remove from the shells and set aside.
3 Add the saffron and thyme to the pan and cook for 1–2 minutes, stirring. Adjust the seasoning and transfer to a large, flameproof casserole dish.
4 Use a small sharp knife to remove the octopus heads. Grasp the bodies and push the beaks out with your index finger; remove and discard. Slit the heads and remove the gut. Mix the octopus, prawns, fish and potatoes into the stew. Cover and cook gently for 10 minutes, or until tender.

Add the mussels, cover and heat through. Garnish with fennel greens and serve.

MOROCCAN SEAFOOD WITH CORIANDER PURÉE

Preparation time: 50 minutes
Total cooking time: 50 minutes
Serves 6

2 tablespoons olive oil
2 red onions, roughly
   chopped
1 red capsicum (pepper),
   chopped
4 garlic cloves, crushed
2 teaspoons ground cumin
1 teaspoon ground coriander
2 teaspoons sweet paprika
½ teaspoon dried chilli flakes
250 ml (9 fl oz/1 cup) chicken or
   fish stock

425 g (14 oz) can chopped
   tomatoes
4 tablespoons orange juice
1 tablespoon sugar
3 tablespoons seedless raisins
375 g (12 oz) baby new potatoes
12 raw king prawns (shrimp)
500 g (1 lb 2 oz) baby octopus,
   cleaned
1 kg (2 lb 4 oz) thick white fish
   fillets, cut into chunks

Coriander purée
30 g (1 oz/1 cup) coriander
   (cilantro) leaves
2 tablespoons ground almonds
4 tablespoons extra virgin olive
   oil
½ teaspoon ground cumin
1 teaspoon honey

1 Heat the olive oil in a large pan and cook the onion over medium heat for about 5 minutes, or until soft. Add the capsicum and garlic and cook for another minute. Add the ground cumin, ground coriander, paprika and chilli flakes and cook until fragrant.

2 Pour in the stock, tomatoes, orange juice, sugar and raisins and bring to the boil. Add the potatoes, reduce the heat to low and gently simmer for 20–30 minutes, or until the potatoes are just tender. Season to taste.

3 Peel and devein the prawns, leaving the tails intact. Use a small sharp knife to remove the octopus heads; slit the heads open and remove the gut. Grasp the body firmly and push the beak out with your index finger; remove and discard. Add the prawns, octopus and fish to the pan and cook, covered, for 10 minutes, or until the fish flakes when tested with a fork.

4 To make the coriander purée, place the coriander leaves and ground almonds in a food processor. With the motor running, drizzle in the oil and process until smooth, then add the cumin, honey and salt to taste. Process until well combined.

5 To serve, dish the stew onto serving plates and drizzle a spoonful of purée on top. Serve with couscous and a green leaf salad.

Peel and devein the prawns and cut the cleaned octopus into bite-sized pieces.

Process the coriander leaves and ground almonds, gradually drizzling in the oil.

OSSO BUCO WITH GREMOLATA AND MILANESE RISOTTO

Preparation time: 40 minutes
Total cooking time: 2 hours 20 minutes
Serves 4

Gremolata
1 tablespoon finely shredded or
   grated lemon zest
1–2 garlic cloves, finely chopped
3 tablepoons finely chopped
   fresh parsley

Osso Buco
4 veal shank pieces, each 5 cm
   (2 inches) thick
plain (all-purpose) flour,
   seasoned with salt and
   freshly ground pepper
2 tablespoons olive oil
2 large onions, sliced
6 Roma (plum) tomatoes, finely
   chopped
2 tablespoons tomato paste
   (concentrated purée)
375 ml (12 fl oz/1½ cups) white
   wine
1 tablespoon cornflour
   (cornstarch)
2–3 garlic cloves, crushed
30 g (1 oz/1 cup) finely chopped
   fresh parsley

Milanese risotto
1 litre (4 cups) chicken stock
50 g (1¾ oz) butter
2 tablespoons olive oil
1 onion, finely chopped
1–2 garlic cloves, crushed
¼ teaspoon saffron threads
250 g (9 oz/1¼ cups) arborio rice
50 g (1⅔ oz/½ cup) freshly
   grated Parmesan cheese

1 To make the gremolata, combine the lemon zest, garlic and parsley and set aside.

2 Coat the veal with seasoned flour, shaking off any excess. Heat half the oil in a heavy-based pan large enough to fit the meat in a single layer. When the oil is hot, brown the veal well on all sides. Remove and set aside.

3 Heat the remaining oil in the pan and cook the onion for 2–3 minutes, or until soft but not brown. Add the meat in a single layer, sitting snugly in the pan. Season to taste.

4 Mix together the chopped tomatoes, tomato paste and wine and pour over the meat. Bring to the boil, reduce the heat, cover and simmer for 1½ hours.

5 Remove 250 ml (9 fl oz/1 cup) of the cooking liquid and allow to cool a little. Place the cornflour in a small bowl and whisk in the liquid, then stir in the garlic and chopped parsley and add the mixture to the dish. Simmer, uncovered, for about 30 minutes, or until the meat is very tender and the sauce has thickened. Sprinkle with the gremolata just before serving.

6 While the sauce is simmering, make the risotto. Heat the stock in a pan and keep it at a simmer. In another heavy-based pan, heat the butter and oil. Add the onion, garlic and saffron and cook, stirring, for 2–3 minutes without browning. Add the rice and stir for 1–2 minutes, or until well coated.

7 Add the stock, about 125 ml (4 fl oz/½ cup) at a time, stirring constantly over low heat until all the liquid is absorbed before adding more stock. Repeat until all the stock is absorbed and the rice is tender—this will take 25–30 minutes, and requires constant stirring. Stir in the Parmesan, season and serve at once.

To make the gremolata, combine the lemon zest, garlic and parsley.

When the oil is hot, brown the veal shanks well all over.

Pour the chopped tomatoes, tomato paste and wine over the meat and onions.

In a bowl, blend some of the cornflour with a cup of the cooled liquid.

Add the rice to the fried onion, garlic and saffron mixture; stir until coated.

Add the stock a little at a time, stirring until absorbed before adding more stock.

247

CHICKEN CHASSEUR

Preparation time: 20 minutes
Total cooking time: 1 hour 30 minutes
Serves 4

1 kg (2 lb 4 oz) chicken thigh
   fillets
2 tablespoons oil
1 garlic clove, crushed
1 large onion, sliced
100 g (3¼ oz) button
   mushrooms, sliced
1 teaspoon thyme leaves
400 g (13 oz) can chopped
tomatoes
3 tablespoons chicken
   stock
3 tablespoons white wine
1 tablespoon tomato paste
   (concentrated purée)

1 Preheat the oven to moderate 180°C (350°F/Gas 4). Trim the chicken of excess fat and sinew. Heat the oil in a heavy-based frying pan and brown the chicken in batches over medium heat. Drain on paper towels, then transfer to a casserole dish.

2 Add the garlic, onion and mushrooms to the pan and cook over medium heat for 5 minutes, or until soft. Add to the chicken with the thyme and tomatoes.

3 Combine the stock, wine and tomato paste and pour over the chicken. Cover and bake for 1¼ hours, or until the chicken is tender.

COOK'S FILE

Storage time: This dish may be cooked a day ahead. Refrigerate in an airtight container overnight.

Note: Don't be tempted to use poor quality wine for cooking, as the taste will affect the flavour of the dish.

Brown the chicken in the hot oil over medium heat and drain on paper towels.

Add the garlic, onion and mushrooms to the pan and cook until soft.

Pour the combined stock, wine and tomato paste over the chicken mixture.

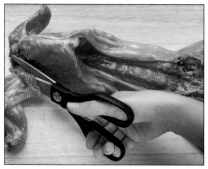

Using sharp scissors, cut the forelegs off the rabbit through the connective tissue.

Cutting where the hind legs join the body, remove the legs and cut in half to separate.

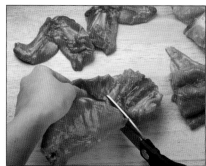

Cut the ribcage and body of the rabbit into 4 even pieces.

Add the peeled and chopped tomatoes to the pan and simmer for 45 minutes.

COUNTRY RABBIT IN RED WINE

Preparation time: 15 minutes
Total cooking time: 1 hour 30 minutes
Serves 4

1.25 kg (2 lb 8 oz) rabbit
125 ml (4 fl oz/½ cup)
   olive oil
2 garlic cloves, crushed
1 sprig of rosemary, finely
   chopped
250 ml (9 fl oz/1 cup) red
   wine
125 ml (4 fl oz/½ cup) chicken
   stock
4 tomatoes, peeled and
   chopped

1 Cut the forelegs from the rabbit by cutting through the connective tissue joining the body. Cut across the back of the rabbit just above the legs, then cut the legs in half. Cut the body (saddle) of the rabbit into 2 pieces, then cut the ribcage and backbone into 4 pieces, to form 8 portions.
2 Heat the oil in a heavy-based pan. Add the rabbit, garlic and rosemary and brown the rabbit over medium heat on all sides.
3 Add the wine and stock; season with salt and freshly ground black pepper. Cover and simmer gently for 30 minutes. Add the tomatoes and cook, covered, for another 45 minutes over low heat, or until the rabbit is tender. Serve with crusty Italian bread to mop up the juices.

COOK'S FILE

Note: To save time, ask your butcher or poulterer to cut the rabbit for you.

Index

Published in 2011 by Murdoch Books Pty Limited.

Murdoch Books Australia
Pier 8/9, 23 Hickson Road, Millers Point NSW 2000
Phone: +61 (0)2 8220 2000 Fax: +61 (0)2 8220 2558
www.murdochbooks.com.au

Murdoch Books UK Limited
Erico House, 6th Floor North, 93–99 Upper Richmond Road
Putney, London SW15 2TG
Phone: + 44 (0) 20 8785 5995 Fax: + 44 (0) 20 8785 5985
www.murdochbooks.co.uk

Publisher: Lynn Lewis
Senior Designer: Heather Menzies
Project Manager: Liz Malcolm
Designer: Kylie Mulquin
Editor: Justine Harding
Production: Alexandra Gonzalez

A record of the Cataloguing-in-Publication Data for this title is available from the National Library of Australia

ISBN: 978-1-74266-314-2

Printed by 1010 Printing International Limited. PRINTED IN CHINA.